SOVIET HISTORY IN THE YELTSIN ERA

By the same author

THE SOCIALIST OFFENSIVE: The Collectivisation of Soviet Agriculture, 1929–1930

THE SOVIET COLLECTIVE FARM, 1929–1930

THE SOVIET ECONOMY IN TURMOIL, 1929–1930

THE DEVELOPMENT OF THE SOVIET BUDGETARY SYSTEM

FOUNDATIONS OF A PLANNED ECONOMY, 1926–1929, VOLUME 1 (*with E. H. Carr*)

SCIENCE POLICY IN THE USSR (*with E. Zaleski and others*)

THE SOVIET UNION (*editor*)

THE TECHNOLOGICAL LEVEL OF SOVIET INDUSTRY (*editor with R. Amann and J. M. Cooper*)

FROM TSARISM TO THE NEW ECONOMIC POLICY: Continuity and Change in the Economy of the USSR (*editor*)

SOVIET HISTORY IN THE GORBACHEV REVOLUTION

THE ECONOMIC TRANSFORMATION OF THE SOVIET UNION, 1913–1945 (*editor with M. Harrison and S. G. Wheatcroft*)

CRISIS AND PROGRESS IN THE SOVIET ECONOMY, 1931–1933

Soviet History in the Yeltsin Era

R.W. Davies
Emeritus Professor
Centre for Russian and East European Studies
University of Birmingham

First published in Great Britain 1997 by
MACMILLAN PRESS LTD
Houndmills, Basingstoke, Hampshire RG21 6XS and London
Companies and representatives throughout the world

> This book is published in Macmillan's *Studies in Russian and East European History and Society*
> General editors: R. W. Davies and E. A. Rees
> Series ISBN 0–333–71239–0 outside the United States

A catalogue record for this book is available from the British Library.

ISBN 0–333–65592–3 hardcover
ISBN 0–333–65593–1 paperback

First published in the United States of America 1997 by
ST. MARTIN'S PRESS, INC.,
Scholarly and Reference Division,
175 Fifth Avenue, New York, N.Y. 10010

ISBN 0–312–17372–5

Library of Congress Cataloging-in-Publication Data
Davies, R. W. (Robert William), 1925–
Soviet history in the Yeltsin era / R.W. Davies.
p. cm.
Includes bibliographical references and index.
ISBN 0–312–17372–5 (cloth)
1. Soviet Union—Historiography. 2. Historiography—Russia
(Federation) I. Title.
DK266.D28 1997
947.084'07'2047—dc21   96–29714
                                              CIP

This book is printed on paper suitable for recycling and made from fully managed and sustained forest sources.

10   9   8   7   6   5   4   3   2
06   05   04   03   02   01   00   99   98

Printed and bound in Great Britain by
Antony Rowe Ltd, Chippenham, Wiltshire

Contents

Contents

Preface

At the time of the XIX Conference of the Communist Party in June–July 1988, Gorbachev's reforms appeared to have entered a period of stability. In the months before the Conference most state enterprises had been transferred to a system of self-management; and the Law on Cooperatives moved the Soviet Union in the direction of a mixed economy. In international affairs the Moscow meeting of Gorbachev and Reagan in May 1988 pointed the way to far-reaching arms agreements and Soviet–American concord.

The rejection by the Politburo of the pro-Stalin 'letter' by the Leningrad Communist Nina Andreeva stimulated radical criticism of the Soviet past. The hero of 1988 was Bukharin, the leading intellectual in the 'Right-wing' opposition to Stalin in 1928–9. By the time of the party Conference, most journalists and intellectuals openly rejected both Stalin's repressive dictatorship and his policies of forced industrialisation and agricultural collectivisation as a betrayal of the spirit of the October 1917 revolution; and they enthusiastically endorsed Lenin's New Economic Policy (NEP) of the 1920s as a humane form of democratic socialism.

The rehabilitation of the mixed economy of NEP, and of Bukharin's advocacy of a peaceful transition to socialism, fitted neatly with a reform programme for the 1990s which would establish the Soviet Union as a modern socialist democracy, a market economy in which both a powerful state sector and small-scale private enterprise played their part.

These hopes soon proved to have been romantic dreams. In 1989–90 the Soviet economic situation gravely deteriorated. Communism in Eastern Europe collapsed. Democratic elections in the Soviet Union exposed the unpopularity of the Communist leaders. Then in August 1991 the coup which attempted to restore the power of the old regime failed ignominiously. It was soon followed by the collapse of the Soviet Union and the tormented efforts to transform Russia into a modern capitalist economy.

The rejection of Leninism and the Bolshevik Revolution in the most popular newspapers and journals in 1989–91 played an important part in the mental revolution. After the failure of the August 1991 coup the Communist past seemed to have been discarded for ever. But the failure of the effort to transform Russia into a prosperous capitalist economy brought great disillusionment. By 1993 the debate about the Soviet past resumed.

Part I of this book tells the story of the politics of Soviet history in the eight years 1989–96. These were years in which the intense interest of the public in their own past rose to a peak – in 1990 or 1991 – and then precipitately declined.

In 1989–96 the archives released many millions of files; and Russian historians began the painstaking work of examining the record of their recent history. Part II considers the stormy and complicated battle for the archives. After vast progress following the defeat of the August coup, advances have proceeded by fits and starts since 1993 – and some documents which were previously available have been withdrawn from public use. This is a revolution; but it is an unfinished revolution.

Russia is now – with some qualifications – a free country. Teachers of Russian history are able to present to their pupils a much fuller and livelier account of the past. The Russian historical profession, no longer restricted to a prescribed account of the Soviet past, has already made striking progress in writing a new history. Part III considers the problems of teaching history, and presents some examples of recent research by Russian historians which have already greatly enriched our knowledge and understanding.

As with my previous volume, *Soviet History in the Gorbachev Revolution* (1989), I have greatly benefited from the assistance and advice of colleagues. I must particularly thank Mike Berry, Nick Baron, Julian Cooper, Oleg Khlevnyuk and Richard Sakwa. Gennadii Bordyugov generously showed me draft chapters from *Istoricheskie issledovaniya v Rossii*, which is forthcoming under his editorship, and sent me recent history textbooks. Patricia Grimsted, Mark Kramer and Sarah Tyacke commented in detail on my chapters on the archives, and provided new material. John Dunstan and Stephen Webber performed the same services for the chapter on the teaching of history, and Yoram Gorlizki for Chapter 17. Melanie Ilič prepared the Appendix Table. Rosalind Marsh's new book has been a valuable source of information on *History and Literature in Contemporary Russia* (Basingstoke and London, 1995), and has obviated the need to discuss literary publications about the past in detail in the present volume. Others who provided valuable comments and information include Edward Acton, Greg Andrusz, Ed Bacon, Francesco Benvenuti, Robin Blackburn, Viktor Danilov, Michael Ellman, Don Filtzer, James Harris, James Laver, John Klier, Taras Kuzio, Bob Lewis, Maureen Perrie, Yurii Polyakov, Silvio Pons, Arfon Rees, Vera Tolz, Nicholas Werth, Stephen Wheatcroft, Andrew Wilson and Matthew Wyman. Betty Bennett and Yvonne Hall helped to prepare the typescript for publication. Some material in Part III has already appeared in *The London Review of Books*; and an earlier version of Chapter 13 was published in *New Left Review*; I am grateful to the editors for permission to use them here. My wife Frances again provided indispensable support.

R. W. DAVIES

Part I
The Politics of Soviet History

INTRODUCTION

My earlier volume dealt with the Soviet historical debate in the period from Gorbachev's election as General Secretary of the Communist Party in March 1985 to the immediate aftermath of the XIX Party Conference, held in June–July 1988.[1] In these years, and particularly in the eighteen months after the beginning of 1987, a vast change took place in Soviet perceptions. By the summer of 1988 the Soviet press discussed the Stalin period quite frankly and freely from many different perspectives. This phase in Soviet intellectual development was more or less complete in itself. I have not returned to it here.

Between the party Conference and the unsuccessful coup of August 1991, the debate about the origins of Stalinism entered a crucial new phase. In 1989–91, disappointed or encouraged by the growing political, economic and social crisis confronting Gorbachev, many writers strongly challenged the whole Leninist heritage, and argued that the Bolshevik Revolution of October 1917 was neither inevitable nor justified. They were supported by the overwhelming majority of the active and vocal intellectuals in Moscow and Leningrad. While the debate of 1987–8 was intertwined with Gorbachev's successful struggle for *glasnost'* against Ligachev and the conservatives in the party, the debate of 1989–91 was an intimate part of the struggle between what might be called the 'free-market democrats' and the Communist Party. The free-market democrats favour parliamentary democracy and Western-style private capitalism, whereas many party officials and ordinary party members sought to maintain their political power, to continue some kind of socialist economic system, and to prevent the collapse of the Soviet Union as a coordinated group of republics. A third force, or middle way, of which Gorbachev was the most prominent representative, advocated a democratic 'socialism with a human face'. In the course of the battle between free-market democrats and orthodox Communists, the third force disintegrated.

Following the defeat of the August 1991 coup, when the old leaders tried to seize power, the Communist Party was temporarily banned and the Soviet Union collapsed. In the Russian Federation the Yeltsin government embarked on its heroic attempt to stabilise the currency and to transform the economy into a capitalist system modelled on the United States and Britain – or on what the economies of these countries were presumed to be.

For a fairly short time – until about the end of 1992 – a euphoric and total repudiation of the Soviet past dominated the media. Apart from a few eccentrics, the publicists who had gained fame as advocates of the New Economic Policy and the Leninist road to socialism now took it for granted that in 1917 Russia had left the road which all civilised countries had to follow. The only question worth discussing was whether it had taken the wrong turning when the February–March Revolution overthrew the Tsar or when the October–November Revolution overthrew Kerensky and the Provisional government. A tremendous nostalgia for the pre-revolutionary past coloured most popular writings about history.

But shock therapy failed – some of my economist colleagues would say 'only partly succeeded' – and widespread disillusionment set in. Yeltsin forcibly closed down the Supreme Soviet in October 1993 and replaced it by a Federal Assembly. The elected Chamber was appropriately named the Duma, after the pre-revolutionary 'parliament' which existed uneasily from 1906 to 1917. Paradoxically, the results of the elections in December were ambiguous. Critics of the free market and nationalists obtained un-expectedly high votes.

In 1993–6, against the background of political pluralism, a genuine plural-ism of historical views was again expressed in the media. The whole range of Russian national history was re-examined. A single issue in 1995 of the most popular history journal, *Rodina*, which still has a circulation of 90 000, dealt with Thirteenth-Century art, Catherine the Great, Eighteenth-Century popular prints, peasant life at the end of the Nineteenth Century, the dearth of food during the second world war, the filming of Sholokhov's novel of the Civil War 'Quiet Flows the Don' in the 1950s, and the failure of Kosygin's economic reform of 1965.[2]

Russian history is only one stream in the teeming flow of accounts of the past which have appeared on the territory of the former Soviet Union. Within the Russian Federation, Tatars, Bashkirs, the peoples of Dagestan and others (including Chechens . . .) are all writing their own history. An acrimonious literature has appeared about the pre-revolutionary and Soviet history of the Cossacks.

The fourteen newly-independent republics which have broken away from the Russian Federation are each re-creating their own national history. Until 1985 the story of the annexation of formerly independent countries by the Tsars was coloured by the knowledge that the Russian Empire was to become the Soviet Union – the model for the future of the world. Russia – with its dominant language, officials and economy – was first among equals, both before and after the Bolshevik Revolution.

Most of the new histories naturally emphasise the struggle of the smaller nations against Russian domination. In Ukraine, the resistance of Bohdan

Khmel'nyts'kyi against Russia is emphasised rather than his eventual
capitulation to Tsar Aleksei in 1654, the central event in the Soviet histories.[3] And in many Ukrainian accounts Stepan Bandera and his followers
turned from villains into heroes. The Banderivtsi were Ukrainian guerrillas, strongly anti-semitic, who were allied with Hitler for much of the
second world war and then fought against Soviet occupation after the war.
Statues of Bandera were erected, particularly in Western Ukraine, and literature favourable to him was widely on sale in Kiev. This intense nationalism lost favour after President Kuchma was elected with the support of
most of the Russian-speaking population, but continued to dominate the
Western Ukrainian view of the past.

In the Crimea the situation is the mirror image of that in the rest of
Ukraine. In honour of the 300th Anniversary of the annexation of Ukraine
by Russia the Crimea was transferred to Ukraine by Khrushchev in 1954,
in spite of its majority population of Russians. In Crimea the Russian
national banner is waved in support of Crimean autonomy. The statue of
Catherine the Great was restored in Odessa, and unveiled with great pomp.
Pro-Russian history textbooks are used in Crimea and in largely Russian-
speaking Donetsk.

In Kazakhstan the story is more complicated. In June 1991 a very senior
Kazakh historian visited my university and spent best part of a day explaining that Russian influence had been harmful to Kazakh progress from
the earliest times to the present day. The new textbook on Kazakh history
is not so one-sided. It describes the colonial regime established by Tsarism
in blunt terms, dwells enthusiastically on anti-colonial Kazakh revolts, and
brings out the horrors of the 'totalitarian system' under Stalin, which were
particularly frightful during the collectivisation of nomad agriculture in
the early 1930s. But its account of cultural and economic progress and
setbacks under both Tsars and Bolsheviks is quite detailed and objective.[4]

In neighbouring Uzbekistan changes have been much slower. According to an American historian, school history textbooks 'still rely to a great
extent on historiography mapped out by Russian and Soviet scholars'.
While the 1873–6 anti-Russian revolt is described in much more detail
than in the Soviet textbooks, the new histories still take the line that in the
long run Russian occupation was good for Central Asia.[5]

In Belorussia the writing of history has undergone two sharp changes
since 1991. In the first years of independence, nationalist interpretations of
the pre-revolutionary and Soviet past were almost universal. But a pro-
Russian president, Lukashenka, was elected in 1995. He promptly stigmatised 51(!) post-1991 textbooks on history and literature on the grounds
that they were nationalistic, 'biassed and politicised', and announced that

for the time being the pre-1991 Soviet textbooks should be used.[6] In practice, an outright ban was not imposed, owing to the textbook shortage. Instead a committee was established to review the textbooks.[7]

In the Transcaucasus, Armenia, Azerbaijan and Georgia are each producing their own histories; and the Baltic republics (Estonia, Latvia and Lithuania), which lost their independence only at the beginning of the second world war, have quickly restored their national pre-1940 histories to centre stage.

In the account which follows I shall not attempt to deal with history in the former Union republics, or on the territories of national minorities within the Russian Federation. And it is possible to offer only brief glimpses of the considerable efforts now being made in many different Russian regions to re-examine their own history. But the reader should be aware that the Moscow and St Petersburg-centred Russian national and nationalist variants of the Soviet past are just one major example of the dozens of national and regional histories which now abound in the former Soviet Union.

1 The Onslaught on Leninism: From the Central Committee Plenum of September 1988 to the XXVIII Party Congress, July 1990

During 1989 and 1990 the triumphal progress of Gorbachev's drive for openness (*glasnost'*) continued. By 1989, major organs of the press had effectively escaped from central control. The number and range of forbidden topics rapidly declined. Then in March 1990 the USSR Congress of People's Deputies removed the clause of the Soviet constitution which proclaimed the 'leading role' of the Communist Party, thus effectively legalising the existence of other political parties. On 1 August 1990, *glasnost'* reached its climax with the abolition, subject to certain reservations, of the censorship system introduced in 1922, which involved preliminary censorship of the press and all other means of communication.

Against this background, the mental revolution spread further into Soviet society, and bit deeper. In the summer of 1989, the number of subscribers signing up to purchase the crucial journals again greatly expanded. The circulation of the weekly newspaper *Argumenty i fakty* increased from 9 million in 1988 to 32 million in 1990. This was a much larger circulation than that of any Soviet daily newspaper, perhaps a larger circulation than that of any other newspaper in the world. (See Appendix 1.)

For Gorbachev and his close associates, the consequences were paradoxical and unexpected. In all his public statements, Gorbachev based his concept of 'reconstruction' (*perestroika*) on a return to a modernised version of several major strands in the Soviet past: the ideals of October 1917; the New Economic Policy of the early 1920s; and, more generally, to Lenin's thought and practice. On this basis, Gorbachev argued, the 'socialist choice' made in 1917 would be reaffirmed and renewed.

Unfortunately for these hopes, *glasnost'* meant that the reconsideration of the past could no longer be confined to Gorbachev's framework – or anyone else's. From the end of 1988, fundamental criticisms of Lenin, the Bolsheviks and their Communist Party, and also of Marxism, were very vocally expressed. Behind the scenes, Gorbachev and some of his principal advisers rapidly lost faith in the renewal of the 'socialist choice'. The debate about history moved beyond the Communist Party framework. The rival pro-Bolshevik views of the past continued to contend bitterly among themselves, but now formed only one school of thought – or group of schools of thought. Desperate efforts were again made to contain the historical debate. However, they failed completely.

THE PROPAGANDA WAR

The first major offensive in the war against Leninism was launched by the publication in the popular science monthly *Nauka i zhizn'* ('Science and Life') of four articles by Aleksandr Tsipko on 'The Sources of Stalinism'.[1] Tsipko is a philosopher who at that time worked in the headquarters of the party central committee. Moscow rumours claimed that Tsipko was protected by Gorbachev's close colleague Aleksandr Yakovlev, just as Nina Andreeva had been protected by Egor Ligachev in March 1988.[2] The general view was that this support was due more to Yakovlev's genuine passion for *glasnost'* than to his complete agreement with Tsipko.

We now know that Tsipko's message was directly inspired by Yakovlev's own views. In his preface to the English edition of Yakovlev's *The Fate of Marxism in Russia*, published in the autumn of 1993, Tsipko reported his first meeting with Yakovlev, which took place in the autumn of 1988:

> Yakovlev impressed me by making his point very clear. He said to me: 'It's time to say that Marxism was a utopia and a mistake from the very beginning' . . . As he spoke, I searched the ceiling for bugs and wondered: 'Why isn't he scared? Is it that Communism is really dead in this country?'

After the Tsipko articles appeared, two historians who had been near-dissidents in the 1970s under party General Secretary Brezhnev, Viktor Danilov and Pavel Volobuev, decided to write a reply. Volobuev was removed from the directorship of the Institute of the History of the USSR in 1972 after advocating fresh interpretations of the 1905 and 1917 revolutions. Danilov was removed from his position as head of the Soviet peasant sector of the same Institute after editing a book on the collectivisation of agriculture which was banned at the proof stage as too critical of Soviet policy. In 1989 they again came up against the resistance of the authorities to their views. But this time they were regarded as too pro-Soviet. They were told that it had been decided (presumably by Yakovlev or someone else very high-up) that replies could not appear in the journal.[3]

Yakovlev was not the only senior member of the central committee staff who had come to the conclusion well before the August 1991 coup that Communism was finished. Danilov has reported an interesting experience at a meeting of Gorbachev with the party Commission on Questions of Agrarian Reform in August 1990. Danilov hoped to give evidence at the Commission, based on his knowledge of collectivisation, about how the collective farms could be transformed into genuine cooperatives:

> I. I. Skiba, the head of the agricultural department of the central committee of the Communist Party, went round those who had assembled in front of the meeting hall of the Secretariat of the central committee, and exchanged two or three phrases with each person separately. He said to me in a confidential manner that I would be called upon to speak if I would speak in favour of private property in land and of permitting trade in land (*vklyuchenie ee v tovarnyi oborot*). When I answered that I was against both, Skiba immediately lost interest in me and immediately in the same confidential manner began a conversation with somebody else. At the meeting those who spoke asserted the necessity of private property in land and declared their unanimous support of the General Secretary, who had expressed regret when he opened the meeting that he did not have the kind of instrument for land reform that Stolypin possessed – land consolidation commissions.[4]

In 1906–11 Stolypin attempted to transform Tsarist Russia into a western-type capitalist economy by agrarian and other reforms imposed from above.

Tsipko's articles caused a sensation among Moscow intellectuals. The main thrust of his argument was that the sources of Stalinism are to be found in Leninist and Marxist doctrine, and its practical application, the October Revolution and the Civil War which followed it. According to Tsipko, the collectivisation of agriculture continued the grain requisitions of the Civil War. And Stalin's view that socialism required the elimination of the market was held in common by all Marxists, from the anti-Bolshevik German socialist Karl Kautsky to the Soviet Left Oppositionist Preobrazhensky:

> In all cases without exception [Tsipko wrote], in all countries including Khomeini's Iran today, the struggle against the market and commodity-money relations has always led to authoritarianism, to the disruption of the rights and virtues of the personality, to the omnipotence of the administration and the bureaucratic apparatus.

In Russia, the entire post-revolutionary process had been a departure from 'the course of development of the whole of human civilisation'.

Tsipko also argued that Stalinism could not have been prevented without a fundamental change in the whole political system which was formed during the Civil War in 1918–20. Indeed, 'the attitude to the tragedy of the Civil War is a measure of the extent to which a person is a true member of the intelligentsia'; the Soviet intelligentsia had accepted Stalinism so easily because of its firm belief that history had been moving in a correct direction since October 1917. This false belief in the Utopian goals of the revolution had profound origins:

> our society was educated in the spirit of the romantic conceptions of the human being held in common with Rousseau . . .
>
> . . . Such messianism and deification of any kind of great idea is more than a weakness and a romantic notion, it is a great sin against humanity and one's own people. Hatred of the routine in life, whatever are the high motives used to justify it, has always been hatred of life.

Tsipko concluded that Left-wing extremism, personified by Trotsky and the Left Opposition of the 1920s, was the greatest danger to *perestroika*. Inability to face up to the whole truth about the deep roots of Stalinism lay behind the failure of Khrushchev. Unless all myth-making about the past and the future were completely eradicated *perestroika* would fail.

Several other influential publications in 1989 challenged the whole course of development since October 1917. Articles about the New Economic Policy (NEP), the mixed economy of the 1920s, by the economist Grigorii Khanin concluded that every phase of Soviet economic policy had almost certainly been doomed to failure. He implied that only a capitalist economy could have been successful. According to Khanin, even as late as 1928 national income per head was as much as 17 per cent below the 1913 level, while the stock of capital was 13 per cent above that level; a 'catastrophic decline' had taken place in the efficiency with which capital was used. These failures were due to the power of the bureaucracy, to the domination of industrial management by ex-workers with low qualifications, and to the elimination of efficient farmers during revolution and civil war. Khanin claimed that the feasible level of capital investment within the framework of NEP was too low to avoid stagnation and military weakness. 'The last chance for alternative solutions was lost, it seems to me, at the beginning of the 1920s; and even then it was small'.[5] Khanin's statistics are strongly disputed by other economists both in the Soviet Union and the West, including myself. We argue that NEP brought about a rapid economic recovery, and by 1928 achieved a level of capital accumulation equal to that of the Russian Empire before the first world war.[6]

The anti-Leninist case was also eloquently presented in two important works published in the Soviet Union for the first time in 1989, but written twenty years previously (and then published in the West). First, Solzhenitsyn's *Gulag Archipelago*. The publication of key sections of this book at the end of 1989 was a major extension of *glasnost'*. As recently as November 1988 V. A. Medvedev, Politburo member and head of the ideological commission of the party central committee, declared at a news conference 'I am against the publication of a number of works of Solzhenitsyn, and in the first place such works as Lenin in Zurich and The Gulag Archipelago. To publish Solzhenitsyn's works would mean, in effect, to undermine the foundations on which today's life rests.'[7] This was a not unrealistic judgment. The central argument of *Gulag Archipelago* was that the spirit and practice of the concentration-camp system can be traced back to Lenin, and to the institutions established during the Civil War under his leadership, and never afterwards relinquished.

Secondly, Vasilii Grossman's bitter essay-novella *Vse techet* ('Everything Flows'). This also treated Stalinism as continuous with Leninism. But, unlike Tsipko and Solzhenitsyn, Grossman believed that Russian historical traditions, and the serf mentality they had produced in the Russian people, played a major part in the triumph of both the Leninist and the Stalinist autocracy:

> Merciless suppression of the personality remorselessly accompanied the thousand-year history of the Russians. The slavish subordination of the personality to the State and its Master.

Both Solzhenitsyn and Grossman are regarded with great respect in Soviet intellectual circles. In surveys enquiring which new publications of 1989 had influenced the respondents, *Gulag Archipelago* and *Vse techet* were the most prominent.

The Bicentenary of the French Revolution, celebrated on 14 July 1989, provided an occasion to discuss – or rather condemn – the October Revolution in a comparative context. The historian Natan Eidel'man claimed that the French Revolution and the Napoleonic dictatorship which followed it had been less bloody than the October Revolution and the Stalin dictatorship because democratic traditions and the rule of law were far more advanced in pre-revolutionary France than in pre-revolutionary Russia. V. Sirotkin condemned both the French and the Bolshevik revolutionaries for their impatient 'running ahead':

The French Jacobins failed in their attempt to build a universal world of liberty and equality. The Russian Bolsheviks failed to bury capitalism by means of a world proletarian revolution. Both attempts to squeeze real life into the Procrustean bed of their doctrines ended in what Lenin described as 'meat-chopping'.[8]

By the beginning of 1990 the view was widespread that, in spite of the Tsars, systematic progress had been taking place in Russia in the decades before the first world war, and had been tragically interrupted by the October Revolution. Influential Soviet intellectuals argued more forcefully and frankly than before that Stolypin's policies had offered a preferable alternative to the revolutions of 1917.[9] Thus Nikolai Shmelev declared: 'I have an extremely positive attitude to Stolypin . . . Stolypin was the hope of the country and he began a very fruitful process. Today the situation is to some extent similar'.

In the course of 1989 and 1990, several prominent figures who had taken broadly Leninist positions in the earlier debate now emerged as strong critics of the whole course of history since October 1917. To some extent, these public figures were now expressing openly views which it had previously been unwise to proclaim; to some extent, their own views changed in the course of the debate. Yurii Afanas'ev, a pioneer of the historical debate at the end of 1986, now came forward as a blunt critic of the October Revolution. Speaking in the summer of 1989, he declared that the Soviet regime 'was brought into being through bloodshed, with the aid of mass murder and crimes against humanity', so that it was a 'hopeless task' to provide a legal foundation for Soviet society.[10] On another occasion he insisted that it was 'necessary to renounce all features of the party which come from Lenin.'[11] And in his speech at the Moscow International Conference of Historians in April 1990, which I attended, Afanas'ev insisted that the true history of the Soviet period could not be written unless the path on which Russia had embarked in October 1917 was recognised to be illegitimate. This was a striking example of an intolerance familiar in Soviet history. But this time it was directed against Leninism, and against Communist doctrine generally. Before the end of 1990, this new intolerance was widespread among both intellectuals and some sections of the general public.

In the spring of 1990 the idealistic image of Lenin universally accepted in the first phases of *perestroika* was thoroughly undermined by the publication in the Soviet press of a letter from Lenin to Molotov. The letter, marked '*Strictly secret*', was written on 19 March 1922, following mass disturbances among Orthodox Christian believers in the town of Shui. The disturbances took place after a local commission, acting on government orders, seized church valuables, on the pretext that they would be sold off to benefit the needy. Lenin cynically argued that the campaign provided a convenient opportunity for a damaging blow against the clergy:

> A wise writer on problems of state said that if a series of cruel actions must be carried out in order to achieve a certain political objective, then they must be carried out in the most energetic fashion and in as short a period of time as possible, because the popular masses will not tolerate a long period in which cruel actions are undertaken . . .
>
> Therefore I have reached the firm conclusion that we must now at this moment undertake a decisive and merciless battle with the Black Hundred clergy and suppress their opposition with so much cruelty that they will not forget it for several decades . . .
>
> The greater the number of representatives of the reactionary clergy and the reactionary bourgeoisie which we succeed in shooting for this reason, the better. It is precisely now that we must teach these people a lesson, so that for several decades they will not even dare to think of any resistance.[12]

*   *   *

What might be called the liberal-democratic anti-Leninist school represented by Tsipko, Grossman, Soloukhin, Khanin and others was opposed in 1989–90 from several different ideological viewpoints. The Russian nationalists were the most strident. In 1989–90 they were divided among themselves to an even greater extent than in 1987–8.[13]

One wing of Russian nationalism was committed to Leninism, and to a nationalistic Communism, in line with the views expressed by Nina Andreeva in March 1988. In September 1989, the newspaper *Sovetskaya Rossiya*, which had published Andreeva's letter, attempted to renew the campaign for nationalistic Communism. An impassioned 'Letter of a Communist', by Ignat Chebukin, who joined the party in May 1941, admitted that Stalin had been responsible for great injustices, but insisted that 'in spite of all Stalin's power he was unable to turn us from the socialist path':

> I, and thousands and millions like me, felt and knew that Soviet power was our power, that it had already succeeded in giving us a great deal. Work and some social protection to the workers. Land and literacy to the peasants. People who were not even considered to be people before watched the cinema, listened to the radio, were called on to the stage, were allowed to experience the arts and the secrets of science . . .

Soviet pride, the new quality of human beings, did not grow up on an empty place.

Chebukin vigorously criticised the 'anti-communists who, disguising their longing for the Russia of the nobility and the landowners, mount their attack beginning with pre-revolutionary times and with Lenin'.[14]

Significantly, no-one paid any attention to Chebukin's letter, while Andreeva's letter had scared the press and most of the intelligentsia into almost complete silence. *Glasnost'* had advanced and become firmly secured in the eighteen months since March 1988.

Other nationalists rejected Lenin, and refused to acknowledge any positive aspects to the Stalin period. The most prominent member of the anti-Leninist nationalists at this time was Solzhenitsyn, living in exile in the United States. Almost alone among nationalist writers, his moral and literary influence was considerable on liberals and nationalists alike.

Both the pro-Bolshevik and the anti-Bolshevik wings of Russian nationalism are tinged with anti-semitism. Nina Andreeva's letter of March 1988 was fairly circumspect in its anti-semitism. In 1989 and 1990 hatred of the Jews was much more openly expressed. The most dramatic example was the long essay 'Russophobia' by the mathematician Academician Igor Shafarevich, published by the nationalist monthly literary journal *Nash sovremennik*. The essay was published in two parts. The first part, which appeared in no. 6, 1989, omitted three sections which dealt directly with the 'accursed question' – the Jewish question. These sections appeared belatedly in no. 11, 1989; the editor apologised for omitting them in the era of *glasnost'*, but remarked that their publication might again lead to 'stupid accusations of anti-semitism'.

According to Shafarevich, the long-isolated Jewish religious communes rapidly disintegrated in Russia at the end of the Nineteenth Century, and as a result Jews in disproportionate numbers had entered the economy and all the opposition groups in society, from the liberals to the terrorists. The difference between the French and the Russian Revolutions was that in the French Revolution Jews had played no role. The influence of Jews on Soviet society continued in the 1920s and the 1930s:

> The situation in the 1930s . . . [was] that while the number of Jewish names declined in the very top leadership, in the next lowest levels the influence expanded and went deeper. In the key People's Commissariats (the OGPU, foreign affairs, heavy industry) Jews occupied a dominant position in the top leadership (People's Commissars, their deputies, and members of the collegia), and amounted to well over half. In some spheres the leadership consisted almost entirely of Jews.

Moreover, ever since the Revolution Jews had been particularly prominent in violent repressive acts: the execution of members of the Union of
Russian Nationalists in Kiev during the Civil War on the basis of membership lists; the murder of the Tsar and his family in 1918; the construction
of the White Sea Canal and the organisation of the GULAG in the 1930s;
and the persecution of the Orthodox Church. Shafarevich concluded:

> [The Jews were characterised by] not merely dislike for the country
> where they were born, but complete alienation from it, and active hos-
> tility to its spiritual principles; not merely a failure to abstain from
> political rights, but the exercise of all their will and strength to influence
> the life of the country. Such a combination was remarkably effective; it
> created a 'Little People', who in their influence exceeded all other vari-
> ants of this phenomenon which have ever appeared in History.

Anti-semitic prejudices are found in other countries, including my
own, but the former Soviet Union is, I think, the only part of Europe in
which such rabidly anti-semitic views would be published in a serious
literary journal. Fortunately, although anti-semitism was widespread in the
Soviet Union, it attracted little public support and few votes as a political
movement.

The advocates of Leninist alternatives to Stalinism – let us call them
'democratic Leninists' – did not fold their tents and depart vanquished
from the battlefield in face of this dual assault from liberals and nationalists. Some historians mounted a vigorous defence of Leninism and of
Lenin's policies in revolution and civil war, and their articles were on the
whole thoughtful and not unconstructive.[15]

The democratic Leninists began to move from general discussion to
serious professional historical investigation of the past. Following the
publication of the Russian translation of Stephen Cohen's biography of
Bukharin in 1988, Soviet historians issued several substantial volumes of
Bukharin's writings and speeches. These included material from the archives such as Bukharin's previously unpublished speech to the plenum of
the party central committee on 18 April 1929, the last occasion on which
he was able to present even to a closed party meeting an extended defence
of his views.[16]

In the course of 1989 and 1990 the democratic Leninists also struggled
to secure the political rehabilitation of Trotsky and the Left Opposition.
For sixty years the most maligned heretic, he was now scornfully dismissed by both liberals and Russian nationalists. The campaign to rehabilitate Bukharin and his allies was led by prominent intellectuals who were
not professional historians; and the historians followed tamely in the rear.

But the liberal intellectuals showed little interest in Trotsky – except to abuse him as being as bad as or even worse than Stalin. The efforts to rehabilitate Trotsky were led by professional historians.

In October 1989 two young historians, Mikhail Gorinov and Sergei Tsakunov, presented to a Soviet–American colloquium in Moscow a carefully-researched paper on Evgenii Preobrazhensky, the principal economist of the Left Opposition; they were assisted in their work by Preobrazhensky's son Leonid.[17] In a sympathetic account, the authors concluded that Preobrazhensky, in his work on the problems of industrialisation in the 1920s, 'disclosed and analysed the main objective tendencies of the period'.

More or less simultaneously, several crucial articles by Trotsky were published in Soviet journals, including *New Course* (1923) and *The Stalin School of Falsification* (1928).[18] This was followed by the publication in substantial editions of a number of volumes of Trotsky's writings.[19] Extracts from the autobiography of Trotsky by Pierre Broué, a French Marxist sympathetic to Trotsky, were published in the Novosibirsk economic journal *EKO*, nos 9 and 10, 1989. Then at the beginning of 1990 *EKO* published an Afterword to Broué by Viktor Danilov.[20] Danilov discovered in the party archives notes by Stalin's secretary Bazhanov on a speech by Trotsky delivered at a party central committee plenum on 16 October 1923.[21]

Previously historians believed that Trotsky was not present at the plenum owing to illness. Trotsky himself had evidently completely forgotten that he had been present when he later wrote about these events. In 1923 he was frequently reproached for his immodesty in refusing Lenin's proposal that he should become deputy chair under Lenin of the top government body, the Council of People's Commissars. Trotsky explained to the plenum that 'I firmly turned down his proposal on the grounds that we should not give our enemies the opportunity to say that our country was being ruled by a Jew.' Danilov argues that in this speech 'Trotsky provided convincing proof that he never sought to struggle for personal power.'

Danilov broadly sympathised with the views of Bukharin, who was in the opposite camp to Trotsky in the mid-1920s. But Danilov held that the lives and opinions of all Stalin's opponents should be presented honestly and fully, including those with which one disagreed. 'The myth that the struggle within the party in the twenties was a struggle for power among all its voluntary and involuntary participants was very necessary to Stalin; with the help of this myth he discredited his opponents and justified his own struggle for personal power.' Danilov also argued that it was important for present-day political reasons to appreciate that there was a much more fundamental divide between Stalin and his opponents than among the opponents themselves. Failure to do so helped those who argued that Soviet history had taken a wrong path ever since 1917:

> As in the case of N. I. Bukharin, the evolution of attitudes to L. D. Trotsky displays a strange shift in historical viewpoints. The main opponents of Stalin, who resisted the establishment of the counter-revolutionary bureaucratic dictatorship, are presented as collaborators in the Stalin crimes, as co-founders of the Stalin regime.

In their publications of 1989 and 1990, a number of Soviet historians, mainly on the staff of the Institute of Marxism–Leninism, the party research institute attached to the central committee, offered a fresh assessment of NEP and of its collapse at the end of the 1920s. Their approach was less superficial than either the uncritical enthusiasm for NEP displayed in the typical writings of 1987 and 1988 or the dismissal of NEP by the anti-Leninists in 1990 as an unsuccessful attempt to prevent the inevitable degeneration of the October Revolution into totalitarianism. Thus the young historian Nikolai Simonov presented the crisis of NEP as fundamentally due to the conflict between two economic formations: 'the traditional semi-patriarchal semi-commodity peasant economy; and the modern industrial economy'. Avoiding this conflict was a difficult and delicate task. In Simonov's opinion, in the mid-1920s the state should have attempted to mitigate this conflict by giving priority to light rather than heavy industry; and it should have acted earlier against rural differentiation, encouraging genuine cooperation in the countryside [how this would have helped with the *economic* problem is not clear]. And in foreign policy it should have been more flexible, so that the Western powers were willing to advance loans for economic development. But according to Simonov even these policies might not have solved the dilemma, in view of the huge expenditures on transport, engineering and chemicals required by the Soviet military.[22]

To sum up. In 1989 and the first six months of 1990, the October Revolution and Leninism were on trial before the country at large. Had Russia been on the wrong path ever since 1917, so that the whole post-revolutionary development must now be superseded? This was the central question about Soviet history which was debated in the Soviet media.

It was also one of the central questions for professional historians, who had cast off the caution which characterised their public activities in the early stages of *perestroika*. At the International Conference of Historians in Moscow in April 1990, Leninism was debated among Soviet as much as Western historians. Some Soviet members of the audience greeted

Afanas'ev's attack on the whole course of development since the October Revolution with enthusiasm, others with hostility. Some Soviet speakers at the Conference took a broadly Leninist approach, but one young historian from the Institute of Marxism–Leninism (previously the shrine of Leninist orthodoxy) criticised Lenin as someone who opportunistically took policies pragmatically from whichever of his pockets seemed suitable. Western scholars who made cautious criticisms of Lenin were enthusiastically slapped on the shoulder by anti-Leninists; those who, like myself, noted that central planning had been responsible for major industrial developments in the 1930s were warmly shaken by the hand by the more orthodox. Historical scholarship proved quite unable to stand outside the general political ferment.

HISTORY AND POLICY

In the months before the XXVIII Party Congress in July 1990 reconsideration of the past was central to several important party or government decisions. First, the Politburo 'Commission on the Further Examination of Materials Concerning the Repressions of the 30s, 40s and Early 50s' vigorously continued to rehabilitate (usually posthumously) the victims of Stalinism, working closely with the Procuracy, the Supreme Court and the KGB. The Commission, established on 28 September 1987, was chaired by Yakovlev from 11 October 1988. It met eleven times between January 1988 and May 1990, and on each occasion rehabilitated large groups of former party members.[23] Its work was greatly accelerated by the Decree of the Presidium of the Supreme Soviet on 16 January 1989, which ruled that all decisions of the special extra-legal committees of the OGPU, NKVD and their successors were illegal. In a statement issued a few weeks before the party Congress, the Politburo Commission declared:

> In 1988–1989 and the first half of 1990 about one million citizens have been rehabilitated. The total number of citizens to whom their good name has been restored now amounts to more than two million. The rehabilitation of citizens in accordance with the Decree . . . of January 16, 1989, is virtually complete.

The statement also declared of the big political trials:

> They were all a result of arbitrariness and extreme violations of legal process. The materials for them were crudely falsified. No 'blocs' or 'centres' existed in reality. They were created artificially.

Some trials had not yet been examined, particularly those of non-party specialists and others. The statement of the Politburo Commission urged the Procuracy, the KGB and the Supreme Court to accelerate their investigation of the Industrial Party, Menshevik and 'Academicians' Trials of 1930–1.[24] But this work was not completed before the coup of August 1991.

Shortly before the party Congress the Politburo Commission published a further list of persons readmitted posthumously to the party. This belatedly included the Left Oppositionists E. A. Preobrazhensky (on whom see above) and I. N. Smirnov.[25] The only prominent Communist opponent of Stalin not rehabilitated by the Commission was Trotsky himself (Trotsky was declared an 'enemy of the people' in the trials of 1937–8, and murdered by an NKVD agent in 1940).

No arrangements were announced for reconsidering earlier trials, including the trials of the Civil War period and the trial of the Socialist Revolutionaries, the pro-peasant revolutionary party, in 1922. The sensitive question of the role of Lenin would inevitably have intruded.

The second important reconsideration of the past in which Yakovlev was closely involved was that undertaken by the Commission of the Congress of Soviets on the Soviet–German Non-Aggression Treaty of 1939, signed shortly before Germany invaded Poland. Yakovlev presented a very thorough report on 23 December 1989. The Congress resolved that the content of the Pact itself 'was not at variance with the international legal norms and the treaty practice of states'. However, it condemned the '"secret additional protocol"'. This divided Eastern Europe into spheres of interest between Germany and the Soviet Union. Soviet spokesmen had frequently expressed doubt about or denied its existence. But the Congress declared that expert analysis confirmed 'the fact of its signing and its existence'.[26] A few months later, the Russian text of this and other secret protocols was published from the copy which had been residing all the time in the Soviet Foreign Ministry archives.[27]

The terms of the Commission were confined to the year 1939, and deputies from the Baltic called for an examination of the entry of Estonia, Latvia and Lithuania into the Soviet Union in 1940.[28] No action was taken.

A third major issue considered by the Soviet government at a high level was the murder of 4000 Polish officers whose bodies were found in Katyn' Woods, and the fate of 17 000 other missing Polish officers. As recently as November 1988, when the USSR Council of Ministers decided to construct a memorial in Katyn', a Soviet official brashly claimed that the Polish officers had been executed 'by fascists in 1943 when our army was advancing'.[29]

However, in the spring of 1990 an enterprising Soviet historian, Dr Natalya Lebedeva of the Institute of General History, provided the final proof of Soviet responsibility for the Katyn' murders. The unit number of a Soviet signal battalion, mentioned in a letter from its commanding officer, enabled her to start tracing the movements of the Polish officers and their Soviet guards between September 1939 and the massacre of May 1940. Much of this material was found in the top-secret Central State Special Archive (on which see p. 87 below).[30] Simultaneously, a military historian followed a parallel trail.[31]

Gorbachev, in his capacity as President of the USSR, apologised on behalf of the Soviet Union to the President of Poland when he visited the USSR in April 1990.[32] The careful research of professional historians had forced the politicians to admit the truth publicly at last. Or rather some of the truth. A further twist to the story became known after Yeltsin took over Gorbachev's archives (see p. 45 below).

2 The XXVIII Party Congress, July 1990

In his report of November 1987 Gorbachev criticised the 'administrative-command system' and bitterly condemned the Stalinist repressions. But in other respects he was more orthodox. He was contemptuously hostile to Trotsky, critical (albeit sympathetically) of Bukharin, and on the whole supported the collectivisation of agriculture. After the XIX Party Conference, Gorbachev slowly moved towards the unambiguously anti-Stalinist position already taken by almost all reformist intellectuals. In an article published in November 1989 his new approach was at last clearly stated:

> Stalin played cleverly on the revolutionary impatience of the masses, on Utopian and equalising tendencies inherent in any mass movement . . .

> In the name of the 'great objective' any means, of the most inhuman kind, were justified . . .

> Instead of the idea of the free development of each as the condition for the free development of all, the concept of human beings as 'little screws' (*vintiki*) appeared.[1]

Three months later, in his report on the 'Draft Platform for the XXVIII Party Congress', presented to the February 1990 plenum of the party central committee, Gorbachev's views on Soviet history seemed to have undergone a further fundamental shift. While he reiterated that 'we remain faithful to the choice made in October 1917, the socialist idea', he silently departed from his previous enthusiasm for Lenin and Leninism, and made only one cursory reference to Lenin.[2] Gorbachev's report led the Western press to conclude that he had abandoned Leninism. Startling headlines appeared such as: 'Farewell, Lenin: three days that shook the Party'.[3]

This conclusion soon proved to have been unwarranted. Gorbachev began his speech of 10 April 1990, to the Congress of the Komsomol (Young Communist League) with a lengthy discussion of the importance of creatively using the Leninist heritage. 'The true Lenin,' he declared, 'is surprisingly up-to-date; don't believe those who claim the opposite'.[4] Ten days later he delivered the keynote address at the meeting commemorating the 120th anniversary of Lenin's birth. He vigorously rejected the view that there was continuity between Lenin and Stalin, and condemned 'philistine slander' of Lenin. But at the same time he argued that Lenin should not be treated as an icon. For Gorbachev 'the principal value in Lenin's thought about socialism, his main contribution to the elaboration of the socialist idea, is to be found in his writings and policy connected with NEP, and of course in his "Testament"' – the 'Testament' refers to Lenin's letter to the party Congress, dictated at the end of 1922, in which he called for the removal of Stalin from the post of party General Secretary.

An aspect of Lenin's character which particularly appealed to Gorbachev, who had himself been battling for a market-oriented reform in the Politburo, was his willingness to push through his policy against the opposition or reluctance of most of the other party leaders. According to Gorbachev, when Lenin proposed the turn to NEP, 'at first perhaps only Krasin and Tsyurupa were fully in agreement' with him, and he threatened to resign. But 'eventually Lenin's arguments and the logic of life prevailed, and NEP became the policy of the party'.[5]

At a reunion with his fellow-students a few weeks later Gorbachev is reported to have spoken as 'a true believer in socialism and Leninism . . . "I can't go against my father or my grandfather", he said.'[6] But he displayed a remarkable ability to adapt Lenin to the needs of *perestroika*.

Among the other members of the Politburo, Ligachev wore Lenin's mantle with far greater assurance. He consistently presented coherent arguments for a more traditional view of the October Revolution and Leninism. At the December 1989 plenum of the party central committee he passionately denounced those who rejected Lenin:

> The Communist Party and Vladimir Il'ich Lenin are the objects of ferocious attacks from political careerists . . .
>
> Yes, comrades, our history is really far from simple and it does of course press down on all of us. But that is not the real question. We have changed much of our outlook in evaluating historical events. I have emphasised, and will continue to emphasise, that we are harvesting the fruits of irresponsible and destructive activity of this kind. We have deprived ourselves of one of the most powerful moral forces, by failing to place all our history, with all its heroism and complexity, at the service of overcoming the difficulties of *perestroika* . . .
>
> I am deeply convinced that attempts are being made, by blackening our history, to weaken the belief of our people in our ideals and to undermine patriotic feelings. If I am wrong, say so.
>
> *Voices*: Correct.
>
> *Ligachev, E. K.*: I am deeply convinced that nihilism towards the past gives rise to nihilism towards the present.[7]

The two unofficial Platforms for the Party Congress, the 'Marxist Platform' and the 'Democratic Platform', took radically different views of the

Soviet past. The Marxist Platform strongly identified itself with the October Revolution and the 'dictatorship of the proletariat', and argued that the tragedy of Stalinism resulted from the historical circumstances of the backwardness of Russian capitalism, plus Utopianism and other weaknesses in Soviet ideology. The Marxist Platform called for a return to socialist ideals, the overturn of the bureaucracy, and the establishment of a society based on self-management.[8]

The Democratic Platform, however, called for 'a fundamental re-examination of dogmatic concepts, including the historical mission of the working class, the dictatorship of the proletariat, and the necessity and inevitability of socialist revolutions'.[9] The supporters of the Democratic Platform included Yurii Afanas'ev, Gavriil Popov, and other reformist intellectuals who reject the Leninist tradition altogether. At first, whether for tactical reasons or through conviction, they supported a mixed economy along Western social-democratic lines, but by the time of the Congress they publicly advocated the introduction of an economy in which private capitalism was overwhelmingly predominant. Afanas'ev resigned from the party a few weeks before the Congress.

The Congress met from 2–13 July. Its proceedings were primarily concerned with the current Soviet political and economic crisis and the crisis in the party itself. But the great debate on history which had raged during the previous three years was a significant sub-theme throughout its proceedings.

The draft 'Programmatic Declaration', published immediately before the Congress, endeavoured to maintain a careful balance between condemnation of the Stalinist system and support for the October Revolution and the Leninist tradition.

The Declaration strongly criticised not only 'the departure from the ideals and principles of socialism in the 1930s to 1950s' but also the 'false conception of socialism as a society based on a monopoly of state property, carried out by the party and state élite (*verkhushka*) in the name of the proletariat'. But it also condemned 'the nihilistic rejection of the ideals of October and the revolutionary and democratic conquests of the Soviet people'.[10] Gorbachev's Report to the Congress took the same line.

At the end of the first day's proceedings, the respect of Congress for the Soviet past was demonstrated when the delegates, led by Gorbachev, placed a wreath on Lenin's mausoleum.[11]

The division in the Politburo about Soviet history appeared more or less openly in the speeches of its members. Yakovlev, bluntly declaring that 'the truth about Stalinism is a sentence on the system it created', spoke about Soviet history in terms critical of the whole of Soviet development, not just the Stalin period. According to Yakovlev, the fundamental trouble was that 'the party of the idea, the revolutionary idea, turned into a party of power'.[12]

In contrast, two Politburo members, while not attempting to defend Stalinism, emphatically opposed the widespread general rejection of the Soviet past. Kryuchkov, head of the KGB, claimed that the present-day KGB bore no responsibility for what he described as 'the tragic pages of the past'. These were in any case not the whole of Soviet history: 'those who try to depict everything in dark colours are either blind, or are acting with intentions that are far from pure.'[13] And Ligachev, in his last speech as a member of the Politburo, rejected the notion that Lenin's outlook had fundamentally changed after the introduction of NEP:

> The example of Lenin inspired me . . . I do not agree with the view that Lenin at the end of his life decisively changed his viewpoint on socialism. He did not change his viewpoint on socialism. He merely changed his view on the methods and means of constructing socialism . . . M. S. Gorbachev stated on the 70th Anniversary of Great October that not one year was lived in vain for our people, but this idea was not developed in the political work of our party, and I profoundly regret this.[14]

The profound differences in attitude to the Leninist heritage appeared even more emphatically in the speeches of other delegates. Yeltsin did not explicitly mention Lenin or the Soviet past. But he fiercely criticised the one-party system and proposed that its leaders should be brought to account for wasting national resources (especially in the anti-alcohol campaign . . .). He still presented himself as a socialist; he called upon the party to rename itself 'the party of democratic socialism', and to join a union of democratic forces together with 'all fractions with a socialist orientation in other parties.'[15] His close associates took a more radical line. V. N. Shostakovskii, rector of the Moscow Higher Party School, who was a prominent supporter of the Democratic Platform, criticised both the October Revolution and Marxism itself:

> The people followed the slogans of the Bolsheviks in 1917. And 73 years later we repeat these slogans again and again: land to the peasants, factories to the workers, power to the soviets, peace to the peoples. We have not put these slogans into practice. Land belongs to the state and is thus without a master. The factories – to government departments. Power – to the party. And there is no peace between the peoples.[16]

The general mood of the Congress was far more conservative. Several delegates sharply condemned the party leadership, and particularly Politburo member V. A. Medvedev, responsible for ideology, for their failure to rebuff the onslaught on Leninism. Thus the party secretary of the Novo-Lipetsk iron and steel combine bitterly complained:

> What is the picture presented to us in the pages of *Izvestiya, Komsomol'skaya pravda, Ogonek* and other publications? The period of the revolution is presented as the debauch of the illiterate rabble, and as genocide in relation to the intelligentsia. The life of the older generation was nothing but a field of blood, the life of the middle generation was a stagnant marsh.[17]

The resolution of the party Congress on Gorbachev's political Report rejected both 'the totalitarian Stalin system' and the attacks on Lenin.[18]

The compromise decisions about the present situation, and the broadly Leninist view of the past, succeeded in retaining both the conservatives and the supporters of the Marxist Platform within the party, as well as the 'centrists' headed by Gorbachev. But towards the end of the Congress both Yeltsin himself, and many delegates who had declared their support for the Democratic Platform, resigned from the party, including figures prominent in the historical debate such as Shostakovskii and Popov (soon to become mayor of Moscow).

As a result of the decisions taken at the Congress, many former members of the Politburo now ceased to occupy any party post. Ligachev temporarily departed from the political stage. Yakovlev left the Politburo, but took on important state responsibilities as a member of Gorbachev's Presidential Council – for the few months it continued to exist. At the time of the Congress Yakovlev, who was responsible in practice for the work of the commission on party history headed by Gorbachev, published in the party journal *Kommunist* an introductory article about the planned (but never completed) multi-volume *Essays on the History of the CPSU (Ocherki istorii KPSS)*. He effectively summed up the state of the debate in critical party circles:

> What was the real significance of Marxism in the Nineteenth Century and how far had this significance changed by the end of the Twentieth Century? Was the historical division of the socialist movement into Social-Democracy and Communism due to the 'irreconcilability' of Lenin or to the 'renegadism' of Plekhanov and Kautsky; and has not Communism returned to Social-Democratic positions? Were there doctrinal 'flaws' in the viewpoint of Marx and Engels, and did these flaws play a pernicious role in the establishment of the historical phenomenon known as 'state socialism'? Did the command-administrative system carry within

itself something from the theory and practice of Leninism and Trotskyism, especially from the 'War Communism' period of 1918–20? Was it not a fatal mistake to create a one-party system instead of a two-party system, which would have enabled natural mutual control? Why did Lenin's colleagues ignore his 'Political Testament'? . . .

Complicated general questions of theory have begun to 'back up' questions which are of a specific character, but also extremely important. What did the 'Stolypin reform' give to Russia in practice and did the Bolsheviks struggle against it in vain? Would it not have been more sensible to stop at February 1917, with its 'freedoms', and not push the country to October, with its 'dictatorship of the proletariat'?[19]

A comparison of this list of questions with the list which Yakovlev presented in his lecture to the Academy of Sciences in April 1987 is instructive.[20] The earlier list was confined primarily to the Stalin period; the new list presented a programme for the reexamination of Marxism and Leninism as well as Stalinism.

The debate about Leninism had found its way into the heart of the discussions within the party. The party was splint asunder, and there was little room for compromise. Before the Congress convened, Yuri Afanas'ev predicted that it would be the 'funeral' of the party. The historical significance of the Congress lay in its failure.

3 The Leninist Counter-Offensive, August 1990–July 1991

In the months following the Congress, the liberal press continued its un-remitting assault on the Leninist past. Previously unpublished documents about prominent figures from the revolutionary period were called into service. Thus reminiscences about Aleksandr Blok, author of the popular revolutionary poem 'The Twelve', described how he gradually turned against revolution in 1920–1; 'he would not even hear "The Twelve" mentioned'.[1] The 1918 diary of the famous writer Mikhail Prishvin, once a Marxist and a revolutionary, records his bitter disillusionment:

> *26 May.* The thought suddenly occurs to me: Napoleon was defeated in Russia by the frost: he wanted to save humanity and was defeated by the frost. Lenin, the saviour of humanity, will also be defeated by fam-ine in that same Russia. . . .
>
> I have something in common with [the small peasant] – a physical feeling for the world of nature, for the land. This is completely inaccess-ible to Lenin. I think that there are similar beings in the countryside, and in nature, and even in the lower world of animals. They transgress this feeling for nature, and they are called criminals . . .
>
> We can count up all our primitive people who will follow Lenin and inform about concealed stocks of grain . . .
>
> In the whole village we can count up about eight such people, they all have a criminal past, they are all criminals, and they are all vigorous people.[2]

An interview with Alexander Kerensky, head of the Provisional Gov-ernment in 1917, never previously published in the Soviet Union, con-firmed the new image of Lenin as the pitiless precursor of Stalin:

> [*Interviewer.*] What was Lenin like?
> [*Kerensky.*] If you met him on the street, you would never think that he was at all unusual. Lenin was a supporter of merciless terror, without the slightest concession. That was the only way in which the minority could enforce its power on the majority, on the country.[3]

On the occasion of the 50th anniversary of the murder of Trotsky, a writer in the literary newspaper condemned both Trotsky's murderers and Trotsky himself, explaining that 'in my opinion Trotsky and Stalin were brothers born from the same womb, sons of the October Revolution . . . They were both ideologists and practitioners of barrack socialism.'[4]

Those who had allied themselves with the Bolsheviks were condemned for their naïveté, notably the Left Socialist-Revolutionaries, who had entered a coalition with the Bolsheviks in the first months after the October Revolution:

> Their compromises, in the name of the 'interests of the revolution', turned the idea of democracy bit by bit into the idea of dictatorship. This had the result that by the summer of 1918 the revolution was headed by a party which was no longer tied down by anything – neither by laws, nor by democratic 'prejudices'.[5]

At the same time public attention turned to the anti-Bolshevik and non-Bolshevik thinkers of the immediate pre-revolutionary period, particularly the contributors to the famous collection of essays *Vekhi* (Landmarks), who called for moderation and compromise in the aftermath of the 1905 revolution. Most prominent among them was Nikolai Berdyaev, who condemned both Right and Left in Russia for allowing slogans to replace truth, and strongly emphasised the need for independent individual thought.[6]

In fact Berdyaev was considerably less hostile than are many contemporary Russian intellectuals to the October Revolution and to the Soviet regime generally – under Stalin as well as Lenin. He saw the October Revolution not as an arbitrary act, but as a natural consequence of preceding Russian history; moreover, he was a socialist. Supporters of Gorbachev came to realise this. Thus an article in *Pravda* cited with approval his view that 'Communism was the inevitable fate of Russia, an internal moment in the fate of the Russian people' and that 'the popular masses were disciplined and organised in the chaos of the Russian revolution via the Communist idea . . . This was the undoubted service of Communism to the Russian state.'[7]

The world outlook of contemporary Russian liberals who advocate parliamentary democracy and capitalism is very different from Berdyaev's. Their view was strikingly summarised in some of their statements for the 73rd Anniversary of the October Revolution:

> *G. Kh. Popov* [mayor of Moscow, and prominent economist]. V. I. Lenin and his party, scared by the absence of a real perspective of remaining at the captain's bridge of Russia, turned force – the midwife

of history – into the child and the father of the new regime, creating as a result the monster of totalitarianism.

The October experiment produced successes in the numerator which were incomparable with the waste and the victims in the denominator.

Nikolai Travkin [co-chair of the Democratic Party of Russia, a former worker]. In my opinion, [October 1917] was a time of a turn into a blind alley, and the Bolsheviks did not lead but drove the Russian people into this blind alley. They considered that they were wiser than everyone else, that the Marxian model of society was the only correct one and could easily be achieved. But life proved more complicated and the model was defective.

If the Bolsheviks can be excused for leading the people away from the path of natural economic and social development – after all, they could genuinely be in error – it is difficult to excuse the elimination of the Church . . .

But reason tells us not to encourage hysteria and political intolerance. Let November 7, 1917 be holy for some people, and February of the same year for others.[8]

The founding congress of 'Democratic Russia', a coalition of parties and movements to which Travkin's party belonged, and which declared itself in opposition to the Communist Party, resolved that 7 November should be declared a memorial day for the victims of Communist terror, and of mass reconciliation.[9] On 7 November 1990, the official parade to commemorate the October Revolution passed off peacefully. But it was followed by an unauthorised anti-Communist demonstration which compelled Gorbachev and his colleagues to leave their podium on Lenin's tomb in Red Square, recorded by the world's television cameras.

The anti-Leninist campaign was accompanied – often quite spontaneously – by the physical removal of many of the ubiquitous symbols celebrating the Communist past. Gorky Street in Moscow (which was named in honour of the famous pro-Communist author) reverted to its old name Tverskoi Boulevard; and the town Gorky resumed its old name Nizhnii Novgorod. The town named after Kalinin (a leading associate of Stalin) was renamed Tver, although less than three years previously the suggestion that Kalinin's name should be removed from some public places in Moscow was rejected by Gorbachev as 'a thirst for sensations'.[10] Simultaneously public monuments to Lenin were removed by the local authorities in the Baltic Republics, Georgia, Moldava and Western Ukraine. The central committee of the Ukrainian Communist Party, and the secretariat of the central committee of the Communist Party of the USSR, both protested vigorously.[11] And on 13 October 1990, a solemn decree 'On Ceasing Outrages against Monuments Connected with the History of the State, and against Symbols of the State' was promulgated by Gorbachev as President of the USSR. This declared that those guilty of vandalism against monuments to 'the founder of the Soviet state V. I. Lenin' and other persons should be prosecuted.[12] But the statues and busts continued to disappear; and the action spread from national areas where passions were inflamed to some towns in the heart of the Russian republic. And in Leningrad a vigorous campaign demanded that the town should revert to its old name of St Petersburg.

Those who remained faithful to Lenin and the October Revolution did not remain idle or silent. In June 1990, shortly before the XXVIII Party Congress, the Communist Party of the Russian Federation was established, with Ligachev's support. In practice it was a virtually autonomous section of the USSR Communist Party. It had strong conservative and Russian nationalist leanings, and was quietly encouraged by the dominant group of officials in the USSR party headquarters. Its views on Soviet history were assiduously propagated in the newspaper *Sovetskaya Rossiya*, which expostulated indignantly about the betrayal of the revolutionary heritage.

More constructively, a number of articles and interviews written from a broadly Leninist perspective discussed the lessons which might be drawn from the experience of the revolution. Two respected historians of the revolution, Volobuev and Ioffe, both victims of the campaign for historical orthodoxy under Brezhnev,[13] rejected the 'noisy campaigns against Lenin, Bolshevism and the October Revolution', and pointed to the historical precedent of the French Revolution:

> After the fall of Napoleon and the restoration of the Bourbon monarchy in France, the revolution and its leaders were anathemised, and the revolution was condemned as a 'frightful plot' of a handful of 'instigators and firebrands.'
> In our days in France . . . different social strata take different attitudes to the revolution. And that is natural enough. But it does not enter anyone's head to demand that the annual celebrations on July 14 should be cancelled.

The authors cited the reflections of the Tsarist General Brusilov, who went over to the Bolsheviks, in support of their own concept of the revolution:

> 'The revolution was a Russian necessity . . . The Bolsheviks to a large extent were proved right. They tore out the decadent Russian aristocracy by the roots, deprived the factory-owners and landowners of the

wealth which they had accumulated over many years at the expense of the Russian people. Finally, the Bolsheviks preserved the integrity of Russia.'[14]

The tension between anti-Leninists and Leninists took place in the context of a general crisis of *perestroika* and *glasnost'*. The anti-Leninist reformers associated with Yeltsin hoped that Gorbachev as President of the USSR would separate himself from the Communist Party and establish a democratic coalition government, which would determinedly carry out the '500 days' economic programme drawn up by Yavlinsky, Shatalin and others. Sometime in November 1990, however, Gorbachev decided not to go down that road, confronted by the prospect of the disintegration of the Soviet Union, which he was not willing to accept, and by the determination of Popov, Shatalin and others that a capitalist economy should be established. Instead, he increasingly turned for support to the Communist Party, much more conservative now that many members of the 'Democratic Platform' had resigned, and to the Army and the KGB.

Gorbachev's own view of Soviet history, which was shared by many party members and ordinary citizens, played a major part in this decision. On 28 November 1990, in his address to his meeting with leading cultural figures, Gorbachev frequently referred to Soviet history, and spoke about his own family history more frankly than in the previous June. He explained that both his grandfathers had been persecuted under Stalin, but one of them had been the head of a collective farm for seventeen years, and 'I never heard that he doubted what he was doing on this earth'. And Gorbachev's father had been wounded as a soldier in the second world war:

> Socialism is deeply rooted in the people, in all of us . . . In renouncing that barracks' system, Stalinism, and in cleansing myself from it, must I renounce my grandfather, and my father, and what they did? Renounce past generations? Did they live in vain? I have often said that we did not grow up on a marsh, we have beneath us a capital point of support . . .
>
> With us everything is black or white. When will we stop seeing everything as red or white, black or white, blue and so on. As someone has already said, perhaps we should act as they did in Spain. They have a memorial to everyone who clashed in the Civil War, when friend was against friend and brother against brother.[15]

With the increasing political tension of the next few months, the note of reconciliation in Gorbachev's speech of 28 November was much more

muted in his later pronouncements. On 16 January 1991, he even suggested to the Supreme Soviet of the USSR that 'as society needs objective
information as never before, it would perhaps be appropriate to suspend
the Law on the Press for these months'. Faced with alarmed opposition,
he partly withdrew the suggestion a few hours later.[16]

On the same day, 16 January, an open letter from Shatalin to Gorbachev
dramatically illustrated the gulf which had now opened up between
Gorbachev and some of his former advisers. With frequent emotional
references to Christianity ('Forgive them, o Lord, for they know not what
they do'), Shatalin, an active party member for many years, and elected a
member of its central committee at the XXVIII Congress, now bitterly
criticised the whole Soviet experiment. While improbably claiming that he
was still a socialist, he declared that Communism had never existed, and
never would exist:

> It must be firmly understood, because it is an axiom, that the crisis
> began in October 1917. If we don't understand that, we are doomed . . . It
> is better to recognise calmly that it would have been better if it had not
> occurred.

Shatalin even claimed quite falsely that 'what we call the Great October
Socialist Revolution, historians throughout the entire world call "the October coup d'état" or "the October adventure of Lenin and Trotsky"'.[17]

In contrast, a few days later, on the anniversary of Lenin's death, *Pravda*
published an emotional appeal by Natalya Morozova, under the headline
'Forgive Us, Vladimir Ilich [i.e. Lenin]'.[18] The plenum of the party central
committee held ten days later on 31 January 1991, was dominated by the
determination of the party leaders to defend the Leninist cause, and to
prevent Yeltsin and his advisers from having their way. Yu. A. Prokof'ev,
one of Gorbachev's close associates, and first secretary of the Moscow
party committee, declared that a 'hidden war' had been waged for two
years against the basic structures of Soviet society. He named eight members of 'a so-called intellectual centre for the opposition forces', five of
whom were active participants in the historical debate – Bogomolov, N.
Shmelev, Popov, Volkogonov and Zaslavskaya.[19] Several other speakers
emphasised that 'the people have been deprived of their past' – 'the continuous subjective re-examination of our own history, discrediting it, re-
ducing it to mocking anecdotes, and dealing only with its shameful aspects,
has meant that the rounded understanding of history has been disrupted.'[20]
The plenum resolved that Shatalin's views were 'incompatible with membership of the Communist Party of the Soviet Union, let alone membership
of its central committee'.[21]

The uncompromising attitude of the traditionalist sections of the party became even more intransigent during the months before the August coup. Power was slipping from their grasp, and they clung to it desperately. In the first election for the President of the Russian Republic, Yeltsin, with 57.3 per cent of the votes, achieved an outright victory. Ryzhkov, the candidate of the moderate reformers, received only 16.9 per cent, and the two nationalist candidates – Zhirinovsky and Makashev – a mere 11.8 per cent between them. Following this victory, there were persistent calls from the traditionalists that Gorbachev should call a state of emergency. On 23 July the notorious appeal, 'A Word to the People', called for emergency measures to secure political and social stability.[22]

Political intransigence was accompanied by insistence on greater orthodoxy in relation to the Soviet past. On 14 December 1990, the Director of the Institute of Marxism-Leninism, G. L. Smirnov, whose reputation was that of a moderate reformer, addressed a remarkable letter to a secretary of the party central committee arguing that the unpublished documents of Lenin should continue to be kept secret. Smirnov's letter was classified as secret, but was published when the new rulers of Russia found it after the defeat of the coup. The following passages show its flavour:

... among [the unpublished documents] are some the publication of which could invoke an extremely ambiguous reaction in the present social-political situation ...

... Some documents reveal certain secret methods of work of state agencies of the Soviet republic (concentration camps for foreign subjects, shadowing foreign delegations travelling in our country, campaigns to discredit them – as happened, for example with the delegation of the British Trade Unions).

Smirnov added that other documents revealed that sections of the Red Army engaged in anti-Jewish pogroms and that 'state agencies made use of the contradictions between nations'. He reached the firm conclusion, which was accepted by the central committee apparatus:

Documents of this kind are unsuitable for publication at the present time.[23]

The attempt to halt the onward march of *glasnost'* reached a thunderous climax on 7 March 1991, at a conference convened at the Ministry of Defence by the Chief Editorial Commission of the proposed 10-volume history of the second world war. The conference, chaired by a deputy Minister of Defence, discussed the draft of the first volume of the history, which had been placed before it. The proceedings were secret, but the verbatim report was leaked to the press, and published *in extenso*.[24]

The conference displayed an extraordinary degree of intolerance. Some criticisms of the book seem justified; but its faults were used as an excuse to denigrate those who did not accept orthodox views of the war. The Minister of Defence, D. T. Yazov, five months later a leading participant in the August coup, insisted, to shouts of 'Hear! hear!' that the book 'must not treat the events of 1939 and the Ribbentrop–Molotov Pact like Yakovlev did' – an astonishing ruling, in view of the fact that the Congress of Soviets had upheld the work of the Yakovlev Commission (see pp. 17–18 above). F. M. Falin, head of the international department of the central committee, bluntly stated that 'such books must not be written with state money'. Volkogonov, then Director of the Institute of Military History, was shouted down; and his treatment led the Director of the Institute of History of the USSR, Novosel'tsev, to protest:

> I am simply frightened by what is happening here. D. A. Volkogonov speaks, and there are shouts of 'Get out' from the floor – it's a riot, and not a scientific conference.

The official military line, and the way in which unorthodox historians should be treated in future, was summed up bleakly by General Moiseev, Chief of the General Staff:

> The manuscript does not need improvement . . . but profound revision . . .
> The whole composition of the Editorial Board must be reviewed, specific people must be made responsible for each chapter, we must consider what kind of human being he is, what his soul is like. Don't send opportunists where the guns are firing. We have not let them into the documents and we will not let them in, we will not give them the archives, because they use them for wrong purposes, to write their own publications in working hours.

In the spring of 1991, both Soviet and foreign historians experienced the attempts of higher authorities to prevent the further spread of *glasnost'*. A young Soviet historian showed me a letter several pages long which he received at this time, listing detailed changes which must be made in his manuscript before he was allowed to cite the party archives. When I attempted to work in the Central Party Archive at this time, the only files I received were those which had already been released to me eighteen months before, and I was not allowed to see any finding aids or new material about the Soviet economy in the 1930s. My request was supported by the Institute of Marxism–Leninism, with which my university had an exchange arrangement, and which nominally controlled the party archives. But it was turned down by the appropriate central committee official in the party headquarters at Staraya Ploshchad'.

Behind the scenes the restrictions on the use of the party archives were supported by V. Naumov, the senior historian in charge of writing the new party history, and a close associate of Yakovlev. He wrote a secret letter to the central committee at this time which was discovered at party headquarters by Yeltsin's associates after the defeat of the August 1991 coup. In the letter he objected to the dangerous practice of providing Xeroxes of party documents from the past to Soviet and foreign historians.[25]

Meanwhile Gorbachev – and his view of Soviet history – had undergone a further abrupt change. At the end of February he had denounced the free-market democrats as 'a typical Right-wing opposition', and firmly rejected the 'capitalisation of society'.[26] But in April, confronted with growing opposition in society, he decided to seek agreement with Yeltsin and the free-market democrats.[27] At the plenum of the central committee, which met on 24–25 April, he again compared the atmosphere in the party to that confronting Lenin in 1921 when he launched the New Economic Policy:

> Lenin was accused of retreating from the cause of the October Revolution and the interests of workers and peasants, and of retreating from the principles of socialism ...
>
> I recall all this because the turning point to which we have all now reached is no simpler than in the 1920s. . . . Communists must learn to construct a legal state and the market.[28]

At this session the hostility of orthodox Communists to Gorbachev was so great that he offered his resignation from the post of General Secretary. The Politburo rejected this proposal, and the central committee concurred. But even the traditionally tame central committee was not quite so obedient this time: 13 members voted against the Politburo decision, and 14 abstained.[29]

The next central committee plenum met on 25–26 July, three weeks before the August coup, and the tense atmosphere reflected the deep divisions within the party. In his report on the draft party programme, Gorbachev described the Soviet system before *perestroika* as a 'totalitarian-bureaucratic system created by Stalin'. His use of the term 'totalitarian', rejected as too crude a description of the Stalin period by many Western historians, indicated how far he had moved since 1985. Gorbachev, speaking to a party audience, invoked Lenin's last writings to call for 'a fundamental change of our whole point of view on socialism', and praised NEP for its 'private entrepreneurship, its cooperatives and syndicates, and the rights for foreign concessions'.[30]

In the discussion, the draft programme was strongly criticised both for its underestimation of Soviet past achievements and for its failure to support socialism with sufficient vigour. General M. S. Surkov, secretary of the army party committee, insisted that the programme should show the role of the party in the defence of the country: 'we should not forget that more than three million Communists perished in the years of the Great Patriotic War'.[31] The head of a research institute attached to the Russian Communist party complained that the programme failed to describe the October Revolution as socialist:

> It should say that [the revolution] posed the task of socialist transformation, not merely the completion of the tasks of the bourgeois-democratic revolution.[32]

An orthodox party official from Lithuania called for a firm statement that 'the peoples of the USSR followed Lenin and these great ideas, selflessly built a new society; defended it with courage and heroism; this was the greatest achievement of the whole of world civilisation'. But even this firm defender of Leninism struck a rather uncertain note:

> Is the fate of the fall of the Byzantine or Roman states waiting for us, or are we capable of continuing the historical upsurge which the peoples of Russia achieved in October 1917? I am deeply convinced that the Soviet people are capable of continuing this upsurge! All that is needed is that the party should find in itself the strength to work out a political line which will enable us to move in this direction.[33]

In spite of these strictures, no challenge was offered to Gorbachev, and his proposal to place the draft programme, after revision, before an Extraordinary XXIX Congress of the party in November or December 1991 was approved. This peaceful outcome astonished the compilers of the programme, who had prepared for a sharp struggle. They later came to the conclusion that the conservatives had already decided to remove Gorbachev from power by force, and therefore did not take the plenum or the programme seriously.

*   *   *

In spite of some threats to *glasnost'* the historical debate still continued uninhibitedly in the rival sections of the Soviet press, though restrictions were imposed on the TV and the radio. By 1991 public interest in the historical debate – and in the general discussion of *perestroika* – had markedly declined. With the increase in prices, subscriptions to news-papers and journals for 1991 fell abruptly. The Soviet reading public gener-ally favoured the 'anti-Leninist' (or 'liberal') press rather than the 'Leninist' press. The circulation of the Leninist *Pravda* halved, while that of the thoughtful and well-edited party theoretical journal *Kommunist* collapsed, even though its pages have been graced by Western historians and social scientists with sharply contrasting points of view, including Alex Rabino-witch, Robert Tucker, R. W. Davies – and Robert Conquest. On the other hand, the anti-Leninist *Komsomol'skaya pravda* and *Argumenty i fakty* lost a much smaller proportion of their readers in 1991. (See Appendix 1.)[34]

The conclusions which the wider public had drawn about history by the end of the Soviet period are more difficult to assess. Opinion polls tend to confirm the hopes of the people organising the polls . . . A survey in Moscow purported to reveal that Lenin, who was the most popular political figure in November 1989, had fallen to second place by the time of the party Congress (the first place was occupied by Sobchak, the mayor of Lenin-grad).[35] However, a survey in November 1990 of 2000 people in ten widely different regions of the USSR (excluding the Baltic States, Armenia and Georgia) claimed that 59 per cent of the population had a positive opinion of Lenin's personality, and only 10 per cent a negative opinion; and as many as 76 per cent evaluated Lenin's activity positively, only 10 per cent negatively (the negative figure rose to 19 per cent among research workers and 36 per cent in Moscow as a whole). These views of Lenin are sur-prisingly positive. This survey was carried out by the party Institute of Marxism–Leninism and the party Academy of Social Sciences, together with the independent Institute of Social Forecasting. In marked contrast, the majority of the population of Leningrad voted to change its name to St Petersburg. It was non-Communist deputies, critical of the central authorities, who usually obtained the majority vote in elections at every level.

4 The Drive against Communism, 1991–2: The Aftermath of the August 1991 Coup

In the first fortnight of August 1991, two documents released to the press reflected Gorbachev's revived determination to press ahead with *perestroika*. The first was the draft party programme already discussed at the central committee plenum in July. The programme, 'Socialism, Democracy and Progress', called for 'a mixed economy' including 'state, collective, private, joint-stock and cooperative forms of property', and confirmed party support for a multi-party system.[1] The party seemed firmly set on the road towards social democracy. The second document was a draft Treaty which proposed to replace the Union of Soviet Socialist Republics by a looser federation, the Union of Soviet *Sovereign* Republics – 'Socialist' had been dropped, but the Russian-language abbreviation, SSSR, remained the same.[2] The draft Treaty had already received the support of Russia, Kazakhstan and Uzbekistan, and most of the other republics seemed likely to join.

With these documents in his pocket, Gorbachev hoped – though with considerable foreboding – that *perestroika* was again under way. He departed on vacation to his sumptuous new summer residence at Foros in the Crimea. He spent much of his leisure time there reading serious books on Russian history. These included Avrekh's study of Stolypin and Robert Tucker's *Stalin: the Road to Power*, the Russian translation of which had been presented to him by the author.[3] His reading must have provided some interesting lessons. We have seen that Gorbachev in a narrow circle spoke favourably of Stolypin (p. 8 above). But Avrekh, contrary to the views fashionable among radical reformers in 1990–1, insisted that Stolypin's reforms had clearly failed and the monarchy was doomed.

Robert Tucker's biography might have been designed to confirm Gorbachev's own view of the past and concept of *perestroika*. Tucker argued that Stalin's personality was the 'decisive trifle' which was responsible for the overturn of the more humane and democratic course being followed by the New Economic Policy in the 1920s.

Both these books were compatible with the pro-NEP and anti-Stalinist view of Soviet history prevalent among Moscow intellectuals in 1988, which Gorbachev had belatedly come to accept in 1989 and 1990, and had then overtaken in the rush towards capitalism.

Meanwhile Raisa Gorbacheva was reading a much bleaker account of Soviet history: Roman Gul's story about Dzerzhinsky, head of the Cheka (the secret police) in the first years after the revolution.[4] Gul's story, written in emigration and first published in Paris in 1935, was republished in New York in 1974, and in Moscow in 1991. It was unambiguously hostile to the Soviet regime.[5] Raisa reflected gloomily 'It is terrible: red terror, white terror. Cruelty gave birth to cruelty'. Even in his Crimean retreat, Gorbachev was confronted with the spectre which was haunting the Soviet Union in 1990 and 1991: the spectre of the overthrow of Communism.

The Gorbachevs' summer reading was rudely interrupted on 18 August. Gorbachev was placed under virtual house arrest, and his powers were assumed by the self-appointed State Committee for the State of Emergency. During its three days of glory, the State Committee and its members made many formal and informal statements about its intentions. All these pronouncements were notable for their almost complete lack of reference to the Soviet past, in contrast to Gorbachev's draft party programme, which included a substantial if banal section on 'The Lessons of History'. The coup leaders did not seek to appeal to the traditions of the October Revolution, or to speak up for the threatened cause of Communism. Their 'Appeal to the Soviet People' referred to the need to 'develop a multi-ownership economy', and even promised to support private enterprise. But it did not even mention Lenin or Marx, and said nothing about socialism, collective ownership or even planning. Its sole reference to the past was an assertion that the ties between the nationalities of the USSR, now being broken asunder by the 'fig-leaf of democracy', had experienced the test of history over many centuries.'[6] These were men without a future, afraid to refer to the revolutionary past in support of their attempt to save a discredited regime.

Yeltsin and his democratic supporters secured an easy victory, and immediately raised high the anti-Communist banner. In Moscow, St Petersburg and many other towns monuments to the heroes of the October Revolution were destroyed, notably the statue of Dzerzhinsky, head of the secret police until his death in 1926, which dominated the Lubyanka square in which KGB headquarters is situated. Many Moscow Metro stations were renamed. And within a few days of the coup, Gavriil Popov, Mayor of Moscow, decreed that the building of the main Lenin Museum, next to Red Square, should be transferred to the Moscow soviet; the Moscow

Duma (town council) was located in this building before the revolution.[7] The Mayor of St Petersburg, Anatolii Sobchak, proposed that Lenin's embalmed body should be removed from the Mausoleum in Red Square and buried next to his mother in St Petersburg.[8]

Within a few days of the defeat of the coup, Yeltsin condemned in a TV broadcast the 'decades of the domination of the Communist regime.'[9] This outright rejection of the whole of Soviet Communism now appeared much more bluntly and frequently in his speeches than before. In support of Gaidar's economic reforms a few months later, he declared that if they failed Russia faced a 'return to the abyss of the last 74 years'.[10]

Yeltsin saw August 1991 as a turning-point in world history. He later wrote:

> I consider that the Twentieth Century finished on 19–21 August 1991 ... the collapse of the August putsch was a global event on a planetary scale.
>
> The Twentieth Century was mainly a century of fear. Humanity had not previously known such nightmares as totalitarianism and fascism, the nightmare of Communism, concentration camps, genocide and the atomic plague.
>
> And in these three days one century finished and another began. Perhaps this assessment will seem too optimistic to some people, but I believe this.[11]

Thus Yeltsin shared the view of the British historian Eric Hobsbawm that the 'short twentieth century' was completed in 1991. But Hobsbawm assessed the century more favourably, holding that this has been an age of human liberation as much as of human suffering.[12]

In their dramatic repudiation of Communism, politicians like Yeltsin underwent the same mental revolution as the majority of Moscow and Leningrad intellectuals. Yeltsin later described his 'agonising' transition from Communist to democrat: 'gradually, gradually, especially when I got into the Politburo [in February 1986], I began to understand that ours was not the way'.[13] Finally, in the autumn of 1989, following the strong Soviet press attacks on him for alleged drunkenness and disloyalty during his visit to the United States, 'I changed my point of view, understanding that I was a Communist by historical Soviet tradition, by inertia and by up-bringing, and not by conviction'.[14]

In such sweeping changes of outlook, contemporary experience of So-viet politics and economics was no doubt more important than rethinking about the Soviet past. The reformers were infuriated by the stubborn re-sistance to change of most party and KGB officials. They were persuaded by the failure of Gorbachev's economic policy that mere modifications to the existing system would not work. They accepted the naïve view that prosperity would follow almost immediately after the switch to a capitalist market economy. At the same time the collapse of Communism throughout Eastern Europe at the end of 1989 showed that the old regime could easily be overthrown.

But the rethinking of history also played its part. Yeltsin has described how in 1989–91 he was strongly influenced by the group of deputies who surrounded him in the Supreme Soviet, including Academician Sakharov and Yurii Afanas'ev. Long before the August 1991 coup Afanas'ev had been transformed from a Young Communist League official and scourge of French social historians of the Annales school into an uncompromising anti-Communist (see p. 11 above). By 1990, if not before, he had already come to the view which he reiterated on the 74th anniversary of the October Revolution in November 1991: the revolution had 'a wholly negative influence on the fate of Russia and the rest of the world'.[15]

The grim facts about the Soviet past which filled the press in 1988–91 destroyed for ever many long-held assumptions. Every Soviet citizen already knew something about past repressions; but most did not appreciate their pervasiveness and scale (see Chapter 13). And many people learned previously unknown details about how the repressions had affected their own family. Yeltsin himself described the traumatic effect of reading KGB-file no. 5644. These yellowing documents reported that his father went to work on a building site after his family was expelled from their land as rich peasants ('dekulakised') in 1930; then in 1934 he was sentenced to three years in a labour camp for 'anti-Soviet agitation'. Yeltsin tells us that 'my father never spoke to me about this; he crossed this piece of his life out of his memory.'[16]

There is a striking parallel between the abrupt changes in world outlook in 1989–91 and the conversion of many Russians to Communism after the October Revolution. At the end of the Civil War, Korolenko, a prominent revolutionary writer, himself disillusioned with Bolshevism, summarised the outlook of his compatriots in a letter to the People's Commissar for Education:

> In just two or three years a kind of logical screw has suddenly been turned in millions of heads. From blind devotion to the autocracy and complete indifference to politics our people have instantaneously gone over – to Communism, or at least to the Communist government.[17]

Many of the heterogeneous group surrounding Yeltsin in 1991 were converts of this kind, including his former associates when he was party secretary in Sverdlovsk. Burbulis, perhaps the most zealous advocate of the new cause, had been a professional exponent of Marxist–Leninist ideology in Sverdlovsk. Other influential converts came from the Moscow Higher Party School, whose rector, Shostakovskii, played a prominent role in the democratic opposition at the XXVIII Party Congress (see p. 23 above). In September 1991, Kuleshov, a prominent member of this group, explained to me that the strength of world Communism in the past 70 years had all been the fault of the English: they should have brought Soviet Communism to an abrupt end in 1919 by giving strong military support to the White armies. Only four years before, Kuleshov had published a revised version of his doctoral dissertation, entitled *Great October and the Triumph of the Leninist National Programme of the Party.*[18]

Such turns of the 'logical screw' were usually quite sincere in the stormy years before the August coup, when new ideas and unknown terrible facts about the past were destroying long-held prejudices. But now – for a time, and in certain important institutions – anti-Communism had become a new orthodoxy, adherence to which was a condition for prestige and publication. Vladimir Buldakov, a leading independent-minded historian of the revolution, commented in 1992:

> If earlier it was impossible to refer, for example, to Trotsky or speak positively about Milyukov [the liberal Constitutional-Democrat Leader of 1905–17], now the editors firmly cross out citations from Lenin from manuscripts and demand unhesitating praise of Stolypin. To simplify, what was earlier treated as 'White' is now declared 'Black'. No liberalisation in the sphere of ideas has yet taken place.[19]

New converts and long-established dissidents vied with each other in condemnation of the Soviet past. A letter signed by fifteen prominent intellectuals, including Academician Likhachev and Zalygin, the editor of *Novyi mir*, attacked 'the ideologists of Leninism from Bukharin to Emel'yan Yaroslavsky', and even claimed that 'the 1920s were years which were perhaps more terrible for the human spirit than the 1930s'.[20]

Many of the more extreme Russian nationalists had previously been ambiguous in their attitude to the Soviet past, realising that Lenin, Stalin and their successors had established a powerful Russian state. Now they joined in the almost universal condemnation of the October Revolution. Viktor Astaf'ev, outstanding novelist of the second world war, nationalist and anti-semite, declared that the second world war would not have taken place if no October Revolution had occurred. Without the October Revolution:

Russia would now have occupied a leading position in the world . . . In
a moral and economic respect, and in the sphere of culture, the Nineteenth
Century gave such an impulse that things would only have gone forward.
And we all at once descended from such heights and hurled ourselves
into a pit.[21]

Zhirinovsky, who sprang to fame as an unsuccessful Russian presidential
candidate with a respectable vote in the June 1991 elections (see p. 32),
condemned the October Revolution as a 'tragic mistake', the consequence
of Lenin's fanaticism.[22]

On the other wing of the political spectrum, Gorbachev's former close
associate, Aleksandr Yakovlev, already hostile to Marxism and the Soviet
system behind the scenes (see pp. 7–8 above), frankly declared a few days
before the August coup:

> I come more and more to the view that our trouble is the result of the
> dogmas of Marxism. What Marxism postulated, Stalin carried out in a
> distorted fashion. But he did carry it out.

Criticising Marxism for its attitude to the peasantry and its emphasis on
class struggle and the role of force, he explained that 'I came more and
more to reject Marxism as a guide to action, to recognise the defeat of
socialism', and described Stalinism as 'the child of Marxism, the logical
continuation of Marxism, and one part of it'.[23]

Following the coup, Yakovlev, who like many other prominent Communist intellectuals had never sympathised with workers' democracy, and
still less with socialist notions of equality, even more bluntly asserted that
'Marxism led us to the abyss, to the loss of conscience and morality, and
the restoration of hierarchical values will save us' (my italics – RWD).[24]
Another of Gorbachev's former allies, Stanislas Shatalin, one of the authors of the 500 days programme, criticised the Mensheviks as well as the
Bolsheviks for their lack of democratic traditions.[25]

In the first few months after the coup, the hostility to the Soviet past
voiced in the press knew few bounds. In the former party journal
Kommunist, now renamed *Free Thought*, the head of the Independent
Service for the Study of Social Opinion condemned the Soviet Union as
'a *totalitarian society* . . . a special civilisation which has never had and
does not have any analogues on the European and American continents'
(not even, apparently, Nazi Germany):

> In a couple of words this was a society of the absurd, the basis of the
> existence of which was not the production but the distribution of goods,

or (in that part of existence which nevertheless concerned production) not the production of the means of life, but of the means of its physical extermination. This was a monster-society, tirelessly fattening itself on depriving the national home of a countless number of its children.[26]

These were mild strictures compared with those of another prominent publicist, V. Topolyansky. He cited the example of Nikolai Ezhov, 'the Russian Marat', notorious head of the NKVD during the Great Purge, to demonstrate that the Bolsheviks were 'inborn instinctive criminals'. According to Topolyansky, their 'robber-brigand psyche' meant that like children or animals 'their main feature, their fundamental characteristic, is their thirst for destruction, their anti-social attitude'.[27]

The post-coup period also saw a swing towards the rehabilitation of the monarchy. Yeltsin tactfully adopted as the flag of the Russian Federation the red, white and blue flag used both by the Provisional Government after June 1917, and by the White armies during the Civil War. It now became fashionable to dismiss not only Lenin's road to socialism via NEP but also Kerensky's road to parliamentary democracy via the Constituent Assembly. One writer even defended not only Stolypin's agrarian reform but also his use of coercion to repress peasant disturbances. When peasants seized the land and burnt down the manor houses after 1905 this was a 'pogrom', 'blind coercion by the crowd'. The redistribution of the land of the nobles among the peasants was less than one step away from the seizure of peasant land during dekulakisation. ' "Black" redivision of the land of the nobles', he claimed, was the equivalent of the ' "red" redivision of kulak land'.[28]

This rosy view of late Tsarism was popularised in Govorukhin's film *The Russia We Have Lost*, which was widely shown in 1992. The film 'depicts Lenin as an amoral demagogue and the last years of pre-revolutionary Russia as a period of unprecedented economic growth and idyllic well-being which were tragically arrested;'[29] it shows 'happy snaps of the last Tsar and his family on their country estates and old newsreels of eager peasants and workers busily toiling in fields and factories or building railways across a country bursting with the energy of early capitalism'.[30]

This was not the only film in praise of Tsarism shown on TV at this time. As one historian put it, 'episodes from the life of the Russian Tsars appear in the press and on radio which in style and spirit are indistinguishable from the stories about how Grandpa Lenin stroked children on the head and gave them sweets'.[31]

The media were flooded with features exposing the Soviet past. On the occasion of the 50th Anniversary of the Battle of Stalingrad in the autumn of 1992, a seven-part documentary on Stalin prepared in conjunction with an American TV company was entitled 'Monster: a Portrait of Stalin in Blood'. The blurb flatly declared that 'Neither Chingis Khan nor Hitler can be compared with him for cruelty and breaking their word.'

Many symbols of Communism were removed during the first year after the coup. More Metro stations were renamed. As new notes were issued, Lenin's image was removed from them, starting with the 1000 ruble note in March 1992. The Lenin Library was renamed the Library of the Russian Republic (though everyone still called it 'Leninka').

The newly-opened archives played a significant role in the anti-Communist campaign. Well-publicised press conferences, sometimes attended by senior officials from the archives, were accompanied by the release of damning material to friendly newspapers and journalists. Much of this material was released by the Russian authorities in defence of the ban on the Communist Party, against which some Supreme Soviet deputies had appealed to the Constitutional Court. Copies of these archival documents have been placed in a special collection of which a catalogue has been published.

The campaign covered the whole period from the October Revolution to August 1991, and was directed particularly against Lenin and Gorbachev. I have a record of more than a dozen mini-campaigns in which previously secret archival documents were used to discredit the role of the Communist Party throughout the 74 years of Soviet history. Here are some well-publicised examples:

On Lenin

In the edition of Lenin's *Collected Works* published before *perestroika*, an apparently innocuous sentence in a letter to Trotsky dated 22 October 1919, reads as follows:

> Should we not mobilise another 20 000 Petrograd workers and obtain a
> mass attack on Yudenich [the White Army commander]?

But the editors of the *Collected Works* spared us a chilling phrase which appears in the original letter in the archives:

> Should we not mobilise another 20 000 Petrograd workers, *plus about
> 10 000 bourgeois, put machineguns behind them, shoot a few hundred,*
> and obtain a mass attack on Yudenich?[32]

On Stalin

Numerous documents published in 1992 showed the direct responsibility of Stalin and the Politburo – and hence of the Communist Party – for the Great Purge of 1937–8 and later repressions (see Chapter 12). The archives also revealed that Stalin personally, together with the Politburo, was responsible for the execution of the Polish officers at Katyn' and elsewhere. Nearly all Western historians who wrote about these murders concluded that the Soviet Union and not Nazi Germany was responsible for them. But it was often suggested that they were carried out by the NKVD through some kind of misunderstanding of Stalin's orders, or that the NKVD had executed the officers not in 1940 but in 1941 during the panic of the retreat after the German invasion.[33] In fact it was the Politburo which, on 5 March 1940, on a proposal from Beria, head of the secret police, decided that they should be executed without trial, and without any charges being presented. The Politburo minute was signed by Stalin as Secretary of the central committee.[34]

The publication of this further material about Katyn' from the archives was designed to discredit Gorbachev rather than Stalin. The assistants to Yeltsin who presented the documents to the Constitutional Court claimed that as early as 1989 Gorbachev had seen the Politburo decision of March 1940 and had concealed it. This charge was repeated by Yeltsin on Russian TV. A Western historian pointed out that 'the entries on the usage list do not, however, bear any indication that Gorbachev saw it before December 1991'.[35] But Boldin, head of the general department of the central committee under Gorbachev, and later a supporter of the August 1991 coup, claims in his memoirs that Gorbachev obtained from him the two sealed envelopes from the top-secret archives which contained the Politburo documents about Katyn'. He unsealed them, read the contents, resealed them and handed them to Boldin telling him not to show them to anyone without his permission – 'it's all too hot'.[36] It does seem unlikely that Gorbachev resisted the temptation to look inside the sealed envelopes; but Gorbachev insists that this was the case. Perhaps I judge this with an historian's prejudices.

The Katyn' case was one of a series of episodes in which the Presidential side at the Constitutional Court attempted to demonstrate that Gorbachev as General Secretary of the party was no better than his predecessors. Yeltsin's information chief Poltoranin assured the Italian Communist Party newspaper *L'Unità* that 'today we can bury Gorbachev with one blow', and denounced the Gorbachev Foundation as 'a second Zurich' (Lenin lived in Zurich during the first world war) and 'a Bolshevik center'.[37]

The Soviet Party and Foreign Communist Parties

A great deal of material was published to show that state money was secretly squandered on financing foreign Communist Parties. The archives have certainly revealed some astonishing facts – for instance that the American party was the most generously financed. Between 1971 and 1990 Gus Hall received $40 million on behalf of the CPUSA while the French party received only $34 million.[38]

The publicity for such material was often carefully timed, if inept. When the then South African President de Klerk visited Moscow in June 1992, *Izvestiya* published documents from the archives which sought to discredit the ANC. The documents purported to reveal that the South African Communist Party with which the ANC was closely associated had been a 'fifth column controlled by Moscow ever since the 1920s'.[39] In fact the documents showed that the South African party was split into factions in the early 1930s, and that Moscow failed to reconcile them.

The case before the Constitutional Court about the ban on the party was concluded in November 1992. The court ruled that the ban on the ruling bodies of the party was justified, but that Yeltsin had acted unconstitutionally in banning its local branches. The main successor to the old party, headed by Zyuganov, soon emerged with an elaborate structure of local branches, but without its vast Moscow headquarters on Staraya Ploshchad' or its archives. The historical documents presented to the Constitutional Court were largely irrelevant to the case for upholding the ban on the Communist Party – the court had ruled quite early on in its proceedings that it had authority to deal with Communist Party activities only for the period after March 1990. But the publication of this material in the press played an important part in spreading further disillusionment about the past. The practice of releasing selective sensational material from the archives has continued until the present.

In the first year after the coup, the new orthodoxy about the Soviet past overwhelmingly predominated. But not completely. With the abolition of censorship in August 1990, the Soviet Union had become a free country. Lack of money and power greatly hampered freedom of publication, as in Western democratic countries. But there was little or no administrative restriction on freedom of expression, and some bold spirits continued to advocate unorthodox views. The Communist Party was banned; but new Communist Parties were soon established. *Pravda* and some other newspapers were closed down after 23 August 1991, but, following protests from journalists and others, they resumed publication on 31 August. For the time being *Pravda* dropped the picture of Lenin on its banner-heading, but its title continued to proclaim, and in a larger font than before, that 'The newspaper was founded on 5 May 1912, on the initiative of V. I. Lenin.'

Gorbachev – to his own great political disadvantage – continued to proclaim his adherence to a kind of socialism, and, for a short time, to retain a vestigial faith in the Communist Party. In his press conference held on the day after his return to Moscow, he even spoke hopefully of the possibility of regenerating the party. He characterised October 1917 as a 'genuinely popular revolution'. While defining socialism rather vaguely, he commended the 'Leninist principle that socialism is the living creativity of the masses'.[40]

A minority of intellectuals determinedly held aloft the banner of democratic socialism. On 13 September 1991, four signatories to a letter to *Pravda* called for the 'formation of a democratic party of socialist orientation'. They included Academician Volobuev and Viktor Danilov, the historians who had unsuccessfully tried to reply to Tsipko's criticism of Marxism in 1988–9 (see pp. 7–8 above).[41] In the introduction to their letter, the authors gently pointed out that they had devoted many decades of their lives to the Communist Party, but 'its bureaucracy did not treat us kindly'. In the body of the letter, they insisted that 'the idea of socialism will continue as long as there is a basis for social and economic inequality, as long as the exploitation of man by man continues,' and defended the October Revolution:

> Knowing history we dare to affirm: the October Revolution was an expression of the age-old striving of the mass of the people for social justice and freedom; it was an attempt to pull the country out of the profound crisis of Russian society. October welded together the idea of socialism and the historical fate of our multi-national country.

And Govorukhin's cheerful view of Tsarism did not go entirely unchallenged. In 1992 a four-part television series on Stolypin, based on Avrekh's critical assessment, was entitled 'The Reform Based on Blood'.[42]

Within a year of the defeat of the August coup, many of those who vehemently opposed the break-up of the Soviet Union had come together in the sinister 'Red–Brown alliance'. In the autumn of 1992 former Communists joined with the nationalists Prokhanov, Sterligov and the notorious anti-semite Shafarevich to form the National Salvation Front (NSF).[43] The stage at the initial meeting of the NSF was decorated with two flags in juxtaposition: the red flag of the Soviet Union with its hammer and sickle and the black and gold flag of the Tsarist Empire with its double-headed eagle.[44]

Before the end of 1992, the Russian authorities began to handle the images of the old regime with some discretion. The process of renaming slowed down. In spite of Popov's decree of August 1991, the Lenin Museum remained in its old building (see, however, p. 59 below), and Lenin remained in his Mausoleum.

In spite of the revelations and the propaganda about Lenin, he did not entirely lose his popularity. In April 1992, an opinion poll among Muscovites revealed that 47 per cent held a positive opinion about Lenin, 22 per cent were indifferent, and only 22 per cent held a negative opinion.[45] But Lenin's popularity had certainly declined. In a nationwide opinion poll in February 1993, only 15 per cent named Lenin as 'Russia's greatest politician', as compared with 44 per cent for Peter the Great – six per cent voted for Stalin, three per cent for Stolypin and only two per cent for Gorbachev.[46]

5 The Mental Revolution after the First Decade

In January 1992 the liberal economist Gaidar launched his major attempt to dismantle the old economic system and replace it by a free-market economy. It resulted in a huge increase in prices, a continuing inflation, and the impoverishment of many Russian citizens. The velvet revolutionaries of 1991, like the Bolshevik revolutionaries of 1917, proved quite unable to honour their pre-revolutionary promises.

Most Russian citizens, increasingly disillusioned about the economic reforms, soon became cynical about the new generation of politicians. The poet and critic Yevtushenko aptly summed up a popular view: 'too many good people today are in a state of depression and too many bad people are flourishing.'[1] Cultural facilities precipitately deteriorated. Most people, apathetic and in dire financial straits, no longer found the money to buy or the energy to read the publications in which the revelations about the past had appeared. The table in Appendix 1 shows that the rapid increase in the sale of quality newspapers and serious journals in 1988–90 was followed by an even steeper decline in 1991–5.

The impression conveyed by the table is a little too bleak. After 1991 many new newspapers and journals appeared, and prominently featured material about the past (for example *Nezavisimaya gazeta* and *Rossiiskaya gazeta*). And newspapers of every point of view – from the liberal-democratic *Izvestiya* to the Communist and nationalist *Pravda* and *Zavtra* – continued to publish far more articles about the past than their British or American equivalents. It is true that sex and religion dominated the bookstalls. But important new books on history, although in much smaller print runs than before, continued to appear, and to be read. A survey of young people's reading in Moscow found that the four most popular books in 1993 were Bulgakov's *Master and Margarita*, Solzhenitsyn's *Gulag Archipelago*, the Bible and Tolstoy's *War and Peace* – all of which might be described as works about history . . .

In an enquiry into popular knowledge of and interest in history in the United States, Britain and Russia, the Russians would undoubtedly score the highest marks.

1993, 1994, 1995 and 1996 were years of unresolved deadlock between President and parliament. In a referendum on 25 April 1993, 54 per cent of those who voted supported 'the social policies since 1992' of Yeltsin and his government. This result provided the moral justification for Yeltsin's decree in September 1993 dissolving the Supreme Soviet. The Supreme Soviet was located in the White House, from which Yeltsin had organised the defeat of the August coup two years before. On 4 October, by an irony of history, Yeltsin's tanks and troops enforced the dissolution decree by storming the White House.

No-one anticipated the eventual outcome. The December 1993 elections to the new Duma (parliament) resulted in renewed deadlock. Gaidar's party, 'Russia's Choice', received only 15.4 per cent of the votes in the section of the Duma elected by party lists; the three parties favouring a more leisurely route to capitalism received between them a further 20.7 per cent, a total of 36 per cent. The three left-wing parties (left-wing in the sense of more critical of capitalism) – the Communist Party of the Russian Federation headed by Zyuganov, the Agrarian Party, and 'Women of Russia' – received between them 28.4 per cent. The most sinister and unexpected result was that Zhirinovsky's right-wing nationalist so-called 'Liberal-Democratic' Party received 22.8 per cent of the votes in the party-list section of the Duma, more than any other party.

The supporters of Yeltsin and the free market were in a minority, and the struggle between President and parliament continued. The new situation profoundly influenced the attitudes and propaganda of many politicians and publicists, and their view of the past.

Several trends may be distinguished. The free-market democrats continued the anti-Communist campaign of 1991–2 before, during and after the December 1993 elections. The tenuous anti-Yeltsin 'Red–Brown' alliance of influential Communists and nationalists failed to find a common language about the past, and collapsed after the December 1993 elections. But Communists as well as nationalists sought support through demagogic appeals to patriotism and even chauvinism. In the course of 1993–5 many politicians and publicists who had previously unreservedly rejected the whole Soviet past began to take a more measured approach to the 74 years of Communist rule – influenced partly by their discovery that free-market capitalism was no Utopia, partly by an expedient need to accommodate to public attitudes. Yeltsin was by no means exempt from this trend.

THE RENEWED ANTI-COMMUNIST CAMPAIGN

The Inheritance from Tsarism

The free-market democrats were not united in their view of the pre-revolutionary past. Almost all of them sympathised with Stolypin's economic programme. But some of them went much further. A deputy to the Duma, Valerii Batkin, in an emotional article entitled 'Communism is the Fascism of the Poor', described at length the tremendous and consistent successes which the last Tsar, Nicholas II, had achieved in popular education as well as in economic development.[2] The Tsarist regime received much favourable publicity. In June 1993 the reign of Nicholas II was the subject of a lavish exhibition organised by GARF, the State Archive of the Russian Federation, in the Manezh Hall – the former Imperial stables – in the centre of Moscow.

Writers hostile to the Tsarist regime attacked it with equal vigour. Batkin was criticised for ignoring its continued backwardness, exemplified in the huge 'tax on drunkenness' (the excise on vodka), and for saying nothing about the very high rate of illiteracy.[3] A long article took the example of the Beilis case of 1911–13 to illustrate the reactionary nature of Tsarism. Beilis was a Jew who was accused of ritual murder, and eventually found innocent by a jury. The author claimed that the case was trumped up by the Minister of the Interior, Shcheglovitov, who had demonstrated his anti-semitism by submitting no fewer than 325 petitions to the Tsar to secure the release of participants in pogroms. Four newspaper editors were arrested and 22 editions of newspapers confiscated in an attempt to silence those who questioned Beilis' guilt. Such was the Tsarist regime.[4]

An intermediate position was taken by Eduard Radzinski, the author of a popular biography of Nicholas II. He argued that Witte, Nicholas and Stolypin between them had saved Russia by establishing a dynamic economy; but the Court, including Nicholas, had delayed political change at a time when the people thirsted for freedom. 'It is clear,' Radzinski concluded, 'that Vladimir Ilich [Lenin] did not import revolution in his sealed railway coach'. But Nicholas had ultimately triumphed over Lenin. At the time of his death he had been popularly regarded as 'Nicholas the Bloody', while Stalin at the time of his death was seen as 'father and teacher'. This had now all changed:

> Suddenly today in front of our eyes both Stalin and his teacher Ul'yanov [Lenin] are turning into monsters in people's eyes while Nicholas is returning, and is becoming one of the most popular figures in the Russian historical pantheon. In the last resort what really mattered was that he was a good man and not that he was a bad politician.[5]

Many articles appeared in the general and the business press on Stolypin's economic policy, and on the operation of the banks and the stock exchange on the eve of the first world war. An unpublished representative bibliography prepared by Nicholas Baron lists books and articles published on this subject: 1989: 0; 1990: 4; 1991: 10; 1992: 16; 1993: 9.

Most free-market democrats did not support the view that Tsarism was firmly on the road to a modern civilised society. They argued that, while Stolypin had the right economic policy, it was the Provisional Government of 1917 which set Russia on the road to democracy. Dmitrii Volkogonov appealed for support for Yeltsin in these terms in April 1993:

> Russia is trying to move onto a democratic and civilised path for the second time in the Twentieth Century. The first time was in February 1917. Then the weak inexperienced Russian democracy lost to the Bolsheviks . . .
>
> Now, 75 years later, Russia has another chance to become a civilised democratic society.[6]

At this time parallels were frequently drawn in the press between the dual power of soviets and Provisional Government in 1917 and the relationship between the Supreme Soviet and the President in 1993; the free-market democrats emphasised the danger that the Supreme Soviet would repeat the success of the 1917 soviets.

Yeltsin took the same line in an interview which took place between the storming of the White House in October and the elections to the Duma in December 1993:

> If you are looking for historical parallels, I would compare the present time with the period in which the Provisional Government was in power, especially after June 1917. In spite of all its mistakes and faults it sought to establish a democratic republic in Russia. Then the Bolsheviks prevented this and led the country into a bloody Civil War. Now, 76 years later, the Russian people has the first real possibility of a free choice of the way forward.

By this time Yeltsin did not share the socialist views held by most members of the Provisional Government after June 1917. He bluntly stated that 'we have said farewell to the illusion of giving socialism a human face'.[7]

Lenin and Leninism

The thrust of popular historical writing continued to be directed unremittingly against Lenin. Every phase of his career was condemned. One author presented evidence that Lenin had been unsuccessful as a defence lawyer as a young man in the early 1890s. She went on to suggest (without evidence) that his failure to win cases brought against peasant thieves might explain his contemptuous attitude both towards legal justice and towards peasants' proclivities to petty theft.[8] Dozens of articles appeared about Lenin's ruthless cruelty and arbitrariness during the Civil War, in matters large and small.[9]

In 1988 the Lenin of the early 1920s had been presented, with the support of new archival evidence, as a progressive reforming figure who quarrelled bitterly with Stalin's Great-Russian chauvinism and high-handedness. But in 1993 readers were confronted with another Lenin: Lenin the friend and admirer of Stalin throughout 1922.[10]

Both the 1988 Lenin and the 1993–5 Lenin were firmly based on fact. But in each case evidence unfavourable to the author's point of view was ignored. Each Lenin was constructed for a political purpose, and the resulting portrait was profoundly untrue. Anatolii Latyshev, once a prolific writer in favour of Lenin, now an even more prolific anti-Leninist, frankly argued that it was not possible to be objective about Lenin:

> For us the time of calm scholarly discussion about him has not yet come. Those who justify him and exalt him are not seeking truth but a symbol for a banner with which again to go into battle for power.[11]

One aspect of Lenin's biography received much attention at this time: his ancestors. Back in 1938 Marietta Shaginyan wrote a novel about Lenin and his family which revealed that one of his father's ancestors was a Kalmyk; Shaginyan's indiscretion aroused Stalin's wrath, and on 5 August 1938, the Politburo condemned the novel.[12] An even more deeply-held secret was that one of Lenin's maternal great-grandfathers, Aleksandr Dmitrievich Blank, was Jewish (Aleksandr's father Dmitri changed his first name from Abel' when he converted to Christianity). Lenin's sister Anna discovered this fact about her family in the police files. In 1932 she proposed to Stalin that this information should be published to assist the struggle against anti-semitism. Stalin told her that 'the present moment is not the time', and ordered her 'to maintain absolute silence about it'.

Thirty years later, in the mid-1960s, diligent investigators, including Shaginyan, rediscovered Lenin's Jewish ancestors. But the party again decided that this was not the time for publication. All the relevant archival papers were transferred to the Institute of Marxism–Leninism, where they were concealed until after the defeat of the August 1991 coup.

One of the virtues of Yeltsin and his supporters, and of the Russian democratic intelligentsia generally, is that they have no taint of anti-semitism. So, unlike the right-wing Russian nationalists, they did not attack Lenin for his Jewish origin. Instead, they convincingly berated Stalin and his successors for their lack of honesty.[13]

The climax of the anti-Leninist campaign was the publication in 1994 of Volkogonov's two-volume biography of Lenin. As late as May 1987

Volkogonov's public image was that of a hard-line conservative: as deputy head of the Political Administration of the army he viciously attacked Soviet writers for their lack of patriotism. But in the course of the next twelve months he began to criticise Stalin and his system with increasing vehemence. At this time he argued that Stalin had destroyed the democratic potential of the Lenin period.[14] His four-volume biography of Stalin, published towards the end of 1989, was also consistent with the view that Stalin had betrayed Lenin's progressive socialist policies at the end of the 1920s.[15]

But Volkogonov's biography of Lenin is uncompromisingly hostile to Lenin and his politics. It is extremely one-sided; thus it largely ignores Lenin's reformist activities during his 'last struggle'. Stalin is treated not as the betrayer of Lenin but his natural successor.[16] 'Stalin', Volkogonov wrote, 'was a most faithful Leninist, carrying out Leninist behests as faithfully as possible'.[17]

Lenin's image in Russian theatre and TV has also been recast. Shatrov's play *Onward . . . Onward . . . Onward!*, a major sensation in 1987, portrayed the later Lenin as a valiant supporter of democracy against Stalin.[18] Seven years later in 1994 Alfred Schnittke's satirical opera *Life with an Idiot* presented Lenin as a red-headed lunatic who destroyed the library of the dissident hero, spread excrement on his walls, and decapitated his wife with a large pair of secateurs.[19]

Stalin's Successors

The anti-Communist campaign also impugned the successors to Lenin and Stalin. After the August 1991 coup the archives were used to censure Gorbachev. In 1994 the heat was turned on Khrushchev. Some free-market democrats endeavoured to topple him from the pedestal on which he had been installed as a democratic hero by the 'people of the 1960s' (*shestidesyatniki*), for whom 1956–64 was a golden age of freedom. His denigrators claimed that in Stalin's day he was one of the worst oppressors. Thus Khrushchev, not Malenkov, had been responsible for the Leningrad affair in 1949–50, which had led to the execution of Voznesensky, the head of the State Planning Commission Gosplan.[20]

But influential free-market democrats still supported Khrushchev. The older generation were nostalgic about the days of their youth, even those who had lost all sympathy for socialism or even for Social Democracy. In April 1994 a conference in Moscow commemorated the centenary of Khrushchev's birth. Its verdict was on the whole favourable. A Russian historian who was present wrote:

Those whose voices were louder than others at the Moscow conferences were intellectuals who recalled the spirit of the 'thaw', former Gulag denizens who gained their freedom under Khrushchev, people who worked with Khrushchev, and members of his family and their children.[21]

(It is worth adding that in contrast very few 'people who worked with' Stalin spoke up for him on the centenary of his birth, and I imagine that Brezhnev will share the same fate.)

Communism, Fascism and the Second World War

The claim that Communism was no better than Fascism, often made after August 1991, was frequently repeated during the election campaign in the autumn of 1993. Not just the Stalin period was compared with Hitler's Germany, but the whole 74 years of Communism. 'The Fascist and Communist regimes are like twins,' declared a writer in *Izvestiya*, 'Both have grown up out of hatred'.[22] Mark Zakharov, the well-known theatre director who had staged Shatrov's favourable play about Lenin six years before, now declared in a banner headline 'Renunciation of the Leninist Heritage is not Extremism, but Necessity', and ironically attacked those who claimed that the Communist system had positive aspects:

It would be sensible to call on our German friends to recognise publicly at least a few merits of the former Fascist leaders. Hitler was a bold man, an outstanding speaker with a brilliant economic intuition, who quite rapidly led the German working class away from the threat of 'democratic' unemployment and idle chatter. If Hitler had not existed, Germany would not have built first-class roads in record time, substantially influencing the development of transport throughout the world. And Goering! . . . Goering with his R-1s and R-2s was undoubtedly a pioneer of the space era. This should not be forgotten. (Incidentally, Beria's services in creating the Soviet nuclear weapon are also undeniable.)

I therefore want to condemn the German people publicly and impartially for their hasty and sudden dismantling of the sculptural models and portraits of Hitler, Ribbentrop, Himmler, Goering and other outstanding statesmen of the Third Reich.[23]

This was a telling satire on 'balanced' views of Stalinism. But there is one obvious awkwardness about the attempt to equate the Soviet and Nazi regimes – quite apart from the immense contrast between the Soviet ideology of racial and sexual equality and political democracy (albeit unrealised) and the Nazi ideology of the Master Race, the Superman and the inequality of women. Nazi Germany conquered and subordinated the whole of Europe, and physically exterminated Jews, gypsies and many Slavs. Stalin's Soviet Union opportunistically seized former territories of the Tsarist Empire, and established the inhuman Gulag system. But it was not the aggressor against Nazi Germany and fascist Italy but the victim of aggression; and Soviet resistance was the major factor in the destruction of Nazism and the restoration of democracy in Europe.

Hitler himself realised that Nazi aggression seemed rather uncivilised to many people outside and inside Germany; he therefore always sought to present Nazi acts of aggression as preventive responses to the aggression planned by his opponents. Such excuses were used to justify in turn the invasion of Austria, Czechoslovakia, Poland and the Soviet Union. In the mid-1980s some Right-wing German 'revisionist' historians, including Topitsch and Hoffman, resuscitated the dubious thesis that the German invasion of the Soviet Union was a preventive strike against Stalin's planned attack.

In 1992 and 1993 the discussion burst out in post-coup Russia with the publication of two books by the Russian émigré former intelligence officer Viktor Suvorov – *Ice-Breaker* and *Day-M*.[24] According to Suvorov, Stalin saw German Fascism as the 'ice-breaker' which, by launching war in Europe, would clear the way for the victory of Communism. Day-M – 13 June 1941, 'one of the most important dates in world history' – was the date on which Stalin allegedly started to mobilise his troops in preparation for the invasion of Poland 19 days later on M+19, 6 July. Suvorov claims that this plan was frustrated by Hitler's preventive invasion on 22 June 1941.

Suvorov's books were very widely circulated in Russia. The print-run of *Ice-Breaker* was 320 000,[25] and *Day-M*, in addition to its large circulation in book form, was serialised in *Nezavisimaya gazeta* in six full-page spreads during the election campaign of 1993.[26] They played an important political role in supporting the thesis that Soviet Communism was as bad as Hitler's Fascism – and that Stalin's regime was distinctly worse.

In the autumn of 1993 a leading historical journal, *Otechestvennaya istoriya*, rather surprisingly gave support to the thesis that Hitler's attack on the Soviet Union was preventive in character. It published an article by the German revisionist historian Joachim Hoffman, provocatively entitled 'The Preparation of the Soviet Union for an Offensive War, 1941'.[27] Hoffman argued – on the slightest of evidence – that Stalin had sought to unleash war in Europe in 1939 and that Hitler's attack in 1941 'anticipated Stalin's attack' on Germany.

Two years previously a Russian historian, M. I. Mel'tyukhov, had published an informative article which demonstrated that in June 1941 Soviet weapons were more numerous and possibly of better quality than was previously believed.[28] This appeared to add some credence to the Suvorov–Hoffman thesis. Following the publication of Hoffman's article Mel'tyukhov submitted an article to *Otechestvennaya istoriya* which purported to sum up the Suvorov discussion. Mel'tyukhov argued that Hitler and Stalin both independently planned to invade each other's territory. Both their intentions were aggressive.

Mel'tyukhov's article aroused a storm on the editorial board of *Otechestvennaya istoriya*. The editors approved its publication by majority vote, but they also took the very unusual step of publishing a verbatim account of their discussion. Publication was supported, among others, by A. N. Sakharov (who later became Director of the Institute of Russian History) and by Academician Yu. Kukushkin, principal author of the notorious orthodox pre-*perestroika* school textbook on Soviet history, who had evidently undergone a fundamental change of heart.[29]

This was an odd episode. I do not agree with Mel'tyukhov's conclusions, but as a discussion document his article deserved publication. *Otechestvennaya istoriya* should, however, have been thoroughly ashamed of publishing Hoffman's article, in which the evidence is quite inadequate to sustain the argument.

The view that Stalin was intending to attack Germany in 1941 was supported by another historian, V. A. Nevezhin, who published a repetitive series of articles in a variety of journals arguing that Soviet propaganda before June 1941 had emphasised the expansionist objectives of the regime.[30]

Many Soviet documents on this issue have been published, including Stalin's speech to Red Army graduates of 5 May 1941, and the strategic plan drawn up by Timoshenko and Zhukov in the same month.[31] So have the main German documents for 'Plan Barbarossa', prepared at the end of 1940.[32] My own view is that the new literature provides no serious evidence for revising the long-established view: Hitler had long planned to invade the USSR; Stalin mistakenly believed he could postpone the invasion until the Soviet Union was ready; Soviet military doctrine was based on the assumption that any invasion would be met immediately by a Soviet counter-attack on enemy territory, and its unjustified optimism greatly hindered Soviet defence.

Unfortunately no Russian historian has yet published a detailed refutation of Suvorov. But fortunately this task was undertaken by an Israeli historian, Gabriel Gorodetsky, whose book published in Russian was one of the major Moscow historical sensations of 1995.[33]

A bizarre further twist to the story was provided by the competent but misguided Mel'tyukhov. In an article published in mid-1995 he held to his view that Stalin was preparing to invade German-occupied Poland in 1941 (he argued that the invasion was planned for some time after 15 July, as against Suvorov's claim that it was planned for 6 July). In previous publications Mel'tyukhov's main emphasis was that Stalin's 'planned invasion' was not preventive but aggressive in character. But in the new article, perhaps in honour of the 50th anniversary of victory in the second world war, he shifted his ground, and reproved Stalin for not invading German-occupied territory earlier:

> If a blow had been dealt against the enemy from dawn on June 21, 1941, when the German armies had completed their concentration and disposition, this would have caught him in a trap, because he did not have plans for defensive action . . .
> The application of the measures proposed by the Soviet military command on June 13–14, 1941, would have led to the disruption of the German incursion into the USSR and would have facilitated victory in the war. The Red Army could have been in Berlin not later than 1942 . . . Unfortunately Stalin rejected this proposal.[34]

The Autumn 1993 Crisis

Denunciation of the Communist past was particularly vociferous when Yeltsin dissolved the Supreme Soviet in the autumn of 1993, and the Khasbulatov government refused to relinquish the White House. The head of the Mir TV-Radio Company denounced this as 'the last hours of the totalitarian Communist Empire baring its teeth in spite'.[35] Yeltsin accused his opponents of attempting to establish a joint 'Communist-fascist dictatorship': 'the Fascists joined ranks with the Communists . . . in this dark deed'.[36]

The crisis of October 1993 led some influential supporters of Yeltsin to search for favourable authoritarian precedents in Russian and Soviet history. Leonid Nikitinskii, an *Izvestiya* correspondent, admitted that Yeltsin had undertaken a 'coup' (*perevorot*) against the Constitution, but argued that this was 'entirely necessary for the future course of Russian history'. In the former Soviet Union there were 'objective historical tendencies to authoritarianism'. Yeltsin therefore could not objectively renounce the use of force; instead, he must learn from Lenin's example in different circumstances. Nikitinskii was contemptuous about the Communist 'turncoats and double turncoats' who now appealed to the law and the Constitution after their 70 years of contempt for all legality:

Their Lenin laughs at them. History simply mocks at them and says: 'Yeltsin is Lenin Today'.[37]

Yeltsin himself claimed that strong Presidential power was essential in view of the weakness of democracy 'in a country accustomed to Tsars and leaders, in which clear group interests are not yet established'. But to his credit he insisted on grounds of both principle and expediency that the Communists and other opponents of reform must be not be forbidden to participate in the elections unless they could be shown in open court to have engaged in criminal acts:

> If we were to follow this path [of bans], we would be hardly distinguishable from the Bolsheviks, who at first banned and then repressed opposition groups because they did not accept Soviet power...
> Moreover, a ban on the participation of Communists in the pre-election campaign would increase tension in society.[38]

Yeltsin did, however, insist that 'the vestiges of the Communist and Soviet past, the vestiges of Soviet power, can be done away with.'[39] The successful storming of the White House in October 1993 was immediately followed by strenuous efforts to remove the symbols and appurtenances of Soviet Communism. On October 5 the Public Committee of Russian Democratic Organisations called for the banning of all Communist and Fascist symbols and trappings, and the closing of the Lenin Museum and its branches in other towns.[40] Within a few days, the main Lenin Museum in Moscow, which had existed uneasily for the last two years, was finally closed.[41] The traditional 7 November parade was cancelled, and all demonstrations were banned in Moscow. On 7 November several hundred people participated in unsanctioned rallies in Moscow, and 76 were arrested.[42]

Meanwhile attention had turned to Lenin's Mausoleum, the Mecca of Soviet Communism. Guard Post No. 1 was removed from the Mausoleum on 6 October 1993, immediately after the successful storming of the White House. The Mayor of Moscow, Yurii Luzhkov, and Patriarch Aleksii II sent a joint letter to Yeltsin claiming that burial was traditional in Russia. Luzhkov prepared a draft decree for Yeltsin's signature, proposing that Lenin's remains should be removed as early as October 15 for burial in St Petersburg. Luzhkov also proposed that the remains of Soviet politicians and heroes in the Kremlin wall should be reburied in Novodevich'e cemetery or in some other burial place chosen by their relatives. Over 300 people had been buried in the Kremlin wall, including all Politburo members who had not been purged, and also leading personalities such as the American revolutionary John Reed, Krzhizhanovsky (long the head of

Gosplan), the notorious prosecutor Vyshinsky, space hero Gagarin, space scientist Sergei Korolev, atom scientist Kurchatov, and military leaders Zhukov, Konev and others. (Khrushchev, under a cloud until long after his death, was already buried in Novodevich'e.)[43]

Various proposals were made for the future use of the Mausoleum. In a letter to the President a war veteran provocatively suggested that Lenin's 'mummy' should be buried in the ground under the Mausoleum, which should be converted into a Mausoleum to the Victims of Revolution and Red Terror. The glass sarcophagus should henceforth contain ashes from Gulag burial-grounds; and on the wall, under the Russian two-headed eagle, should be displayed an Orthodox Christian cross, an Islamic crescent, the Star of David and a five-pointed star with a hammer and sickle.[44]

October 15 came and went, and the proposed date of Yeltsin's decree was postponed to 20 October. For some time there had been few visitors to the Mausoleum, but in the weekend 16–17 October, 10 000 people queued up.[45] In the outcome Yeltsin failed to sign the decree; the decision was postponed until after the convening of the new parliament.[46]

Instead, he took the more constructive step of approving the two-headed eagle as the official National Emblem of Russia. Yeltsin declared that, while his contemporary models were the dissident physicist Andrei Sakharov and Margaret Thatcher, the historical figure on whom he would model himself was Peter the First. But he rejected the Petrine black eagle on a gold background, the National Emblem from the early Eighteenth Century until October 1917, in favour of the more colourful pre-Petrine gold eagle on a red background.[47] The Emblem retained the crowns, orb and sceptre and St George the dragon-slayer on horseback which were added in pre-Petrine days after the original emblem had been adopted by Ivan III.[48] Some medieval historians viewed the return of the two-headed eagle with alarm. A. L. Khoroshkevich wrote that after its original adoption it 'quickly – as soon as Ivan the Terrible – lost its character as a national emblem and became a symbol of the oppression of the Russian people themselves, and the peoples of Eastern Europe, and later of Central Asia.'[49]

Yeltsin and his entourage, and many local politicians, have made heroic efforts to reconcile their regime with the Orthodox church and to identify it as continuous with the pre-revolutionary past. The huge and rather ugly Church of the Redeemer, built in the mid-nineteenth century to celebrate the defeat of Napoleon, was razed to the ground on Politburo orders in 1931 with the intention of replacing it by the much larger and almost equally ugly Palace of the Soviets. The Palace of the Soviets was never constructed; and in Khrushchev's time an open-air swimming pool was built on the site. The swimming pool has now been removed in its turn;

and, with the support of Yeltsin and the Mayor of Moscow, it is being replaced by an exact replica of the nineteenth-century church, constructed in Soviet-style breakneck speed. It is planned that it should be completed for the 850th Anniversary of the foundation of Moscow in September 1997. One of the sensations of 1993 was the identification of the remains of Tsar Nicholas and his family by British and American scientists, with the help of the Duke of Edinburgh's DNA. Yeltsin, in Brezhnev's time, was responsible as party secretary in Sverdlovsk for the razing to the ground of the house in which the Tsar and his family were executed. The remains are to be reburied with due pomp and appropriate Orthodox rites in St Petersburg. Yeltsin, God willing, will be the principal honoured guest.

INTELLECTUALS AND SOCIAL EQUALITY

With the exception of 'Women of Russia', political parties strongly favouring greater social equality failed in December 1993 to receive the minimum votes required to obtain representation in the Duma. The old political leaders, whether they supported Gorbachev or tried to undermine him, were committed to the state social welfare system. But they strongly opposed all calls for greater equality of incomes, and regarded the measures of 1987–8 which had briefly encouraged workers' democracy as an inexcusable anomaly. In his memoirs published after the August 1991 coup, Ryzhkov, Gorbachev's Prime Minister, and the official Communist opponent of Yeltsin in the June 1991 election of the Russian president, inveighed against 'equalisation' (*uravnilovka*). According to Ryzhkov, while Marx was in favour of people having an equal start in life, he would not have supported the 'general equalisation' favoured by Lenin and Trotsky, or 'the reduction of equalisation to the mere equality of the poor' undertaken by Stalin.[50] This is of course entirely unconvincing, in view of Lenin and Trotsky's caution about 'equalisation' and Stalin's outright hostility to it.

The vast majority of the Soviet intelligentsia shared this opposition to social equality and workers' democracy. All agreed on this: the advocates of a reformed socialism along the lines of NEP; the conservatives who favoured the retention of the old system; the free-market democrats who supported capitalism. V. Iordanskii, criticising this dominant view, claims that Bulgakov's play about a dog turned into a man, 'The Heart of a Dog', was so popular among the intelligentsia during *perestroika* not only because of its trenchant satire on the Bolshevik attempt to create a new kind of human being but also because of its pitiless and high-handed mockery of people who had come up from the 'lower depths' of society.[51]

The 'democrats' attacked Lenin's famous slogan that 'every cook shall learn to govern the state' with particular ferocity. Kozyrev, Minister of Foreign Affairs until the end of 1995, joined in. An anonymous poet in the literary newspaper summed up the whole history of the Soviet state in a lampoon directed against Lenin's cook:

> The cook is buried near the Kremlin –
> Her children now retired.
> Her grandsons snooze at the wheel of state –
> And we to fight them are inspired.[52]

The buzz-word reflecting this hostility to social equality, both before and after 1991, was 'Lumpen' (*lyumpen*, plural *lyumpeny*). According to Marx, the Lumpenproletariat (the 'ragamuffin' proletariat) were 'the scum and offal and detritus of all classes' on whom Louis Napoleon relied for his victory in Paris in 1850–1:

> Side by side with broken-down profligates . . . [and] decayed adventurers who had dropped out of the ranks of the bourgeoisie, there were vagabonds, disbanded soldiers, discharged prisoners, fugitives from the galleys, sharpers, jugglers, professional beggars, pickpockets, conjurors, gamesters, pimps, brothel-keepers, porters, men of letters, organ-grinders, ragpickers, knifegrinders, tinkers.[53]

In the years of *perestroika* and after the term 'Lumpen' was used to refer both to louts and hooligans of all kinds and also to those in the poorer strata of society who wanted to improve the standard of living of their social group, and objected to the wealth and privileges of those who had power over them. In 1990 a Russian historian with whom I am acquainted had a slight quarrel with a young man on a bus, and remarked to me 'you see what we have to put up with from our Lumpens.' The same evening he assured me that people who favoured a currency reform which would reduce the savings of the better-off were 'Lumpens'.

The use of the term was exemplified in November 1993 in an article by Otto Latsis, who like many other leading intellectuals was a Gorbachev supporter who had gone over to Yeltsin:

> The phrase 'earns a lot' has an irresistible influence on a proletarian consciousness of a certain kind: the mass consciousness of the Lumpens and the caste consciousness of the bureaucrat . . .
> We must accept it as a fact: there is a very sensitive aspect of mass consciousness: *social envy*.[54]

Thus the Russian intellectuals' hostility to 'Lumpens' was combined neatly with a Thatcherite contempt for the 'politics of envy'.[55]

Aleksandr Yakovlev condemned the Soviet system and its 'Lumpenisation' in terms not entirely different from British Right-wing Tory and American Republican criticisms of the welfare state:

> If human beings renounce the struggle for existence, and seek to retain the state as a philanthropic institution and a, distribution office, this leads to mass Lumpenisation in all social strata and groups.

> The crisis in society, in industry and agriculture, resulted from a lumpenised ideology; senseless conflicts among the intelligentsia result from the conceit of untalented people at the top; . . . Chernobyl' was the result of the activity of lumpenised engineers and a lumpenised leadership, who had lost the habit of independence . . . The Stalinist model of socialism was also born of a lumpenised understanding of the world.[56]

When the staff of Ostankino TV protested about the sudden secret transfer of Ostankino and its all-important Channel 1 to a new company of doubtful origins, Yakovlev, who was then in charge of Ostankino, described their protest as 'a revolt of the Lumpens'.[57]

Stalin at the end of the war tactlessly referred to the Russian people as the 'little screws' (*vintiki*) on whom the leadership depended.[58] Russian intellectuals after 70 years of Soviet rule blamed the 'lumpen' lower depths of society for the faults of the system and dismissed as lumpens the many ordinary Russians who opposed the drive to the free market. This is perhaps the crucial difference between the Russian intelligentsia today and the democratic and revolutionary intelligentsia before the revolution, who strongly supported greater social equality and spoke up for the underprivileged. Vadim Rogovin, who has defended socialist values throughout *perestroika*, suggests that 'a genuine Communist mentality was destroyed by the flames of Stalinist terror together with several generations of Bolsheviks'.[59] This is not, of course, the whole story. The provision of privileges for the new political élite was well under way during the Civil War, twenty years before the Stalinist terror.

COMMUNIST NATIONALISM

The Communist Party of the Russian Federation (CPRF) hardly deserves to be described as 'left-wing'. It includes the main leaders of the August 1991 coup, and is more concerned with bringing down Yeltsin and his policies than with socialism. Its leaders find it ideologically acceptable and tactically convenient to seek historical precedents in Russian nationalism, and in the powerful industrialised super-state created in the Soviet period, rather than in the socialist spirit of the October Revolution. The future leader of the re-emerging Communist Party, Gennadii Zyuganov, signed the notorious nationalist 'Word to the People' document in July 1991 (see p. 32 above), and in the autumn of 1992 he was one of the founder members of the National Salvation Front (NSF).

After the elections of December 1993 the CPRF increasingly separated itself from the nationalist Right; the 'Red–Brown Alliance' largely ceased to exist. But in his political credo of 1994, appropriately entitled *Derzhava*, which roughly means State Power, Zyuganov unremittingly presents himself and his party as Russian patriots, with a strong chauvinist tinge. The first section is entitled 'I am from the party of Korolev and Zhukov'.[60] Korolev was the chief space and rocket scientist; Zhukov the Marshal who led the Red Army in the second world war. Between them Korolev and Zhukov stand for the military-industrial complex and Soviet triumph over fascism – for Russia as a super-power and the USSR in its finest hour (in that order . . .).

Zyuganov bitterly criticises *perestroika*, claiming that the mass of the people were deceived into 'abandoning their support for the Soviet socialist system and accepting "the Utopia of capitalism"' – according to Zyuganov, this was a 'very great historical mistake'. He calls instead for a mixed economy in which ownership by the people predominates, and in which the economy is controlled by a combination of planning and the market.[61]

The heart of his credo is that it is essential to reconstitute the Soviet Union. Zyuganov describes the pre-revolutionary Russian Empire with approval as 'the historically and geo-politically conditioned form of development of the Russian state', and praises Peter the Great as the inheritor of the Imperial tradition of Rome and Constantinople which present-day Russia must not renounce. Although 'Autocracy; Orthodoxy; Nationality' was a conservative Tsarist maxim it also had a 'broader cultural and historical meaning' which was taken over into the Soviet period in the form of a new maxim, 'the all-Union multi-national state'.[62]

After insisting on this essential continuity between Imperial Russian nationalism and Soviet patriotism, Zyuganov then offers us his own peculiar history of the Soviet period:

> For some people, independently of its name – the USSR – and in spite of ideological changes, revolutions and wars, Russia remained the Fatherland, their own beloved country, for the good of which they

intended to work to the extent of their ability, using the state power conquered during the Civil War. For others Russia was a mere bundle of brushwood for the bonfire of world 'permanent' revolution, a jumping-off point for the preparation of new international cataclysms, a testing-ground for inhuman experiments . . .

The first group strove to restore the ruined paralysed economy, to arrange food supply, to modernise the economy, to build new factories, to revive the armed forces. The second group signed savage orders on mass 'deCossackisation', exterminated hostages in thousands, advocated 'death by shooting as a method of education', organised concentration camps, starved to death millions of people and blew up the holy places of the nation. The inner-party struggle of these two groups . . . did not cease for a moment over long decades.

The great creative work of the Communist Party had been damaged by the 'deliberate and malicious Russophobia of groups within the party and the blasphemous campaign for the "deChristianisation" of Russia'.[63] Later in his book Zyuganov claimed that in practice throughout Soviet history two parties existed. One could be called '*Our Country*', and included Sholokhov and Korolev, Zhukov and Gagarin, Kurchatov and Stakhanov. The other could be called '*That Country*', a much smaller but very influential group, and included Trotsky and Kaganovich, Beria and Mekhlis, Gorbachev and Yeltsin, Yakovlev and Shevardnadze.[64]

Readers will notice that the first group, the good patriots, consists entirely of Russians; the second group, the bad cosmopolitans, includes three Jews and two Caucasians. Lenin and Stalin are missing from both lists; the author achieved the feat of not mentioning either of them throughout his book. He would have found it impossible to place them in either his first or his second group. Lenin restored the economy *and* he eagerly sought world revolution. Stalin built factories and strengthened the armed forces; *and* at the same time he organised concentration camps and bore a great deal of responsibility for famine.

This obviously untenable version of history would not have been worth reproducing at such length if it had not been written by so influential a politician. The Platform for the December 1995 Elections adopted by the Third Conference of the CPRF set out a revised version of Zyuganov's lessons from history. The Platform presented the CPRF as essentially the latest stage in a historical continuum from Muscovy to the present day, and argued that the party must emulate past patriots who fought for the independence of Muscovy and Russia: 'Our forebears teach us this lesson above all: *Without a Strong State There Will Be No Strong Russia.*'

The CPRF Platform castigated Gorbachev, Yakovlev and Yeltsin, together with their predecessors Trotsky, Beria and the Nazi collaborator General Vlasov, as 'the party of national treachery', which had sought to destroy Russian achievements. It also praised the leaders of the August 1991 coup for their 'unsuccessful attempt to defend the Soviet Union and socialism.'[65]

The pro-Communist newspapers, *Pravda* and *Sovetskaya Rossiya*, also combine advocacy of a form of state socialism with a nostalgia for the Soviet past which is strongly tinged with Russian nationalism. *Pravda* on one occasion even repeated the old charge that the Hasidim Jews practice ritual murder. An article explained that there is a simple explanation for the desperate efforts of the Lubovicher Hasidim sect to recover from the Lenin Library the Rebbe Shneerson collection, which was confiscated in the 1920s: the collection contains manuscripts justifying ritual murder! Some weeks later the newspaper apologised for its error in publishing the article, stating editorially that *Pravda* 'as always stands for an internationalist position, opposed to attempts to incite race hatred'.[66]

Although the CPRF sought and seeks to present itself as an advocate of democracy and moderate economic reform, nostalgia for the Soviet past – and for Stalin – is widespread among its members. In September 1995 *Pravda* even published a letter from a factory worker seeking to defend the execution of 755 000 people in the Stalin years. 'Do not hurry to say it was a lot', he insisted; 'a large part of the repression took place during the war and post-war years up to 1951: [pro-German] traitors, police and so on'.[67] What is remarkable about this incident is not that an eccentric individual wrote a silly letter but that *Pravda* thought it appropriate to publish it.

In December 1995 – for the first time for many years – a serious collection of Stalin's writings was published, edited by R. I. Kosolapov, chief editor until 1986 of *Kommunist*, the main party theoretical journal.[68] Kosolapov's book included some fairly mild criticisms of Stalin. But in Stalin's home town Gori in Georgia – now an independent country – the Stalin Museum, closed in 1988, reopened in 1993; and presented a bland portrait of the leader. In October 1995 the Georgian government decided that a Centre for the Study of the Stalin Phenomenon should be opened at the museum; a British journalist concluded after his visit that this would celebrate Stalin's life in a spirit of uncritical enthusiasm.[69] Shevardnadze, now president of Georgia, greatly assisted the uncrowning of Stalin a decade previously with his support for the film 'Repentance' while party secretary in Georgia. He now acquiesced in his rehabilitation.

RUSSIAN NATIONALISM

If Zhirinovsky's eccentric 'Liberal Democrats' are not included, the Far Right received very few votes in the December 1993 elections. But it is extremely vociferous. Some leading Right-wing nationalists continue to offer a crudely anti-semitic version of Russian history. Aleksandr Sterligov, a former KGB General, stigmatised the 1917 revolutions as 'Zionist–Masonic', *perestroika* as seeking to establish capitalism 'under the control of an anti-national Zionist–Nazi bourgeoisie', and 'the Jew Yeltsin' (Yeltsin is not Jewish) as 'a servant of international Zionism': 'the Jews planned the complete elimination of Russian statehood'.[70]

Zavtra describes itself as 'the Newspaper of the Spiritual Opposition', and Aleksandr Prokhanov plays a major part on its pages. It combines a militant nationalism with a strong injection of nostalgia for the Soviet past. Its anti-semitism is also blatant. In one issue it praised two newly-published anti-semitic books. *Satrap* is a viciously anti-Jewish biography of Kaganovich, the only Jew in Stalin's Politburo – it even describes the Protocols of the Learned Elders of Zion as a genuine work. I met its author, the late E. S. Evseev, in the former Central Party Archive a few months before the August 1991 coup. He boasted that he had very good access to archival material on Kaganovich (then closed to everyone else). Russian friends told me to keep away from him because of his close connections with the KGB.

The other anti-semitic publication praised in the same issue of *Zavtra* was Henry Ford's notorious book on International Jewry, written in the 1920s and published in Russia for the first time. According to *Zavtra*:

> This book is popular with some people and hated by others. The secret is simple: it openly investigates the question of the role and place of International Jewry in international civilisation; it traces its pre-history and genesis, and its position at the time the author wrote the book.

In the same issue two new books on the role of the masons in provoking the 1905 and 1917 revolutions are also singled out for praise.[71]

Vicious anti-semitic literature is openly on sale in Moscow and St Petersburg of a kind which is hardly seen at all elsewhere in Europe. In June 1995, the publisher of the Russian translation of Hitler's *Mein Kampf* was arraigned in a St Petersburg court for calling the Jews 'human garbage ... who are not needed by mankind'; he was acquitted.[72] In a public opinion poll in Moscow in October 1993, 17 per cent of those questioned admitted to being anti-semitic; the percentage was twice as high among supporters of the CPRF and three times as high among supporters of the national Salvation Front.[73]

The most difficult historical problem for the nationalist 'Browns' in coming to terms with the Communist 'Reds' is of course their assessment of the Bolshevik Revolution of 1917 and of the Soviet regime. Zhirinovsky, whose support in the country greatly declined in 1994 and 1995, but who remained the most influential nationalist politician, continued his earlier unwillingness to come to terms with the Bolshevik Revolution. In March 1995 four members of the Duma from Zhirinovsky's party unsuccessfully proposed a draft law entitled 'On Recognising the State Coup in Russia on 7 November (25 October) 1917 as Illegal'.[74]

Zhirinovsky continued his condemnation of the Soviet past in his election campaign in the autumn of 1995. In a TV broadcast in November 1995 he compared the October 1917 revolution with rape, Stalin's one-party system with 'homosexuality where there are relationships between representatives of the same sex', and Khrushchev's policy with 'masturbation where a person satisfies himself alone'. The Brezhnev and Gorbachev periods were 'a time of political impotence; they wanted to perform but they could not'.[75]

Some monarchists and other enthusiasts for the pre-revolutionary system hoped that the 1990s would see a return to the allegedly peaceful Russia before 1914. But Zhirinovsky believed that the collapse of Communism could enable the renewal of the Tsarist policy of Southwards expansion into Afghanistan, Turkey and Iran, which he claimed had been broken off by the revolutionaries after 1916 (in fact the expansionist drive virtually ceased after the 1905 revolution). Zhirinovsky argued that Russia should now advance to the Indian Ocean, and all the inhabitants of the southern flank should see themselves as Russian and speak the language . . . [76]

In the context of his expansionist nationalism, even Zhirinovsky, so unwilling to compromise with Communism, praised the Soviet development of Siberia, the intervention in Poland in 1939, the post-war Warsaw Pact, and Soviet success in developing atomic weapons. He argued that it was the presence of Soviet 'offensive armies' in Europe after the second world war which enabled peace to be maintained, and criticised Soviet policy at the beginning of the war only because it was too defensive:

The position of the Red Army in the first year of the second world war is the most tragic example of forgetting the 'offensive defence' elaborated by Russian military leaders. The support of the Soviet government for an exclusively 'defensive' military strategy led to the lack of preparedness of the Red Army for pushing back and destroying the carefully-prepared German-fascist invasion.[77]

(This interpretation of the events of 1941 is the polar opposite of Suvorov's, and equally untenable.)

The political party of the nationalist former General, Aleksandr Lebed', the Congress of Russian Communities, included some serious politicians and economists. But, like Zhirinovsky, Lebed' placed his main emphasis on the need for continuity with the pre-revolutionary past. According to Lebed', in the millennium of its existence Rus' has been based on 'the spiritual power of the Orthodox Church, the creative genius of the Russian people and the valour of the Russian army'. The Church had been attacked ever since 1917, and independent thought by the Russian people had been suppressed since the end of the 1920s, but the attempt to destroy the spirit of the Army in 1937 had failed.[78] But Lebed' also firmly opposed the total renunciation of the Soviet past:

> It must always be clearly remembered that we are the inheritors of 1000 years of orthodox Rus', 300 years of the House of the Romanovs, and almost 75 years of Soviet power. We do not have the right to renounce anything or anyone in our history. Without the past there is not and cannot be a future. It is not necessary to shoot at the Past with a pistol. The Future would answer with a cannon. Ivans who do not remember their national origins (*rodstva*) deserve only to be slaves.[79]

'Ivans who do not remember their origins' are Lebed''s equivalent of the liberal intellectuals' Lumpens.

Lebed' called for a national reconciliation between Tsarism and Leninism. In a nation-wide ceremony, Nicholas II and Lenin should be buried simultaneously – the royal family in the burial place of the Russian Tsars, Lenin next to his mother:

> To the sound of bells throughout the land. Under furled banners. To an artillery salute. To the sound of a funeral orchestra with a thousand wind instruments. One of our national (it must be national) directors of genius, like Nikita Mikhalkov, must create (yes, create) this tragic and mighty ceremony like a sculpture. It must strike at nerves, souls and hearts! . . . This will be a great symbol of universal reconciliation and purification, which will bring about a breakthrough into the future![80]

Some other politicians also returned to the attitudes prevalent in some nationalist circles before the August 1991 coup. They were prepared to swallow their distaste for the Bolsheviks and Soviet Communism in the interests of unity against Yeltsin, and dealt with Lenin and the revolution ambiguously or by polite silence.

RECONCILIATION WITH THE SOVIET PAST

Gaidar's attempt to introduce shock therapy soon met with the hostility of many prominent intellectuals, including economists with rival programmes for transition to the market, such as Yavlinsky and Shatalin.

Shatalin always tried to place his current political views in a historical context, and his withering if extravagant attack on Gaidar's policies was no exception:

> If economic policy is not changed, the collapse in output will continue and Russia may lose half its industrial production. This is comparable only to the combined results of the first world war, the revolution and the Civil War.[81]

The same critical attitude was taken by the economist Grigorii Khanin, who in 1989–90 came to prominence for his strong criticism of the official statistics of Soviet economic growth, and his rejection of the popular view that the New Economic Policy could have provided a sound road to rapid industrialisation.[82] Khanin did not retreat from his earlier criticism of Soviet statistics, but came to the conclusion that the 'administrative-command economy' had been relatively stable and successful as compared to the chaos after 1992.[83]

Alexander Zinoviev, exiled from the Soviet Union following the publication in the West in 1976 of his brilliant satire on Soviet society, *Yawning Heights*, and living in Munich, was contemptuous of *perestroika* from its inception. He argued that it was entirely inappropriate for Soviet reality, and would lead to the restabilisation of the Communist system in a more oppressive form.[84] Unexpectedly for many of his admirers, within eighteen months of the collapse of Communism he emerged as a passionate defender of the Soviet system:

> The 1917 revolution [he wrote in March 1993] was truly Great. And the Soviet period in the life of Russia was the summit of its greatness – so far at least. During the war, although I was an anti-Stalinist, I went into battle as a Communist . . . I am ready to fight to the last drop of my blood today for this Russia – socialist Russia. The Russia of merchants and monarchs is deeply alien to me.

He argued that a 'new Stalingrad' was needed to prevent privatisation and the sale of Russian wealth to foreigners.[85] Two years later, he criticised the Communist Party for its parliamentary compromises, and called for revolutionary action against the Yeltsin regime.[86]

The most famous Russian exile, Alexander Solzhenitsyn, in no way abandoned his hostility to the revolution and Communism. In September 1993, on the occasion of the 200th anniversary of the counter-revolutionary peasant vendée in France, Solzhenitsyn was the guest of honour, and told his audience that it was the defeat of the vendée in 1793 which started the Red Wheel which ended in the establishment of the Soviet Gulags.[87] In a further condemnation of revolutions three months later, he declared that 'those moments in history threaten catastrophe in which personalities are put in second place, and the decisive word is given to the crowd on the street'.[88] But he was equally hostile to the developments after 1991, attacking both Gorbachev and Gaidar for handing over state property to the *nomenklatura* (the former party élite) and for the chaotic inflation.[89] Ever since his permanent return from exile in May 1994, he has campaigned against shock therapy and the free market.

The prominent historian Akhmed Iskenderov, editor of the leading historical journal *Voprosy istorii*, played a significant role in the rethinking of history which led to the rejection of Communism. But by the end of 1994 he had come to the conclusion that Russia was faced with a crisis of state power, in which 'the negative, or destructive, features of Russian statehood predominate over its positive, or constructive, functions'. The crucial mistake of the democratic forces was that they had based their strategy on personalities rather than on the creation of a functioning method of governance. Iskenderov argued that they had followed the deep-rooted Russian tradition of confining decision making to a narrow circle of individuals – the mistake of the Provisional Government in 1917.[90]

Solzhenitsyn and Iskenderov criticised the present in the light of the past without softening their view of the Soviet period of Russian history. But some leading political figures began to reconsider their blanket hostility to the past. In the midst of the political crisis at the end of 1993, Alexander Yakovlev, in the article in which he was so scathing about Lumpens (see p. 63 above), also presented the myths of Communism in a certain positive spirit:

> Romantic dreams of a better life charmed the consciousness of insulted and humiliated people, who had been left behind by life.
> The hungry child dreamt of candies, the homeless – of beautiful Cities of the Sun, those tortured by endless work – of distant blue lands

of rest, those ground down by injustice – of a realm of equality and fraternity.

These myths must now be given up, but Russia now faced a new choice. The notion that it was possible simply to move from 'A' to 'B' was naïve; 'the experience of European civilisation, its material and spiritual development, have led us to a new frontier where a new synthesis is required both in concepts and in the mode of conduct.'[91]

Immediately following the December 1993 elections, in which Zhirinovsky's party obtained such an alarmingly high vote, Kozyrev, then Minister of Foreign Affairs, recalled the Communists' anti-fascist past and spoke about them in conciliatory terms:

> We can look [in different ways] at our communist past in the Soviet Union, but nobody can take away the fact that communists were fighting against fascists in the second world war . . . It would be strange indeed if the communists were standing aside from an anti-fascist movement.[92]

Reconciliation between Communists and the newly-established Yeltsin–Chernomyrdin government proved utterly impossible. But, faced with hostility to economic reform, nostalgia for the Soviet past, and nationalism, Yeltsin and his advisers, and their supporters in the regions, sharply modified the passion of their anti-Communism. Their shift in approach was made easier by the dismissal of the intransigent Burbulis, Poltoranin and Gaidar before the new Duma assembled at the beginning of 1994.

The authorities now dealt much more circumspectly with the symbols of the Soviet past. Even before the December 1993 elections, complaints had appeared of the 'sharp reduction in the tempo (or even complete cessation) of the deBolshevisation of the toponymy [the names etc.].' of streets, towns and settlements.[93] After the elections, both changes of name and the removal of Soviet monuments were undertaken even less frequently. In Moscow at the end of 1995 the huge statue of Lenin remained in place in October Square, although the square had lost the name which it received in honour of the October Revolution. In spite of frequent rumours that the Lenin Mausoleum was to be closed, it continued to operate, and the bodies of the revolutionary heroes remained in the Kremlin wall. The main Lenin Museum in the centre of Moscow had been closed before the results of the elections. But together with the Lenin Museum at Gorki it was administratively attached to the Historical Museum. Its contents were not dispersed or stored as was originally intended, but transferred to Gorki, together with Lenin's flat in the Kremlin, and an unused building was set aside for them.[94]

From time to time leading politicians called for the removal of Lenin's body from the Mausoleum. In August 1995, Patriarch Aleksii again proposed that Lenin and other persons buried in Red Square should be removed to cemeteries, but now added the qualification 'without inflaming political passions' – a counsel of perfection.[95] In St Petersburg, while only two of the ten(!) Lenin museums continued to operate, the only major statue of Lenin to be dismantled was at the Moscow railway station, where it was replaced by Peter the Great.[96]

On the other hand, the former honour guard at Lenin's mausoleum, removed in October 1993, has now been refitted as a ceremonial Presidential Regiment. It wears uniforms based on the 1907 dress of the Russian Imperial guard, manufactured at a cost of $900 each. The designer, Oleg Parkhayev, a monarchist military book illustrator, explained that he had chosen the royal blue of the breastcloth because this is 'the traditional colour of the KGB', to which the unit once belonged. He also reported that the guardsmen must be at least 5ft 10ins tall, and be 'of Slavic type':

'Can you imagine what it would be like if an English Guards regiment had Africans in it?', chortled Mr Parkhayev.[97]

The British military authorities have at least tried unsuccessfully to recruit some of our black citizens for the Guards.

THE 50TH ANNIVERSARY OF SOVIET VICTORY IN THE SECOND WORLD WAR

In the course of 1994, the Yeltsin–Chernomyrdin administration decided that the Anniversary on May 9, 1995, must be an occasion for national unity and reconciliation, rather than for the denunciation of the heavy war losses for which Stalin and his system had been responsible. While Suvorov's preventive war thesis continued to raise its head in historical journals and in parts of the press, it was ignored by the official celebrations. For Yeltsin, the need for a patriotic commemoration was reinforced by the involvement of the Russian army in the unpopular war in Chechnya from the end of 1994.

On 23 February 1995, several months before 9 May, a large banner straddled a main Moscow road reading 'Congratulations on Your Holiday, Dear Servicemen, the Conquerors of Fascism'. 23 February 1918 was the day on which the Red Army was founded. It was an important Anniversary in the Soviet calendar, but virtually ignored in 1992, 1993, and 1994. But Yeltsin now announced that 23 February would be a national holiday henceforth, renamed 'Day of the Defenders of the Motherland'.[98] It was duly celebrated in 1996. Both in the Soviet period and under Yeltsin 23 February was celebrated without reference to Trotsky, founder of the Red Army.

In preparation for 9 May, the Russian and Moscow authorities constructed a huge war memorial park at Poklonnaya Gora, a few miles from the centre of Moscow. The memorial had long been planned, but had been drowned for several years in a sea of bitter dispute about the form it should take. In 1994–5 an enormous column and war museum were erected, and tanks, planes and other wartime weapons were located in the park. The construction was afforded top priority in typical Soviet fashion, and the Mayor of Moscow frequently appeared there to goad on the builders. The Army newspaper fiercely insisted that there must be no delay: a front-page banner headline six weeks before 9 May read 'No More Disorder and Dissension! We Expect the Poklonnaya Gora Complex to Open on the 50th Anniversary of Victory'.[99]

The construction was completed on time, together with the Orthodox Church 'St George the Victor', a prominent building next to the main monument. The authorities announced that a mosque and synagogue would follow. But five months later, in October 1995, 58 per cent of Duma deputies voted for a resolution which declared:

> Do not establish a hearth for national and religious conflicts on Poklonnaya Gora . . . The construction in addition to the national memorial complex which already exists, of a mosque and synagogue, and of a 'separate memorial to the memory of the Jews who perished during the Great Patriotic War', is completely unacceptable in view of its extreme social danger.

Journalists scathingly described this resolution as 'a posthumous victory for Hitler'.[100]

In other ways the authorities went even further with reconciliation in honour of the victory than might have been reasonably expected. Marshal Zhukov had frequently been held up as a hero figure by the parties opposing Yeltsin. But, following a protest by Zyuganov, a large statue to Zhukov was erected in Manezh square near the Kremlin; and a prominent Zhukov on horseback featured in one of a series of commemorative stamps in honour of the Victory. Moreover, while many exposures of Stalin continued to appear in the press, another postage stamp in this series bore the heads of Stalin, Roosevelt and Churchill; this is the first time Stalin has appeared on a stamp in over forty years.[101] At a conference devoted to the war Prime Minister Chernomyrdin announced:

While noting all the talent and good deeds of our Soviet commanders, we must not stay silent about the importance of the actions in the Great Patriotic War of Josef Vissarionovich Stalin. It would not be fair or just.[102]

The same line was taken by Zyuganov a couple of months later.[103] Gorbachev had made a similar gesture to Stalin almost exactly ten years previously.[104] At the height of *glasnost'*, no-one would have guessed that the gesture would be repeated within a few years.

On the morning of 9 May, a march-past of veterans in Red Square was addressed by President Yeltsin, who referred movingly to 'the terrible price we paid to prevent the world from sliding into the abyss of fascism.' This was a slightly odd event. Yeltsin was standing in customary fashion on Lenin's mausoleum, a large official placard in the square read 'POBEDA SSSR' ('VICTORY–USSR') as if the Soviet Union was still in existence, and the veterans' march was organised by a committee headed by General Varennikov, one of the supporters of the August 1991 coup.[105]

But these moves failed to achieve national unity and reconciliation. In the afternoon two large demonstrations commemorated the victory. The official army and civilian demonstration marched to Poklonnaya Gora. Simultaneously, an unofficial pro-Communist march, bearing anti-government banners, made its way from Belorussian station to Lyubanka Square. The popular view in Moscow, among both supporters and opponents of Yeltsin, was that the Communist march was larger.[106]

FILMS

Long before 9 May 1995, TV had begun to cater for the curiosity of the young and the nostalgia of the old by showing and discussing seriously films from the Soviet era. In his memoirs Gorbachev notes that in 1992 almost the whole of Soviet cinema was subjected to relentless abuse, but 'as early as 1993 many films of earlier years began to appear on TV, and were watched by young and old with pleasure'.[107]

One of the most popular, 'Two Warriors' (*Dva boitsa*) (1943) is shown at least twice a year, and songs from it are still sung. The film is far more subtle than the crude patriotism and enthusiasm for Stalin which characterised many wartime and postwar films about the war. War is presented not as a matter of glory but as a difficult and terrible duty. Although many wartime films did not admit that their soldier heroes longed for home, *Dva boitsa* is franker about its two heroes – as a Russian film critic put it, they fight not to the death but 'for life – their own and the lives of those near to them'.[108]

The revival is not confined to war films. The popular film which presented a glowing image of the countryside after the war, 'Cavalier of the Golden Star' (1950), was shown on TV in January 1994. After the showing it was critically but sympathetically discussed. The historian Viktor Danilov pointed out that the countryside was in a very poor state in 1950, and its inhabitants were unhealthy – but there had been a considerable increase since 1947 in the number of villages supplied with electricity, so the huge power station glowing with light with which the film ends was a fantastic image of a certain reality. The commentators agreed that the film would remain popular, because – unlike present-day films – it showed the willingness of men and women to work with dedication for others, not just for themselves.

In December 1993, 'Engineer Kotin's Mistake' (*Oshibka inzhenera Kotina*) was shown on TV and discussed by a panel. Made in 1939 before the Soviet–German pact, this is a well-made and strongly anti-fascist film – a loyal Soviet Jewish family is central to the action. But the film is fundamentally unpleasant and even corrupt; its main objective is to justify the purges. It shows the exposure of Soviet citizens spying for the Germans by a masterly and pleasant NKVD officer. The script was written by two well-known authors, the Brothers Tur, together with L. Sheinis. Sheinis was an assistant procurator for many years, working closely with Vyshinsky on many political trials. In his spare time he wrote popular detective stories.

The panel discussing the film on screen consisted of a film critic, an historian, and a pleasant old man who turned out to have been the deputy head of the technical and scientific department of the NKVD from 1941–1960. This senior NKVD officer claimed that the film, though somewhat primitive, represented the true position at the time. But the film critic and the historian explained quite fully the social function of the film and its thorough misrepresentation of the reality of the purges. After watching this programme I felt that the Russian audience as well as myself would understand much better why many people believed in the guilt of those put on trial, and how the Stalinist system worked.

According to one of the organisers of the series 'Kinopravda' ('Cinema Truth'), some young people thought that such films as 'Lenin in October' were a great joke, and regarded Lenin as 'a comic character – nearly on the level of Charlie Chaplin'. But they were exceptions. Millions of viewers thoroughly enjoyed the films and rejected the 'commentaries and exposures'. The TV authorities, fearing the series would help the Communists,

closed it down. But other channels continue to show Stalinist films –
without any warning commentary . . .[109]

Films made since 1991 – insofar as the industry has been able to make
films at all – when concerned with the past have primarily sought to show
the advantages of Tsarism, as with Govorukhin's film, or to expose the
evils of the Soviet past. In the main Russian film journal, a critic of a
recent war film, 'The General' (*General*), points out that in earlier Soviet
films about the war, whatever their weaknesses, everyone was involved in
the war against an external enemy. But recent films concentrate their attention on the struggle of various generals against Zhukov and Rokossovsky,
with the shadow of Stalin in the background. Stalin and the NKVD troops
are treated as an internal enemy worse than the external enemy, and the
enemy is ignored on an emotional level.[110]

Russian cinema is now, however, beginning to present a more measured
view of the past. Nikita Mikhalkov's film, 'Burnt by the Sun' (1994), has
been widely shown in Western Europe, and received the Academy award
for the best foreign film of 1995. Mikhalkov, the director who was recommended by Lebed' to stage the simultaneous funerals of Nicholas II and
Lenin (see p. 69 above), was at that time a supporter of Rutskoi, the
nationalist vice-presidential running mate of Yeltsin in 1991 who supported
Khasbulatov when Yeltsin's troops stormed the White House in 1993. His
film shows a great military Communist hero of the Civil War and his
pleasant life in the countryside in the 1930s, before in the last scenes he
is arrested and broken by the NKVD. Soviet history is portrayed as neither
black nor white. In a recent interview Mikhalkov commented:

> Then they were making films about the Reds, who were good, and the
> Whites, who were bad. But now they are about the good Whites and the
> bad Reds. [Today's directors] have no sense of responsibility.[111]

THE DECEMBER 1995 ELECTIONS AND THE PRESIDENTIAL CAMPAIGN OF 1996

The deadlock between President and parliament continued as a result of
the second election of the new Duma. The votes showed a sharp swing
away from the pro-market parties. In the section of the Duma elected by
party lists, the votes cast for parties supporting the free market declined
from 36 to 24 per cent of the total. Gaidar's party received a pitiable 3.9
per cent; the main pro-market votes were for Prime Minister Chernomyrdin's party 'Our House is Russia', with 11.2 per cent, and Yavlinsky's

'Yabloko', with 6.9 per cent. The votes for the Communists and their allies increased from 28 to 35 per cent; the CPRF vote increased to 22 per cent, largely at the expense of its allies. The main nationalist vote (Zhirinovsky plus Lebed') declined from 23 to 14 per cent. Unexpectedly, the 'self-government' party of the famous eye surgeon Fyodorov, whose cooperative was very prominent in the first years of *perestroika*, received 4 per cent, but it did not cross the 5 per cent barrier.[112]

The leading contenders for the Presidency immediately began to take their stand in preparation for the June 1996 elections. Zhirinovsky, when nominated as his party's candidate, knelt and kissed the St Andrew's flag, the flag of the Tsarist navy.[113] Zyuganov declared in his post-election statement that his party was based on the three pillars of Orthodoxy, Islam and Buddhism, all of which belonged to the socialist and collectivist tradition.[114] Yeltsin, extremely disturbed by the shift in political attitudes, replaced his foreign minister, Kozyrev, by the more nationalist Primakov, and removed several of his assistants who were strong supporters of rapid market reforms. His message to the Federal Assembly at the time of his nomination as Presidential candidate for a second term strongly emphasised the importance of social welfare and of state regulation of economic reform in the interests of the people.[115]

At the same time throughout the presidential campaign he insisted on the inherently pernicious nature of the Communist past, and sought to associate it with Zyuganov, his chief rival for the presidency, and the candidate of the CPRF and other Communist groups. After the election of December 1995 he uncompromisingly announced that 'the way of Marxist ideology is criminal for Russia and the Russians, and we will not allow it to happen.'[116] In his message to the Assembly in February 1996 he insisted that 'the tragic consequences of the Communist experiment were natural'. Mass repressions and isolation form the external world were 'standard features of a totalitarian regime', and the failure of the Khrushchev thaw had demonstrated the 'inability of the system to reform itself'.[117]

Yeltsin also stressed his adherence to patriotism and religion. Even before the December 1995 elections Yeltsin issued an instruction that 'A New History of the Russian State' was to be written, based on documentary evidence. Its aim should be 'establishing the truth about what we have lived through' – though the nature of that truth was not specified. This revived a notion popular in September 1991 (see pp. 96–7 below).[118] On the occasion of the Orthodox Christmas, on 6 January 1996, Yeltsin and Patriarch Aleksii jointly laid a dedication stone at the church of Christ the Redeemer. On 20 February, in preparation for the first celebration of Armed Forces' Day on 23 February (formerly Red Army Day), he announced that a 'Zhukov medal' would be awarded to meritorious war veterans.[119] In acknowledgment of Yeltsin's strongly nationalist policies, in the same month some of the extreme nationalist parties voted to support Yeltsin as candidate for President. Eduard Limonov, former dissident in emigration, pointed in justification to Yeltsin's 'invasion – er, sending of troops into Chechnya'.[120] Yeltsin repudiated their support.[121]

The principal contenders fervently paraded their rival views of the past throughout the Presidential campaign. Yeltsin and his supporters dominated television. In the run-up to the first vote on June 16 viewers were treated to many films demonstrating the evils of the Soviet past. One lengthy series showed the last months of the Imperial family, including a minute-by-minute presentation of their final brutal execution.

It would be wrong to suppose that the media were entirely one-sided. On the Friday evening before the vote on Sunday June 16, two leading film directors offered rival presentations. Mikhalkov, whom we have met as a supporter of Rutskoi, now emphatically supported Yeltsin. And – an astonishing change of view – the case for Zyuganov was presented by Govorukhin, director of *The Russia We Have Lost*, the notorious film idealising the last days of Tsarism (see p. 43).

Peak time on the eve of the June 16 vote was devoted to Mikhalkov's *Burnt by the Sun* (see p. 77). The film has generally been regarded as anti-Communist (see *The Guardian*, 1 July 1996). But I am not so sure. The hero was a Bolshevik leader who retained his principles. The villain, employed by the NKVD, was a former White. The film was dangerous to Zyuganov not because it was anti-Communist but because it was anti-Stalinist. Zyuganov had increasingly allowed himself to become identified with Stalinism, and even with its post-1945 variant. In an interview which he later attempted to repudiate, he attacked Khrushchev and détente, and stated that Stalin 'gradually became identified with Russian national thought . . . If he had lived another five or six years, the Soviet Union would have become unconquerable for long centuries' (SWB, SU/2638 A/4, June 14 1996).

On 16 June, 35 per cent of voters chose Yeltsin and 32 per cent Zyuganov. Lebed' received a surprising 15 per cent, taking votes from Zhirinovsky. Then in the second round on 3 July only the two main contenders remained. Yeltsin was the clear victor, supported by 54 per cent of voters against Zyuganov's 41 per cent.

* * *

Opinion polls during the past two years indicate that voters supported Yeltsin not because of enthusiasm for his policies, but because he was a lesser evil than Zyuganov. A nation-wide survey in November 1994 which asked the respondents their opinion about Lenin's role in history reported that 44 per cent gave a positive evaluation, 29 per cent a negative evaluation.[122] This was a small shift in Lenin's disfavour as compared with the survey in April 1992.[123] Another survey enquired whether respondents thought that a market or a state-planned system was preferable. The responses revealed a remarkable change in attitude in favour of planning (in percentages of total number of respondents:[124]

	February 1992	December 1994
Market better	52	26
Planning better	27	41
Difficult to say	21	26
[Residual	0	7]

In an opinion poll at the time of the December 1995 elections, 55 per cent of the population said they were not averse to a return to the situation prior to 1985, and only 38 per cent positively rejected such a return.[125] On 16 June 1996, in an exit poll of the voters in the Presidential election, 58 per cent of voters stated that big industrial enterprises should be owned by the state, 26 per cent that they should be owned by the workers, and only 12 per cent that they should have private owners (*International Herald Tribune*, 18 June 1996).

Most Russian voters seem to favour a form of welfare socialism without the repressions and bureaucracy of the past. But neither the victorious Yeltsin nor the defeated Zyuganov offered any prospect of such a future.

It would be wrong to conclude from either of these surveys or the results of the elections, however, that the shift in public attitudes towards the Soviet past had been small. Of the younger age-groups, 70 per cent expressed a negative attitude to Lenin, whereas 70 per cent of the older age-groups were favourable. And perhaps even more indicative of a change in public attitudes is the almost complete abandonment of the everyday use of the word 'Comrades' – the most widespread form of address in 1985. In July 1993 only 20 per cent of respondents regarded 'Comrades' as a natural form of address – and only 5 per cent of respondents under the age of 20.[126] Psychologically as well as politically, Soviet history was a thing of the past.

Part II
The Battle for the Archives

INTRODUCTION

The Soviet archival system taken over by the Russian archives in the autumn of 1991 was vast and complicated. Soviet state archives had been managed centrally by the Chief Archival Administration, Glavarkhiv, which had Ministerial status. The central archives, located in Moscow and St Petersburg, were themselves divided into a number of separate depositories. Every republic, region and large town also had its own branch of the state archives. After the collapse of the Soviet Union, the Russian archives retained control over local archives on the territory of the Russian Federation, but this control was often more nominal than real.

In addition, every government department also had its own archives. As in other countries, the boundaries between central and departmental archives were difficult to draw. Most governmental organisations transferred a large part of their files to Glavarkhiv after a certain lapse of time. But they had the right to determine how far this material was made accessible to historians. And the Ministry of Foreign Affairs, the KGB, and the military retained firm control over their own post-1917 materials, and did not relinquish any of them to Glavarkhiv. (Similar arrangements for foreign affairs and the military exist in many other countries – Britain and the United States are exceptions.)

The Communist Party had always controlled its own archives, independent of Glavarkhiv. The historical material (except for the most secret documents) was deposited in the Central Party Archive, TsPA; the central committee offices on Staraya Ploshchad' held a large current archive, inaccessible to historians. As with the state archives, there were also party archives in every republic, region and large town.

6 Before *Perestroika*: The Historical Background

The Soviet archival system dates back to a decree of the Council of People's Commissars of 1 June 1918, signed by Lenin. This sought to establish a powerful agency to coordinate and control all archives.[1] As in society at large, the influence of the centre, and ultimately of the Politburo, relentlessly increased from 1918 onwards.

Nevertheless, in the 1920s, according to the foremost Western authority on the Soviet archives, Patricia Grimsted, 'scholarship and serious reference work were the order of the day' in the state archives; 'archival inventories and reference compilations prepared in those years extended scholarly pre-revolutionary traditions, and were still on a European standard'.[2]

Many repressive acts were taken against archivists in the early 1930s. But until 1938 Glavarkhiv was a nominally semi-autonomous agency under the Central Executive Committee of Soviets. In that year it was placed under the People's Commissariat of Internal Affairs, the NKVD (later the MVD), which also controlled the secret police and forced labour. It was answerable to Beria's deputy Kruglov (in Chapter 13 we shall meet Kruglov as the principal official responsible for taming the mutinies in the labour camps after Stalin's death).

One of the most unpleasant aspects of both state and party archives was their availability to the security services to disclose the past activities and social origins of individuals under suspicion. These operations became far more extensive after Glavarkhiv was taken over by the NKVD. In 1939, 108 694 'enemies of the people' were disclosed by the state archives. In 1940, with the archives now reinforced by the acquisition of the archives of the Baltic States and Eastern Poland, 'enemies' exposed increased to 1 399 217. But even this number was considered insufficient. On 23 October 1940, Beria signed a secret order 'On the Utilisation of Archival Materials in Cheka Operations' (Cheka is the original term for the secret police). The order claimed that local state archives contained large numbers of documents which had not yet been examined, and warned that 'a considerable number of enemies of the people who appear in the documents are at large, and are undoubtedly continuing their disruptive work'. A recent Russian study plausibly suggests that the wish to exploit the archives in order to expose 'hidden enemies' accounts for their transfer to the NKVD.[3]

In the context of Stalinist terror, what did the Soviet archive system achieve? In George Orwell's *Nineteen Eighty Four* officials are continuously adjusting the archival record so that it corresponds to the latest official falsifications about the past. This is a fair account of the *published* record under Stalin. But the story of the archives is quite different. All of us who work in the archives of the Soviet period have been surprised at the range and vast quantity of information unfavourable to the regime which has been carefully preserved. As collectors of information about their regime, the Soviet archivists under Stalin and after had few equals.

This is of course only half the story. There are occasional examples of the falsification of the records kept in the archives themselves. Some materials were destroyed for political reasons. Very extensive destruction took place in Moscow and elsewhere at the time of the German advance in 1941.[4] And the unexpurgated record of the past, blandly denied in current books and newspapers, was kept under seven seals.

THE KHRUSHCHEV THAW

During the Khrushchev years freedom to use the archives – like other more important freedoms – began to be conceded by the authorities. In 1960 the state archives were removed from the Ministry of Internal Affairs and attached to the Council of Ministers. Even before this welcome transfer, important materials had been made accessible to historians. In 1959, when I began research on economic development in the late NEP period, several volumes of archival documents had just been published and proved extremely valuable.[5]

Following Khrushchev's second denunciation of Stalin in 1961, the stream of archival revelations became a small flood. The authorities stemmed and manipulated the flood, but historians succeeded in publishing archival-based articles with new approaches to such sensitive subjects as the collectivisation of agriculture.

Khrushchev's successors imposed much stricter limits on access. Some sections of the archives of the Council of People's Commissars (SNK) were made available to approved historians in the last years of Khrushchev. In the Brezhnev years they were closed again. Moreover, the economic archives (TsGANKh) 'ceased to admit researchers to all the documents of the Central Statistical Administration of the USSR, Gosplan of the USSR, the Ministry of Finance of the USSR and the State Bank of the USSR, and to many documents of other Ministries and government departments'.[6] As one commentator explained:

At the end of the 1960s and beginning of the 1970s documents which had been released ten years before underwent a second secretisation (*povtornoe zasekrechivanie*). A new classification was introduced – 'limited use' – on the standard grounds that 'the ways in which the information is distributed cannot be controlled.'[7]

V. P. Kozlov argued that, once the incubus of Stalinist terror was removed, the main weakness of the archival system in Brezhnev's time was not only its all-pervasive secrecy but also the great control exercised by government departments:

... Today, although there is an elaborate network of central state archives the situation, in essence, if not in form, greatly resembles that before the revolution. Government departments dictate the weeding, preservation and use of the documents of the State Archival *Fond* [the total collection of state archival material], and this is the main obstacle to the transformation of the archival system.[8]

We shall see in due course that the influence of government departments on their own archives has continued to limit access to archives years after the collapse of Communism. This is to a greater or lesser extent a major problem for state archives everywhere.

ON THE EVE OF PERESTROIKA

In spite of improvements in the Khrushchev years, something resembling a medieval caste system of access prevailed until 1985, and for several years thereafter. Younger historians who are accustomed to working in Russian archives today – for all their awkwardness, discomfort and occasional corruption – find it almost impossible to envisage the working life of Soviet and Western historians in the bad days before *perestroika*.

Historians obtained access to the state archives only if they were provided with a letter of support from an approved establishment; this rule dated back to 1918.[9] When admitted, they had to work on an approved topic, and were not allowed to see files judged to be 'not related to the topic'.

Once admitted, Soviet historians were given access only to files which were classified at the lowest order of secrecy – 'confidential' or 'not for publication'. Access to 'secret' or 'top secret' material depended on obtaining the appropriate personal security clearance. Files at the highest level of secrecy – the so-called 'special files' (*osobye papki*) – were rarely if ever shown even to the most reliable historians.

Access to a 'top secret' file did not mean that the historian had the automatic right to make notes about it and take them out of the building. For one category of files, notes could be made, but the source of the information could not be mentioned in published work. For a second category, notes could be made, but the information obtained could not be published even without attribution. For a third category, notes could be made, but the notes had to be kept permanently in a special safe in the archives. And for files in a particularly secret category no notes of any kind could be made. The last category was of course particularly frustrating. Historians have described to me their efforts to memorise what was in a file and write it down as soon as they got out of the building. Bolder spirits would scribble notes secretly on scraps of paper when the archivists were not looking.

The secrecy categorisations were often arbitrary and confused. But boundaries of 'secret' and 'top secret' were drawn much tighter than in Britain or the United States, or in most European countries.

Security provisions meant that the different archives had little contact with each other. Several of the main state archival collections are situated in the complex of buildings on Bol'shaya Pirogovskaya Street, commonly known as the 'Archive Suburb' (*arkhivnyi gorodok*). A quite senior member of the staff of the international department of the state archives, also located at that time in the 'Archive Suburb', told me that she had spoken to the staff of TsGANKh, the economics archive, on the telephone, but had not been able to visit it until she accompanied our British delegation there in 1984. Our delegation found it very difficult to arrange the visit to TsGANKh. The authorities were afraid that we might happen upon some secret. Eventually, we were allowed a visit which was officially categorised as 'for information' but not 'for observation'. This meant we could talk to the Director in his office but not visit the stacks where the files were kept.

The above account refers to the *state* archives. The party archives, both central and local, operated under a much stricter regime. Only party members were allowed to work there.[10] Notes on all files – however trivial – had to be made in a special bound notebook, in which the pages were numbered; the empty notebook was inspected by the archivist in charge of the reading room, who stamped and signed the back of the last page. Notes had to be made in ink in clear handwriting on one side of the page only (the reason for this will emerge shortly). Overnight the notebook was kept, together with the files which were still being read, in a locked safe personally allocated to each historian; the safe was in a locked room. (This being Soviet Russia and not Prussia, the keys were then hung up where anyone could get at them!) When work was complete or the notebook was full, it was handed in. The responsible archivist read through the notes and crossed out or removed with a pair of scissors those passages which it was thought unwise to have taken out of the building. The archivist was also supposed to check that the notes correctly reflected the original material in the archive(!). Sometimes the notebook returned to the historian was literally cut into ribbons.

This was not all. Draft articles based on the party archives were then scrutinised by the relevant department of the archives, which was well-briefed on the acceptable party line. The article then had to be rewritten in accordance with the comments of the department. (See p. 33 above.)

Some archival repositories were even more restricted than the party archives. The Soviet-period archive of the Ministry of Foreign Affairs admitted a mere handful of trusted historians; until a new reading room opened in mid-1994, only seven seats were available to researchers. In practice publication from these archives was the responsibility of the Foreign Ministry and the historians on its staff. The Foreign Ministry published 21 volumes of documents on Soviet foreign policy up to 1938 (one for each year).[11] The KGB archives were completely closed, though KGB officials occasionally published collections of documents.[12]

And very few people knew about the existence of one large repository: the so-called 'Central State Special Archive', containing millions of documents seized from Germany and German-occupied Europe after the war. This archive included such important documents as the files of French intelligence seized by the Gestapo during the war. Three million files of the NKVD concerned with German and other prisoners of war were also transferred to the archive. Its mere existence could not be mentioned in the press, and very few historians were allowed access to it until 1990.[13]

Parallel with the security arrangements in the archives, dangerous books were also screened from the public in the so-called *spetskhran* (Special Store), found in major libraries. The *spetskhran* of the Lenin Library contained 298 239 books, 521 054 issues of periodicals, and 2 498 800 issues of newspapers. All of these had at one time been on open sale, but were later banned. It also incorporated 473 760 publications issued 'for official use' only.[14] The latter included not only statistical and technical handbooks, but also translations of unacceptable Western books such as E. H. Carr's *History of Soviet Russia*. All 14 volumes of Carr's *History* were translated into Russian, and published in a handsome secret edition of which every copy was numbered. One of these sets was kept in the Lenin Library's *spetskhran*.

Access to the *spetskhran* was strictly regulated: only 4 424 of the hundreds of thousands of readers in the Lenin Library were allowed to use it in 1986. While the existence of *spetskhrans* was widely known, mention of them in the press was forbidden until 1986. The *spetskhran* in the Lenin Library contained a further group of materials (*osobyi fond*) to which access was particularly severely restricted. This consisted largely of works deemed to be dangerously anti-Soviet, including the publications of Academician Sakharov and Solzhenitsyn, as well as Trotsky and Bukharin.[15]

Once Soviet historians had fought their way into and out of these various collections of materials, they were faced with a further obstacle: the censorship. All published matter, including mimeographed documents and posters, was subject to censorship before publication. A large book, frequently brought up to date, informed the censors about what information or ideas could not be published. Here are a few examples of matters which could not be mentioned in the open press, culled from the summary regulations issued in 1933, which continued with minor changes until 1990: data on military matters, non-ferrous metals and foreign trade; 'information on unsatisfactory political attitudes, disturbances and strikes, apart from statements from the government'; suicides; fires, explosions and accidents at industrial enterprises and on the railways.[16]

The use of the archives by foreign citizens presented intractable problems to the Soviet authorities. Their basic dilemma was the obvious one that once a foreigner had made notes on a document and taken the notes out of the country, Soviet officials had no power to control publication. The simple solution was to exclude foreigners from the archives altogether. Until the late 1970s, no foreigner was allowed to use any Soviet archives for the whole period after 1920. But Glavarkhiv was under political pressure, in the bleak days of frozen diplomacy after the Soviet invasion of Afghanistan, to reach agreements for exchange and cooperation with Western archives. It was made abundantly clear to Glavarkhiv that better access for Western historians was a condition for such agreements. Glavarkhiv was also subject to moral persuasion. On the memorable occasion of the visit to Moscow of a British archival delegation in 1981, the senior archive officials were undoubtedly uneasy when we shamed them by pointing out that in the absence of access to Soviet archives we had no alternative but to use the Trotsky archives, deposited by his widow at Harvard, and the section of the Smolensk party archives purloined by the Germans during the war and taken over by the Americans in 1945. The Keeper of the Public Record Office, Freddie Mabbs, shook a reproving finger at the Soviet officials and proclaimed 'I believe in the words of Lenin that "the archives belong to the people"'.

So in the early 1980s, before *perestroika*, a number of British and American lecturers and research students, including myself, were allowed to work in the state archives of the Soviet period. But all foreigners, including citizens of other Communist countries, were placed in a special reading room where there were no finding aids. A large notice on the door to the main archive read 'No Entry for Outsiders' (*Postoronnym vkhod zapreshchen*). To our discomfort, the canteen was located among the archival buildings on the other side of this door (the kindly archivists allowed us to make tea and eat sandwiches in the reading room). We were not allowed to see the inventories of files (the *opisi*). The archivist was told what our topic was, looked in the *opisi*, and passed the files to the senior official whose job it was to vet our access. We then received a small clutch of files once a week or so. But even these concessions were absent in the Central Party Archive. Very few Western historians were allowed to work there before 1989; even senior members of foreign Communist Parties were excluded.

7 The Opening of the Archives

From 1988 onwards bastion after bastion began to fall. On a memorable day in 1989 foreign scholars were moved out of their confinement in their special reading room in the state archives into the normal reading room, and were given access to the inventories of many Soviet commissariats. In the Central Party Archive a selected group of Soviet historians – several of whom we have already met in these pages – was allowed extensive access to formerly secret materials in connection with the preparation of the new party history. The directors of both Glavarkhiv and the Central Party Archive claimed in numerous interviews that all was going well.[1]

The more open regime in the archives was established at a time when public interest in revelations about the past was at its maximum. Historians poured into the archives. The general reading room of the state archives was usually half-empty. But in 1990 there was a 'flood of Soviet and foreign researchers; there are no free places; there is nowhere to keep the files which have been issued to readers'.[2]

These relaxations did not satisfy many archivists and most historians. Vaganov, the Director of Glavarkhiv, was regarded with great suspicion in view of the extreme orthodoxy of his contributions to the historical debates of 1987.[3] By 1990, only a handful of files classified as 'secret' had been released (notably the population census of 1939). Only a couple of historians were given access to the NKVD files about the Gulag, which for the years 1934–60 were located in the state archives. These historians were allowed to cite data extensively from these files, but they were not allowed to state their provenance. Until some months after the August 1991 coup even the reference number for the NKVD *fond* (group of records), 9479, was not mentioned in publications about the camps.[4]

The arguments about openness penetrated deeply into the archives themselves. In the spring of 1989, 324 archivists working in the central state archives addressed a letter to the Supreme Soviet insisting on the urgent necessity of adopting a Law on the Archives.[5] Then in 1990 the head of the secret department of a major state archive argued that 'the time has come to simplify the system for arranging research which uses secret documents'.[6] Tsaplin, Director of TsGANKh, the economic archive, published a pioneering article in 1989 about the mass repressions, based on secret material from his archive.[7] Then in 1990 he pressed hard for greater openness in the state archives generally and addressed a detailed report on their failings to the party central committee. The letter was forwarded from party headquarters to Vaganov, who regarded it as extremely disloyal. Tsaplin had to take early retirement.

Some archives remained under a very tight regime. In August 1990 the Council of Ministers passed a resolution nominally introducing greater access to the archives of the Ministry of Foreign Affairs. Declassification was to be undertaken by *ad hoc* groups, in which retired diplomats predominated. The authorities admitted that 'years will go by' before the millions of documents were declassified; and the archivists in the Ministry insisted:

> the diplomatic archive is not a public library where every schoolboy can receive a copy of a book he needs which exists in many copies. It is a temple, where the sanctuaries – i.e. the documents of which only one copy exists – can be approached only by those who have proved by their publications that they can work, and are able to evaluate primary sources.[8]

Not surprisingly, the security services were particularly insistent on controlling their own archives. In 1990 the Ministry of Internal Affairs even tried to remove the documents of the Ministry for 1934–60 from the state archives (these documents contain nearly all the material about the Gulag which has been published so far from Soviet archives). The deputy chair of the Commission on the Literary Heritage of Repressed Writers, Vitaly Shentalinsky, described their exhausting experiences in seeking to obtain access to KGB files about writers persecuted or executed under Stalin:

> Eighteen months ago we began to knock at the massive doors of the *spetskhran*. A voice was heard 'What do you want?' We explained. A few sheets of paper were pushed through to us under the door. They thought we would go away. We did not go away, we began to shake at the door. They opened it a little on a chain, looking us in the eye, and we began to receive files. A gap in the door appeared. The entrance is getting bigger, but the door is still not wide open.[9]

Shentalinsky eventually published a fascinating account (available in English) of the KGB archives about writers.[10]

Meanwhile the state archives had completed the preparation of an elaborate draft Law 'On the Archival *Fond* of the USSR'. They had been working on the draft since 1987. The work was undertaken in secrecy, and the draft was never published in the Russian press. It incorporated a restricted thirty-year rule.[11] But it was regarded by critical historians and archivists as utterly inadequate. They particularly objected to the stipulation that the 30-year rule did not apply in the case of 'information which concerns state interests of particular importance'. The draft also refrained from explicitly extending its coverage to the Communist party archives.[12]

Simultaneously, an unofficial 'initiative group' of archivists and lawyers, headed by B. S. Ilizarov from the Moscow State Historical Archive Institute, of which Afanas'ev was director, prepared a more liberal draft Law 'On Archival Affairs and the Archive'. This was published in the prestigious journal of the Academy of Sciences.[13] It firmly proposed that the thirty-year rule should apply to all state documents; the only exception, also proposed in the official draft, was a 75-year limit for personal files. The unofficial draft unambiguously proposed that the new law should cover party as well as state archives.

The course of events in 1990 and 1991 mirrored the political tension in society at large between democrats and the old regime. Confronted with the rival draft Law, Vaganov proposed that the two drafts should be considered by a 'round table'.[14] But the Ilizarov group refused on the grounds that their project was 'incompatible in principle' with the official draft, and in February 1990 did not turn up at a meeting on the two drafts convened by the state archives. Both drafts were submitted to the Supreme Soviet in 1990; the official draft was supported by the Council of Ministers.[15] The Supreme Soviet failed to resolve the controversy before the August 1991 coup.

In archival administration, as in other matters, the Russian Supreme Soviet, with Yeltsin in the chair, sought to wrest initiative and power from Gorbachev and the USSR government. On 5 November 1990, the archival administration of the RSFSR (the Russian Federation), which had been subordinate both to the republic and to Glavarkhiv of the USSR, was replaced by a Committee on Archival Affairs attached to the Council of Ministers of the RSFSR, known as Roskomarkhiv. Roskomarkhiv was headed by Rudol'f Pikhoya, a historian of pre-revolutionary Russia who transferred to Moscow from Sverdlovsk, Yeltsin's home region.[16] Pikhoya was a vigorous administrator, and Roskomarkhiv soon asserted its independence. But until after the failure of the August 1991 coup the major USSR archives remained under Vaganov and Glavarkhiv. The Central Party Archive remained outside the control of the governments of both the USSR and the Russian republic, and imposed even tighter controls in 1991 (see pp. 33–4 above).

THE AUGUST 1991 COUP AND ITS AFTERMATH

During the three-day reign of the State Emergency Committee, Glavarkhiv issued firm instructions to the Directors of individual repositories and their various departments that all archival staff were to remain in place. The authorities were afraid that junior archivists might sneak off to participate in the defence of the White House, occupied by Yeltsin and the Russian Federation (RSFSR) government. It was August, the height of the holiday season. Many archivists were not in place anyway. Those department chiefs who sympathised with the democrats were able to turn a blind eye to defections.

On 24 August 1991, three days after the defeat of the coup, Yeltsin signed two revolutionary decrees on the archives in which he assumed that the powers of the USSR would now pass to the RSFSR. The decree 'On the Party Archives' ruled that as the Communist Party had been part of the state machine 'documents created in the course of its activity are to be preserved by the state'. Hence the Central Party Archive, the current archive of the General Department of the central committee and the regional party archives were all to be 'transferred to the management of the archival agencies of the RSFSR together with the buildings and plant they occupy, their staff and their allocation for the payment of wages'. A similar decree announced that the archives of the KGB of the *USSR* were to be transferred to the archival agencies of the *RSFSR*. Both decrees were to 'come into force at the moment of signature'.[17]

Roskomarkhiv and its Director Pikhoya enthusiastically welcomed the arrival of a new era. All the archives would be 'depoliticised', and the public would be granted full access:[18]

> I believe [Pikhoya told the main archival journal] that with the adoption of the Law 'On the Archival *Fond* of the RSFSR and the Archives' the problems of access by researchers to the archives will be removed. The Law will fix a period of restrictions on documents containing state, military, commercial or other secrets protected by the Law (but no more than 30 years from the moment of their creation). Restrictions are possible for particular groups of documents. The Law will protect the researcher from arbitrary decisions by the legal holder of the group of records concerned (*fondoderzhatel'*) or by archivists.[19]

At this time Pikhoya was confidently expecting that a large part of the KGB archives would be transferred to his care. 'After the *fond*s of the KGB have arrived in Roskomarkhiv,' he wrote, 'it is intended to organise historical archives, with the status of central archives, in Omsk, Ul'yanovsk, Penza and Moscow' (some of the places where KGB depositories are located).[20]

One immediate administrative obstacle remained to be overcome. The USSR for the moment continued to exist, and with it Glavarkhiv USSR and its Director Vaganov. In October an RSFSR decree attempted to take over Glavarkhiv.[21] Nevertheless, on 19–20 November Glavarkhiv USSR convened a meeting of the Directors of the archives of the Soviet republics at Glavarkhiv headquarters in the 'Archival Suburb' with the intention of establishing new arrangements at the USSR level. But Roskomarkhiv was naturally unwilling to accept any such proposal. The meeting was dominated by sharp exchanges between Vaganov and Pikhoya, as the following extract from the verbatim report demonstrates:

> *R. G. Pikhoya (addressing F. M. Vaganov).* Can you ensure that the two archival institutes and the state archival administration of the USSR will be financed?
>
> *E. Z. Kuz'mina* [Director of TsGANKh, who replaced Tsaplin]. On the decision of the RSFSR government Roskomarkhiv has taken us over, and it will provide finance.
>
> *R. G. Pikhoya.* We are required to pay you money, we have money, but we need a deed of transfer. I have left the deed with cde. Vaganov.
>
> *V. E. Filippova* (head of financial department of Glavarkhiv USSR). There is a war between governments. The RSFSR Ministry of Finance must take things over from the USSR Ministry of Finance. But the USSR Ministry of Finance has been instructed to continue until January 6, 1992. It will carry out all its obligations. The USSR Ministry of Finance has not refused us.
>
> *R. G. Pikhoya.* We are living from month to month. The USSR Ministry of Finance will not finance anyone.
>
> *V. A. Tyuneev* [Pikhoya's deputy]. The USSR Ministry of Finance is transferring things to the RSFSR Ministry of Finance.
>
> *V. E. Filippova.* So far it hasn't been doing so.
>
> *E. P. Makharadze* [Georgian archives]. Can Glavarkhiv USSR be transferred to Roskomarkhiv without a decree of the USSR government?
>
> *F. M. Vaganov.* No.[22]

A month later the USSR and its state archival administration ceased to exist, and all the activities of the former Glavarkhiv USSR were transferred to Roskomarkhiv. Vaganov's job came an end, and he died an unhappy man in November 1993.[23] The orthodox and bureaucratic Kitaev was removed from his post as Director of the former Central Party Archive immediately after the defeat of the August coup. Early in 1992 Kuz'mina, who strongly supported Vaganov at the 19–20 November meeting, relinquished the directorship of TsGANKh. But this was a velvet revolution. Kuz'mina continued to work elsewhere in the Russian archives. Nearly all the other archivists, senior and junior, remained in place in both the state and the party archives.

In December 1991, Pikhoya was appointed Chief State Archivist of the Russian Federation, and in December 1992 Roskomarkhiv was upgraded and renamed Rosarkhiv – the State Archival Service of Russia.[24]

THE NEW ERA OF OPENNESS, 1992–6

The golden promises made in the weeks after the defeat of the August coup were in large part honoured. A decree of the Council of Ministers of the RSFSR announced that the Central Party Archive was to be reorganised as RTsKhIDNI – the Russian Centre for the Preservation and Study of Documents of Recent History. The current archive of the central committee, which mainly contains post-1952 documents, was to be reorganised as TsKhSD – the Centre for the Preservation of Contemporary Documentation.[25] RTsKhIDNI was duly declared open to the public in December 1991 and TsKhSD in February 1992.[26] In RTsKhIDNI, microfilms of the inventories (*opisi*) were made available in the general reading room; in TsKhSD some of the files had to be assembled from the cupboards and safes of the various departments, and a smooth service took longer to achieve. In both archives the old requirement that readers' notes should be kept in special books for inspection by an archivist was abolished.

Access to the state archives was also greatly extended. The 'confidential' files and their inventories were freely available to all readers; and large numbers of previously secret and top-secret files were declassified for general use. By the end of 1992, for example, the NKVD files for 1934–60 in GARF – the State Archive of the Russian Federation – were available to foreign as well as Russian scholars.[27]

I have worked in both the state archives and the former Central Party Archive (now RTsKhIDNI) in Moscow annually since 1991; and in each year a wider range of materials on the 1930s has been available to me than in the previous year. And in regional and local archives rich collections have often been available with even less restrictions. Access has been more difficult for historians concerned with sensitive issues of foreign policy and with more recent periods. But with this important reservation the story of the archives is a success story. Improvements before August 1991 were transformed into a revolution thereafter.

But this was an unfinished revolution, as the next chapter explains.

8 Persistent Problems

Throughout 1991–6 serious restrictions and problems have marred the considerable achievements, to such an extent that some historians have almost forgotten the advances. By 1996 it has begun to look as if the next chapter in the history of the archives will be entitled 'The Revolution Betrayed'.

Here I shall consider the problems – and the malign influences – under five main heads: (1) Politics; (2) Impoverishment; (3) Privileged Access; (4) Secrecy; (5) Privileged Archives.

POLITICS

In important respects the archives continued to play a political role – but now in the service of Yeltsin and the campaign against Communism.

In the volatile weeks after August 1991, it sometimes looked as if access to the archives was to be a new ideological monopoly. The newspaper *Izvestiya*, often a reliable source on archival matters, reported that on 17 September 1991 Pikhoya had received in Roskomarkhiv Yurii Afanas'ev and the well-known former dissident Vladimir Bukovsky, who was visiting Moscow from emigration. Bukovsky was described as 'representing a number of international organisations'. According to *Izvestiya*:

> An international commission is being established consisting of the most important world specialists on the history of the USSR to study the new archival information: scholars from the Hoover and Kennan Institutes, the International Council of Archives, the 'Memorial' centre, etc. The result of the joint work will be the creation, or more precisely the re-creation, of a full and objective history of the Soviet state, which will finally be presented to the world without gaps, black holes and blank pages, on the basis of the colossal documentary wealth which will be placed in the hands of researchers.[1]

A few weeks later a report appeared in the British *Sunday Times* that Yeltsin had invited Robert Conquest and Norman Stone, Professor of Modern History at Oxford, to join an international commission to examine the Communist Party and KGB archives. For this purpose Norman Stone would take two years' sabbatical leave from Oxford. The *Sunday Times* added rather flippantly that 'the jovial historian may find Moscow congenial', including perhaps 'the sort of conviviality encouraged by Mr. Yeltsin.'[2]

The International Commission did not materialise. No further attempt was made to establish a new orthodoxy based on the archival truth, until November 1995, when Yeltsin ordered the preparation of a new history of the Russian state (see p. 78 above).

Material newly-released from the archives has frequently been used by Yeltsin and his associates for political purposes (see Chapter 5). Writing about the situation at the beginning of 1993, Patricia Grimsted concluded that 'delayed, piecemeal, highly censored revelations are being used or "misused" as pawns in the troubled post-Soviet political and diplomatic arena.'[3]

The practice has attenuated in recent years, but not vanished. Thus on 23 August 1993, a decree of the Council of Ministers 'On the Realisation of State Policy in Archival Affairs' called for the publication of volumes of archival materials during 1994–2000 which would 'show Russia's role and place in the history of world civilisation and world culture and its influence on the world community' and would take into account 'the growth of the national and historical consciousness of the Russians (*Rossiyane*)'.[4] And archival revelations continue to be used in the interests of Russian foreign policy. In June 1994, in the course of his visit to South Korea, Yeltsin presented copies of 216 top-secret documents about the Korean War to President Kim Young-San; these showed the active and perhaps decisive role of North Korea in launching the invasion of the South in June 1950.[5]

IMPOVERISHMENT

Since the collapse of the Soviet Union and the launching of shock therapy, the archives, like nearly all other Russian academic institutions, have received disastrously inadequate budgetary allocations. Staff wages are minuscule; and cheap meals are no longer available. In June 1995 I visited the reopened canteen in the 'Archive Suburb', always packed in the past. Prices were very high in comparison with Russian wages, and the only people eating there were the Director of one of the archives and three foreigners.

Many of the staff have left in search of better pay, including a number of very experienced archivists. Staff in one major archive work part-time. They spend the other half of the week trying to earn enough to feed their families. In consequence some reading rooms are open at irregular and unpredictable hours.

The buildings of the 'Archive Suburb' were already in a very poor state at the end of the 1980s. Since then almost no repairs have been carried out. Lifts frequently break down, so that files have to be carried up and down long flights of stairs to the reading rooms. In some important repositories, there are no bulbs in many of the microfilm readers.

PRIVILEGED ACCESS

Desperately short of money, a few archivists at every level have been tempted to make their services and documents available only in return for bribes and other inducements. Fifty dollars from a foreign historian is more than a month's wages. An American historian with considerable experience in the archives described in stark terms the petty corruption he had witnessed:

> In the second half of 1992 I personally witnessed several disturbing and even sickening manifestations of the economic disaster. One archive demanded five dollars per page for photocopying (because another American had paid it); elsewhere an archival employee wanted payment in dollars to provide documents to an American in the reading room. At another archive, a representative of a European publisher was carrying documents out of the building in his shirt, while a low-level employee in a stairwell offered to sell original archive materials for an airline ticket.[6]

I have discussed this question with many Western and Russian historians, and in my estimation such cases of petty corruption are remarkably rare. Russian archivists are extremely well-trained professionals. Most of them are selflessly devoted to their work, and helpful to both foreign and Russian historians.

At a higher level, Russian archives, and groups of Russian historians and archivists, have made many agreements or deals, large and small, with Western publishers and academic institutions. The Russian press – especially the nationalist press – has frequently expressed suspicion and indignation about these activities.

The principles which the archives are supposed to follow in approving such arrangements are reasonably clear. The archives claim to hold the copyright on their documents. A historian may freely publish short extracts or notes, but a payment must be negotiated with the archive for the right to publish or reproduce a complete document in Russian or in translation. Rosarkhiv has firmly stated, repeating this as recently as November

1995, that such arrangements should not interfere with the rights of historians who are not participating in the arrangements; the documents should be fully accessible except for short periods when they are being examined or microfilmed. This rule, when observed, is a welcome departure from the old Soviet practice that senior historians could have large groups of documents withdrawn from circulation, sometimes for many years, on the grounds that they was preparing them for publication.

Some important projects seem to have abided by the rules, to the mutual benefit of both archives and historians. A prominent example is the Cold War International History Project at the Woodrow Wilson International Center in Washington, financed by the MacArthur Foundation. This project has supported joint conferences, provided fellowships for Russian and other historians, and above all assisted the prompt release of many important top-secret post-war Soviet documents. It has helped Western historians who are not part of the project to work in Russian archives. It publishes a series of Working Papers, and a *Bulletin* which prints translations of newly-released documents and is a rich source of information on Russian and former Communist bloc archives (the *Bulletin* has been frequently cited in the present book).

Many smaller projects have also worked well. A joint Russian–French–Italian programme is supporting the publication in Russian of a series of 'Documents of Soviet History'. The first book deals with the Politburo in the 1930s, and greatly enlarges our knowledge of how central Soviet government worked under Stalin. It includes a full record of the dates of meetings, and of the names of those attending. The core of the book is the reproduction of material related to important items on the Politburo agenda. This includes many vivid letters to Stalin and other members of the Politburo from Ordzhonikidze, Voroshilov, Kaganovich, Kirov and Mikoyan.[7]

The University of Pittsburgh Russian Centre is issuing valuable research guides to RTsKhIDNI, RGAE and other depositories.

An agreement between RTsKhIDNI (the former Central Party Archive) and the Feltrinelli Foundation has resulted in the production of a lavish well-edited and scholarly volume containing the verbatim reports of the Cominform conferences of 1947, 1948 and 1949, with a full English translation, and articles by eminent specialists such as the Russian Grant Adibekov and the Italian Anna di Biagio.[8] However, in this case many of the Comintern materials were temporarily closed to other historians.

The agreement made in 1992 between the Russian Federal Intelligence Service, one of the successors to the KGB, and Crown Publishers, a United States firm, is even less satisfactory from the point of view of historical research. It provided for the publication of up to ten volumes in English, based on the KGB archives, and covering such important topics as the Berlin crisis, the Cuban missile crisis, and British espionage. A fee of $1 million is being paid by the publishers, including translation and other expenses. The most objectionable feature of the agreement is a clause which requires that the documents concerned should be withheld from all historians except those taking part in the project. The ban will operate at least until the publication of each English-language volume; according to some accounts, it will operate for much longer.[9]

An even more serious disadvantage of the Crown project is that Russian intelligence will itself decide what documents the historians working on the project are entitled to see. Major-General A. Belozerov, head of the Archive of External Intelligence (AVR), the main repository involved, boasted in December 1995 that 'outsiders extremely rarely cross our threshold', and that only Russians would have access to some of the materials involved in the Crown agreement.[10] An American historian concludes that 'the version of history that these books yield will be the KGB's own'.[11]

The first volume has already been published and partly confirms this pessimistic conclusion. The British author of this volume did not apparently know Russian; his joint author is a senior member of the Russian Intelligence Service. The book presents Alexander Orlov, a senior Soviet intelligence officer, as a 'professional to the end of his days', who remained a 'steadfast adherent of the Communist vision'. Orlov had been responsible for the Stalinist purge in Spain, and defected to the United States in 1939, concealing the unpleasant aspects of his activities from the American authorities. I think it is fair to say that in this volume he is presented in far too rosy a light. Appropriately, the book jacket assures us in large letters that it contains 'the KGB secrets the British government doesn't want you to read'.[12]

Major-General Belozerov has recently played down the significance of the agreement with Crown. He claimed that it was made not with his archive but with the 'Association of Veterans of External Intelligence', and that it would result in four rather than ten books.[13]

Another agreement which has aroused controversy was concluded between Yale University Press, RTsKhIDNI and other archives. It provides for the publication in both English and Russian versions of nine volumes of documents jointly edited by Russian and American historians. One of the first three volumes, *Stalin's Letters to Molotov*, is extremely well annotated by the Russian editors (see Chapter 12). A second volume, on the fall of the last Tsar, is a sound work of scholarship.[14] A third volume in the series, *The Secret World of American Communism*, has received most publicity. It consists of 92 documents from the Communist International (Comintern) archive on the clandestine activities of the American Communist Party.[15] The publishers presented it as a major historical sensation, and the editors claim that it demonstrates that the party was 'a conspiracy financed by a hostile foreign power that recruited members for clandestine work, developed by an elaborate underground apparatus and used by that apparatus to collaborate with the espionage services of that power'. Most reviewers have assessed the volume favourably. But a senior American historian, Alfred Rieber, who has worked in the Comintern archives, criticises the book for its 'accusatory tone, the use of innuendo and the stretching of thin evidence'. He strongly rejects its claim that the documents demonstrate the reliability of Whittaker Chambers, who accused the American diplomat Alger Hiss of spying for the Soviet Union.[16]

Even if Rieber's strictures on this volume are true, however, the Yale series is much more satisfactory from the point of view of objective research than the Crown series. The Yale project, apart from a hiccup in the early stages, has not apparently prevented access to these materials – though historians are required to obtain permission from Yale for publishing citations from documents which are in process of publication.[17] And until recently all the Comintern material on the American Communist Party was available for research, including those documents which were not included in the book. Unfortunately, some of this material has now been withdrawn from public access through no fault of Yale.[18]

The largest project, and the one which aroused most anxiety, was the agreement reached in 1992 between the Hoover Institution, Rosarkhiv and the British microform publishers Chadwyck–Healey to microfilm at least 25 million pages of documents (25 000 reels) from RTsKhIDNI and other archives, including about 3000 reels of inventories. The project was expected to cost $3–5 million over five years. Copies will be deposited at the Hoover and in Moscow, and are being placed on sale to the public by Chadwyck–Healey.[19]

The project was ferociously criticised in the Russian nationalist press: a typical angry article was entitled 'The Archives – Everything is on Sale'.[20] But strong objections also came from far outside nationalist circles. Yurii Afanas'ev claimed that the Hoover deal meant that 'the most valuable blocks of our historical memory' were being sold in secrecy and haste. The result would be that the centre of research into Russian history would be moved from Moscow to the Hoover Institute, where Westerners would find it easier to work.[21] The fear that Western historians would stop coming to Moscow, and hence damage the usefulness of the Russian archives, was very strong among archivists. In my opinion, the availability of basic documents in the West for their dissertation or book is far more likely to encourage postgraduate students and teachers to take up research on Russian history, and visit Russia for more material.[22]

Afanas'ev also inadvertently revealed that he had not shaken off the mentality of a Young Communist official by advancing a nationalist argument taken straight from Soviet practice in the Brezhnev years:

> historians from our fatherland (*otechestvennye istoriki*), who have for so long been deprived of access to the most important archival stores in the USSR, have the full right to be the first to enter the fatherland's archival stocks.

He also proposed that foreign historians should be required to pay a fee in foreign currency in return for the use of the archives. Fortunately Yeltsin's legislators have so far been more enlightened than the 'democrat' Afanas'ev, and archival legislation has specified – as is normal practice in state archives throughout the civilised world – that all historians irrespective of nationality have equal rights to use declassified documents. Admission to most archives remains free of charge.

The files for prominent revolutionary leaders, including Ordzhonikidze and Molotov, prepared as a result of a previous agreement with Chadwyck–Healey, have already been placed on sale. And more than 5000 reels are available from the main agreement. Their most alarming deficiency is the extremely high price, $41 695 for 355 reels on revolutionary leaders, and over $300 000 as a special reduced price for the bulk purchase of the 5000 reels. These prices will preclude nearly all British and most American libraries from purchasing these important microforms.

Many commentators in both the Russian and Western press have given the impression that such arrangements often result in the export from Russia of original archival documents. This is explicitly forbidden by Russian law. Some documents have been smuggled out of the archives and the country since 1991. But almost every specific sensational revelation which I have been able to follow up has turned out to be based on some misunderstanding. Thus Russian Central TV falsely reported, evidently with reference to the Hoover agreement, 'facts of the sale of documents from the CPSU and the KGB to various foreign organisations'.[23]

In December 1995 the Board of Rosarkhiv, in a dramatic move, voted unanimously to cancel the agreement, against Pikhoya's advice.[24] This is a striking example of the increasing general hostility to 'Western interference' in internal Russian affairs. A few weeks later, on 17 January 1996, Yeltsin accepted Pikhoya's resignation from the post of Chief Archivist of the Russian Federation.[25] Unconfirmed rumours abounded in Moscow of new archival scandals, financial and political. Pikhoya has been succeeded temporarily by V. E. Tyuneev, a professional archivist.

Another form of privileged access which rightly aroused great indignation among Russian historians has been that afforded to certain individuals by virtue of their political influence – or in the case of certain foreigners as a result of their powers of financial persuasion.

The most notorious privileged individual was the late Dimitri Volkogonov, who received unparalleled access to all kinds of secret archives in the Gorbachev years in view of his authority as General Volkogonov, at first the deputy head of the Political Administration of the Army and then the director of the Institute of Military History. For his four-volume study of Stalin, published in 1989 when most archives were still closed to other historians, Volkogonov was able to use the Central Party Archives, the military and foreign archives, and the particularly inaccessible archives of the Ministry of Defence (TsAMO) in Podol'sk.

Russian historians had already referred to Volkogonov scathingly as 'the General Writer' (*General'nyi Pisatel'*), and when his books appeared their hostility increased. His appointment at the end of 1991 as chair of the parliamentary Commission for the Transfer and Acceptance of the Archives of the Communist Party of the Soviet Union and the KGB added insult to injury. In this role he undoubtedly accelerated the release of many documents. But the general feeling among Russian historians remained, and was summed up by Vladimir Buldakov:

> Volkogonov over several years essentially came into monopolistic possession of the documents of Stalin, Lenin and Trotsky. He used this situation in accordance with political circumstances, and the 'exposure' of Lenin helped to consolidate him in his anti-Communist stance.[26]

Some sensational cases of exceptional access to the archives remain obscure. In 1992 the British right-wing historian David Irving was shown copies of the Goebbels' diaries in the former Special Archive; the Soviet authorities had seized the diaries in Berlin in 1945 and concealed them from the world. The *Sunday Times* is reported to offered $145 000 for the acquisition of the diaries. But it is quite unclear how much of the fee was paid, and how much of it went to Russian archives or Russian archivists. According to a statement by the head of the international relations' department of the Russian archives, they were the victims of a deception by David Irving. He was given permission to publish only 90 of the 80 000 pages of the 1941–5 diaries, but made copies of many more pages without permission.[27]

The most notorious controversy about access was 'the Morris affair'. In January 1993 an Australian researcher, Stephen Morris, who was working in the post-1952 party archive, TsKhSD, with support from the Cold War Project, acquired the Russian translation of a speech by the North Vietnamese deputy chief of staff, delivered in September 1972. The document stated that North Vietnam was holding 1 205 American prisoners of war rather than the 368 officially admitted; the true total was kept secret for tactical reasons. Morris reported his discovery to American officials, and the story appeared on the front page of *The New York Times*.[28] Hell broke loose in the archives. The director of TsKhSD, Usikov, was dismissed, and accused of shady financial dealings, including the sale of the offending document to Morris. All the Russian historians and archivists with whom I discussed this matter believed these accusations. But a circumstantial account by Mark Kramer, a senior member of the Cold War project, who was present in the reading room when the document was issued, claims that 'Morris had ordered the document in the same way as he would have requested any other document, and the archival staff delivered it to him in a perfectly routine manner . . . At no point did Morris even meet Usikov, much less buy documents from him.'[29]

Following the Morris affair, archival procedures were tightened up. Usikov's immediate successor, Prokopenko, has often been helpful to Western historians, including the present author. But a month after this incident, in May 1993, he made his notorious comment 'Yes, these documents have been declassified, but that doesn't mean people should be allowed to look at them'.[30]

There have been many sensational publications from the archives in recent years. Some of them are part of a political campaign (for examples see Chapter 4). Some are facilitated by bribes to archivists. Some, as in the Morris affair, are lucky finds which the historian for reasons of conscience or ambition feels bound to publicise. Such publicists are all scathingly described by more serious or less entrepreneurial Russian historians as 'marauders'.

Soon after TsKhSD opened its doors, Tim Sebastian, former BBC correspondent in Moscow, published in the *Sunday Times* a dramatic account of secret reports sent to Moscow from the Soviet Embassy in London about meetings between Soviet officials and Neil Kinnock, Denis Healey and other prominent members of the Labour Party. Writing in *Izvestiya*, a Soviet journalist formerly based in London insisted that these were normal diplomatic contacts, magnified into an attempt to smear the Labour Party in an election year. Sebastian's report made no mention of Soviet contacts with Conservative politicians. *Izvestiya* asked how a Western journalist had managed to penetrate an archive 'inaccessible to the ordinary Soviet journalist'.[31]

The Western penetration of the archive on this occasion eventually proved politically impartial. A few days later *The Guardian* correspondent in Moscow went to TsKhSD and asked to see the same set of files. He discovered reports, some of which Sebastian had seen but ignored, of Soviet meetings with Reginald Maudling, Lord Home, Edward Heath, Geoffrey Rippon, St John Stevas and other Conservative MPs, and with Mrs Thatcher's policy adviser Sir Alfred Sherman. Sherman's interview with the *Pravda* correspondent in London, which took place in 1984, was more outspoken than those by the Labour leaders. He told the *Pravda* correspondent in London that he favoured cuts in pensions and unemployment pay, noting that 'the unemployed and the lumpen [yes, that word again – RWD] never have been a revolutionary force'.[32]

Parliamentary elections were taking place in Italy as well as Britain in 1992; and a second archival sensation, involving the other former party archive, RTsKhIDNI, concerned the Communist leader Togliatti and his attitude to Italian prisoners of war.[33] RTsKhIDNI had signed a project with an Italian publisher, Ponte alle Grazie, for the publication of a book of documents on 'Comintern and the Italian Communist Party [the PCI]'. At the end of January 1992 RTsKhIDNI issued a letter written by Togliatti to an Italian historian, Professor Franco Andreucci, who was working on the project. Togliatti's letter, dated 15 February–3 March 1943 (the middle of the second world war), was addressed to a fellow Communist, Vincenzo Bianco (the two Italians were both in Moscow). Togliatti rejected Bianco's complaints about the harsh conditions under which Italian prisoners of war were living in the USSR:

> I am not a cruel man, as you know. I am just as humane as you are, or as the ladies from the Red Cross may be . . . In practice, however, if a large number of prisoners of war die because of the bad conditions which exist, I see nothing at all in this that is worth discussing. On the contrary. And I will explain why. There is no doubt that the Italian people are poisoned with the imperialist brigand ideology of fascism. The poison has penetrated the peasants and the workers, not to mention the petty bourgeoisie and the intelligentsia – in general, it has infected the people. The fact that for thousands and thousands of families the war unleashed by Mussolini, and particularly the expedition against Russia, will finish in tragedy and personal grief is the best and most effective antidote.

In his reply, dated 20 March, Bianco rejected Togliatti's harsh attitude to the prisoners of war, and four days later raised the issue with Dimitrov, the

General Secretary of Comintern, and with the section of the NKVD responsible for the prisoners. Bianco argued that they should not be treated
as unredeemable enemies but should be re-educated so that they would
return to Italy as allies.[34]

Andreucci promptly passed the letter to the Milan weekly *Panorama*.
Panorama published an extract from the letter on 9 February 1992. The
letter was printed with some inaccuracies; most of these were minor, but
at least one resulted in Togliatti appearing as even more pitiless than he
actually was.[35] *Panorama* also omitted passages in Togliatti's letter which
looked forward to an anti-fascist movement of the Italian people supported
by the invading British and American troops. And it failed to mention
Bianco's memorandum to the NKVD, which showed that another important Italian Communist in Moscow was more humane than Togliatti (Bianco
was the representative of the PCI at the Comintern).

The publicity which followed was of course extremely damaging to the
Italian Democratic Party of the Left – the successor to the PCI. The President of Italy even proposed to establish a special State Commission of
historians to examine the document. The Director of RTsKhIDNI told a
press conference held in Moscow on 20 February that Andreucci had been
issued with the letter for research purposes and did not have the right to
publish it; 'the violation of the rules for utilising the document has caused
moral harm to RTsKhIDNI'.[36] Later, however, the archive journal stated
that 'the publication of an extract is not a violation of the existing archive
rules'.[37] But the president of Ponte alle Grazie apologised to RTsKhIDNI,
and Andreucci resigned from the project.[38]

The archival sensation most potentially harmful to the openness of the
archives was the publication in the Russian journal *Questions of the History of Science and Technology* of a series of documents, not from any of
the state or former party archives under Rosarkhiv but from the Russian
Archive of External Intelligence. These documents were offered to the
journal for publication by a former KGB agent who had been involved in
atomic espionage. The publication, entitled 'The Atom and Intelligence',
consisted of reports prepared in 1941–6 by the NKVD and by Kurchatov,
the scientific head of the Soviet nuclear bomb project, on intelligence
received about the United States bomb from the physicist Klaus Fuchs and
others. It included a 14-page description of the design of the American
bomb sent to the Soviet government by Kurchatov in March 1943.[39]

When the journal was already in print, it was shown to Yu. B. Khariton,
who had been in charge of weapons research and development at that
time. Khariton persuaded the Ministry of Atomic Power that publication
would contravene the nuclear proliferation treaty.[40] But the ban came too

late. Although the offending issue of the journal was withdrawn from circulation, copies had already been sent out to a number of foreign and Russian subscribers.

SECRECY

In the euphoric days immediately after August 1991, it seemed as if all secrecy about the Soviet past would be completely set aside. Archival officials frequently repeated the provisions of the legislation drafted before August 1991: a thirty-year rule would apply to secret documents, except for personal files, to which a 75-year rule would apply. These provisions were included in legislation about the archives approved in June 1992 and July 1993.[41]

But there was of course a snag. As in many other countries, including Britain and the United States, the legislation specified that certain documents could be exempted from the thirty-year rule. In practice there were no clear procedures for declassifying the vast number of documents in the archives which were more than thirty years old and were categorised as secret or top secret. The various archives took it upon themselves to establish arrangements for declassification; and very large numbers of important documents became available. By the end of 1993, the State Archive of the Russian Federation (GARF), for example, had declassified 1.5 million files. This was about half the total of three million files declassified within the state system as a whole.[42] RTsKhIDNI, the most liberal of all the archives at this time, assumed that normally all documents in its files were no longer secret, having been created by the now defunct Communist Party before 1953 (it should be noted, however, that the 'special files' (*osobye papki*) were not at this time located in RTsKhIDNI but in the Presidential Archive).

But by the end of 1993 the process of declassification had markedly decelerated. By this time at least three obstacles to declassification had emerged. First, in July 1993 the Law on State Secrecy had been approved. This provided that an Interdepartmental Commission on the Preservation of State Secrecy should be responsible for declassifying all documents of government departments and other agencies for which successors did not exist (these included the Communist Party and various Ministries). But the Commission was not actually established until over two years later (see p. 108 below). The process of declassification was ambiguous and confused.

Secondly, various Ministries and other government departments acquired – or rather re-acquired – the right to decide which documents created by their predecessors and deposited in the state archives should remain inaccessible to historians. Post-war documents were a particular cause of anxiety. Older officials had worked in the Ministries for decades before the fall of Communism, and were most unwilling that their activities should be exposed to the searchlight of post-Soviet criticism. And Russian officials generally continued to be influenced by the Soviet ethos of secrecy, which as we have seen set the bounds of confidentiality far wider than in most other advanced countries.

Thirdly, the security services began to resume part of their traditional authority. They acquired the right to visit archives to check how far their internal processes of declassification had violated the needs of state security. Several Western historians have told me that their research was interrupted because the reading room in which they were working was temporarily closed for an inspection by the security services. The *International Herald Tribune* reported that 'secret-police agents have recently reappeared at top archives and major research institutes'.[43]

Procedures for declassification adopted since the beginning of 1994 have introduced much more severe restrictions. A Directive issued by Yeltsin on 22 September 1994 gave a formal role to the security services and the Ministry of Foreign Affairs in the process of declassification generally. However, it ordered that the declassification procedure should be elaborated together with Rosarkhiv. The most encouraging provision of the Directive was its insistence that decisions about declassifying documents created before 1963 should be reached before the end of 1994.[44]

Alas, this provision was not achieved in practice. A further Law on Information, passed by the Russian parliament and approved by Yeltsin on 20 February 1995, appeared to leave individual Ministries and agencies with full discretion over their own records management.[45] And a new 'List of Information Deemed to be a State Secret', approved by Yeltsin at the end of 1995, is a most elaborate Soviet-style document, including both defence data and matters relating only indirectly to defence.[46]

An Interdepartmental Commission on the Defence of State Secrecy (see p. 107 above) was finally established on November 8, 1995.[47] The Statute on the Commission, approved on 20 January 1996, entrusted it with all decisions relating to the extension of the 30-year rule on grounds of secrecy. It also confirmed that decisions about secrecy in relation to those archival collections for which successor organisations did not exist should be made by 'interdepartmental expert groups' responsible to the Commission. The Commission consists of senior representatives of the security services, the Ministry of Defence, the General Staff of the armed forces, the various economic and defence industry ministries, and of Korzhakov's

Presidential security service. But unlike all previous arrangements for declassification the Commission does not include a representative from the archives – neither from Rosarkhiv nor from the individual depositories.[48] This is an ominous development.

Many historians have reported some tightening up of access in the course of 1994–6. American historians on the Cold War project have been refused access to documents which they had already seen in 1992.[49] Russian and Western historians working on the Comintern files in RTsKhIDNI have found that their access has been restricted, on grounds of both state secrecy and personal confidentiality.[50] At the International Congress on Central and East European Studies held in Warsaw in August 1995 Pikhoya was strongly criticised by Russian historians for allowing the new restrictions to be imposed.[51]

Other historians, Russian and Western, including the present author, report that formerly secret files have continued to be released, albeit intermittently. What is certain is that vagueness about secrecy provides the opportunity for favoured treatment to particular individuals. As a Russian historian puts it:

> The boundaries [of secrecy] operating at the present time are incomprehensible to the ordinary historian. These 'boundary zones' are wide open for all kinds of special rights to documents and to double standards in resolving the question of access.[52]

The issue of privileged access is inextricably bound up with the question of secrecy.

PRIVILEGED ARCHIVES

In autumn 1991 the plan to place all archives of government departments under Roskomarkhiv was launched with great enthusiasm. Following Yeltsin's decrees of 24 August, *Izvestiya* announced in a banner headline 'The Archives of the CPSU and the KGB are being Transferred to the Ownership of the People'. In the case of the KGB, for example, its archival buildings and staff would be divided up, and only files classified as secret under new laws would remain closed.[53] In November 1991 the parliamentary commission headed by Volkogonov announced that the mechanism for transferring the archives was being worked out.[54] In January 1992, the parliamentary commission discussed a liberal draft law 'On the Archives of the KGB', which proposed that more than two-thirds of the files should be transferred to the normal archive system. Regional

KGB archives would form part of the normal regional archival system, and in Moscow a special Russian Centre for the Preservation and Study of Documents of the State Security Services – RTsKhIDSG – would be established.[55]

These proposals were exceptionally liberal. It is perhaps not surprising that they failed almost entirely – except in the case of the former party archives RTsKhIDNI and TsKhSD. The departments of state stubbornly clung to their special archival privileges. This applied even in the case of those archives which were already formally part of the state archival system before August 1991, but had a special status, such as the military archives. Three military archives which contain pre-1941 material are in principle open to historians. But these archives often follow the practice of providing lists of appropriate files to foreign historians and arranging declassification only after a substantial fee is paid for the archivists' work. And the military archives containing material for the post-1941 period, as well as the military intelligence archive, have remained largely inaccessible.[56] In March 1995 the Ministry of Foreign Affairs was also granted the formal right to retain all its archives.[57]

But it is the KGB archives and the so-called 'Presidential Archive' which have retained a particularly privileged status in spite of the 1991 decrees.

The KGB Archives

These remain firmly under the control of its successor organisations. As early as June 1992 the parliamentary commission and the external intelligence service were in deadlock, when the latter announced that all their 340 000 files, dating from 1920, were 'working papers', and could not be released.[58] Discussions continued throughout the year.[59] But in 1996 the position still remains as it was in 1991. The security services exercise their own discretion about what materials to release and to whom. As we have seen, substantial amounts of material are made available for publication – but at the discretion of the security services and for a high fee.

Since 1991 the security services have made strenuous efforts with the aid of selective releases from the archives to demonstrate that, while their repressive activities went a little too far, their intelligence work was extremely useful to the state. Documents have been released and interviews given to show the crucial role of the atomic spies in the development of the atom bomb, and the small contribution made by Soviet scientists. In response, Soviet scientists have persuasively argued that Soviet science and technology could not have used the intelligence material without a high degree of competence; and that the hydrogen bomb was developed without intelligence assistance.[60]

The security services have also published a wealth of material demonstrating that they were extremely well-informed, and in detail, about Hitler's preparation for invasion of the Soviet Union in 1940–1. They claim that Stalin was taken unawares owing not to the fault of the intelligence services as such but to his own stubbornness, and the unwillingness of the top security officials, Beria and Merkulov, to take a firm line.[61]

The 'Kremlin', Politburo or 'Presidential' Archive

The Archive of the President of the Russian Federation originated as the archive of the VI Sector of the General Department of the Central Committee. It contained material which Pikhoya described as of 'tremendous interest to historians and political scientists'. Its most important section was the original protocols of the Politburo from 1919 to 1990, with the verbatim reports of the meetings where these existed, and the associated memoranda and other working papers. It also included the personal archives of the General Secretaries of the party, including Stalin, of leading figures such as Mikoyan, Kaganovich, Trotsky and Maxim Gorky, and of many officials working for the Politburo, the Secretariat and elsewhere.[62]

The archive was established on the initiative of Boldin, who had been head of the General Department. Boldin was appointed head of the presidential Chancellery following Gorbachev's appointment as first President of the USSR. He then arranged to transfer the archive to Presidential jurisdiction (June 1990).[63] (In August 1991 Boldin went over to the side of the plotters.) On 10 September 1991, after the defeat of the coup, Gorbachev issued a Directive retaining the archive; this claimed that the Politburo materials (from 1919!) were 'important for information and reference'. When the USSR was dissolved he issued a further Directive on 23 December stating that 'the archive of the President of the USSR, including the documents of the archive of the Politburo . . . shall be transferred to the archive of the President of the RSFSR'.[64] This was not a smart move. Apart from the endless trouble the transfer caused for historians, it also provided Yeltsin with an abundance of material which he was able to use selectively against Gorbachev.

In the first year after the defeat of the coup everyone, including Pikhoya and his colleagues, thought that the transfer of the historical material, at least up to 1952, would be a straightforward matter. In June 1992 Poltoranin, then Minister for the Press and Information, announced that on the occasion of the newly instituted Independence Day, 12 June, the secret documents from the former party archives would be open to the public, initially those more than 50 years old.[65] A few days later the official government newspaper, under the headline 'Stalin's Personal Archive will be the Property of Society' printed an ITAR–TASS announcement that the archive was being declassified by a Presidential special commission and systematically transferred to the normal archives. The announcement whetted our appetites with extracts from top-secret documents, including a memorandum from secret police chief Ezhov to Stalin offering him information about Khrushchev, Vyshinsky (the chief prosecutor), Malenkov and Beria.[66]

The following September I arrived in Moscow and demonstrated my naïveté to Russian colleagues by eagerly enquiring how I would get access to the Stalin files. 'Nothing has been transferred,' they told me, 'the whole story was a smoke-screen'. A few weeks later the Russian press published a letter sent from the Presidential Archive to V. P. Kozlov, one of Pikhoya's deputies, who had suggested that archivists from RTsKhIDNI should visit the Archive in order to acquaint themselves with the Politburo documents from 1919 to 1941 in preparation for their transfer. This was a modest request from a quite high official who is also a respected historian – it said nothing about the post-war section of the Presidential Archive. But it was brusquely rebuffed:

> To Deputy Chair of Roskomarkhiv V. P. Kozlov . . . The Archive of the President is in a formative stage, and a Commission is working to prepare a list of its documents . . . Until the Commission has completed its work and the status of the Archive of the President has been finally established, access to documents is limited, unless it is directly related to the provision of information to the President and to the structures of the supreme executive authority of Russia.
>
> For these reasons we consider it inexpedient for staff of RTsKhIDNI to work in the Archive of the President. In our opinion this work is not required for any practical purpose; the Archive of the President does not plan any joint work with RTsKhIDNI either at present, or in the near future . . .
>
> Director of the Archive of the President of the Russian Federation A. Korotkov.[67]

This letter was written five days after the official ITAR–TASS announcement about the transfer of the Stalin archive. By this time a few privileged historians like Volkogonov had already been admitted to the Presidential Archive, and it had been extensively mined for material to use against the Communist Party in the case before the Constitutional Court.

The issue dragged on. In November 1992 the press announced that 'in

two or three months the whole of the historical section will be transferred
to normal archives (the former party archives); the President will retain
only documents which he needs for current work'.[68] But this did not happen. Even by the spring of 1994 only a limited number of papers had been
transferred to RTsKhIDNI, the most important being second copies of the
'special files' of the Politburo for the pre-war years; the files contained
Politburo decisions, but none of the accompanying material. Meanwhile
the archivists of the APRF published many interesting documents in the
new archive journal *Istochnik*, and an important booklet of documents
from the Stalin archive (see Chapter 12). The Archive remained almost
completely closed to scholars. In the spring of 1994 I was told that I
should apply for access to the head of the Presidential Administration, but
that my application would be refused. In the spring of 1996 I was told that
no foreigners were ever admitted to the archive.

Historians, archivists and Rosarkhiv itself found this permanent pro-
crastination intolerable. In July 1994 *Izvestiya* published a savage article
entitled 'Purveyors of Sensations from the Archive of the President', by
their well-informed correspondent Ella Maksimova. She reported that
Tatiana Pavlova, the respected head of the publications department of
Rosarkhiv, condemned APRF for 'privatising archival information by
usurping the possibilities provided by one's official position'. Maksimova
concluded:

> The Presidential Archive continues to be an oasis of the socialist system
> of privileged information.
> It is shameful that all this is done in the name of the President, on his
> premises and with his help. I would like to believe that this is unin-
> tended, a result of his lack of information.[69]

There was a six weeks' delay before Korotkov, Director of the Archive,
replied to these charges in the government newspaper.[70] He asserted that
while access to the archive was limited, it was not closed to 'scholars,
journalists and society' – and cited in proof the names of three historians
who had worked in the archive (they were all conservatives who had held
high positions in the history profession in the Brezhnev years of stagnation[71]). Korotkov claimed that the Archive was essential to the President's
work. Thus documents from the 1920s had been used to provide material
about the division of the Black Sea Fleet between Russia and Ukraine, and
material had recently been prepared for the President about the Katyn'
murders and the Kronstadt revolt. The Archive had been used to expose
misrepresentations about the past by Beria's son. (Suppose the President
of the United States insisted on holding on to government archives of the

1920s and 1940s on the grounds that he needed them for information about Saccho and Vanzetti, the Ford strikes and the activities of J. Edgar Hoover . . .)

At this point Yeltsin, who still retained some democratic instincts, decided that he could not be a party to this nonsense any longer. On 22 September 1994, he issued a directive that the 'Presidential Administration jointly with Rosarkhiv shall organise the transfer by stages in the course of 1994–5 of those original documents of the former Politburo archive which were created up to and including 1963; they are to be transferred to the archival establishments of Rosarkhiv'.

He also established a Commission for the Declassification of Documents created by the CPSU, which was to report quarterly to the President about its work.[72] The Commission included representatives of the security services, and the transfer involved a much stricter declassification procedure than had hitherto prevailed. Transfers included the working papers of the Politburo (excluding those classified as special files), the personal files of Politburo members Kaganovich and Mikoyan, and the confidential papers of Molotov as head of government in the 1930s. Molotov's papers had been taken by Boldin from the main state archive, GARF, but now ended up in the former party archive RTsKhIDNI . . .

You may think that the historical part of the Presidential Archive was now secured for the normal state archives. Not a bit of it. In the first issue of *Istochnik* for 1995, a 46-page insert was entitled *Vestnik* [Journal] *Arkhiva Prezidenta Rossiiskoi Federatsii*, and reprinted documents from APRF. The editors announced that their journal was being published on the basis of a Presidential directive dated 25 July 1994 (twelve days after Maksimova's critical article), that it would cover the whole Soviet period, and that they hoped that it would soon appear as a separate publication.[73]

By this time it was abundantly clear that there was no intention of transferring the whole of the historical part of APRF. In particular, the archives of the successive General Secretaries, including the crucial Stalin archive, were not to be transferred. The battle for the archives has not yet been won.

Part III
The New Soviet History

INTRODUCTION

History teaching and research have been seriously impaired by the severe reduction in central and local government expenditure since 1991.

School teaching is in general crisis. Teachers' pay is very low, and often received only after great delay (this led to a teachers' strike in January 1996). Many young teachers with families have left their jobs in search of better pay; after training, many graduates do not go into teaching at all. Schools often have to appoint teachers immediately after they leave school at the age of 17 or 18 without any professional training. The arrangements for retraining teachers in the course of their career have considerably attenuated.

History teaching is in particular jeopardy because pupils' interest in history has greatly declined as compared with the excitement of 1987–91. They take much more seriously subjects which will help them to earn a living in the new brash commercial world of post-Communist Russia. A teacher who surveyed pupils in the top forms of Moscow schools found that in 1995 only 34 per cent knew what 'Gulag' meant as compared with 82 per cent in 1992. A mere 7 per cent knew that Babii Yar was a place where fascists exterminated people during the war as compared with 48 per cent in 1992.[1]

At first sight the state of historical research seems equally bleak. Many historians appointed in higher educational establishments and research institutes in Brezhnev's day were sons and daughters of the *nomenklatura*. Lacking merit and enthusiasm, they were indelicately described as *ballast*. Historians in research institutes were nominally inspected ('attested') every five years. But in practice they often failed to undertake serious research once they had received their higher degree. For those concerned with the Soviet period, the absence of access to archives provided a perfect excuse for merely regurgitating well-known dogmas.

These traditions die hard. A month after the defeat of the August 1991 coup I went to the main reading room of the 'Archive Suburb' and naïvely expected to find it packed with Russian historians, curious to see what was in the files and anxious to show that they could contribute to historical knowledge in the new atmosphere. But the reading room was almost empty.

Since 1991 the real earnings of historians in higher education establishments and research institutes have continuously declined. Many talented historians, particularly in the provinces, live in conditions of severe hardship.

Like school teachers and archivists, they often seek jobs in other fields in order to feed their families.

Both specialist and popular historical journals have suffered a drastic fall in circulation (see Appendix table). At the peak of *perestroika*, the print-run of the leading journal *Voprosy istorii* was over 100 000. Not only research historians but also many school teachers and members of the public read it, and even subscribed to it. But its circulation in 1995 was only 11 000, two-thirds of the level ten years previously in the days of Chernenko.

Book publication has been even more seriously affected. In 1990 a bumper 768-page volume appeared in Russian containing the first two volumes of E. H. Carr's *History of Soviet Russia*, first published in English in 1950 and 1952. The new edition was based on the secret Russian translation prepared for the élite (see p. 87 above).[2] The print-run was 100 000 – several times the circulation of all the English-language editions published since 1950 in the whole of the rest of the world (including the Penguin paper-back). But since 1990, as a result of the financial crisis, no further volumes have been published, not even in a small circulation.

The fate of the translation of Carr's *History* is quite typical. Oleg Khlevnyuk's book on the 1937 purges went to press in September 1991 – just before the publishing crash – with a print-run of 100 000 copies.[3] But his next book, on Stalin and Ordzhonikidze (see Chapter 12), appeared in only 1000 copies, and even this required a subsidy from a Russian Fund to assist young scholars.[4] Yurii Goland's study of currency regulation during NEP (see Chapter 11) appeared in only 300 copies.[5]

In spite of these very serious obstacles to teaching and research, a great deal has been achieved. Chapter 9 discusses the new textbooks and other historical materials which have been prepared for schools, which for all their faults are a great advance on all previous textbooks since the 1920s.

Research has also progressed. In Moscow, St Petersburg and elsewhere the profession has been assisted by the financial support of many Russian and Western institutions. Russian historians now participate in joint projects with North American and European historians, to our mutual advantage. Historical publications have also benefitted. For example, the important series of 'First Monographs' edited by Gennadii Bordyugov has been supported by an enlightened Russian entrepreneur, and by the Carnegie Foundation, Jesus College Cambridge, the University of Lodz, and the centres for Russian and related studies in Birmingham, Bochum and Stanford. Work on local history is sponsored by enterprising local authorities. The Tambov Mayor's office supported the study of the Antonov movement (see Chapter 10). The Moscow Mayor's office and government subsidised the major volume on Moscow in the second world war (see Chapter 16).

However, the main reason for the survival and success of research on Soviet history is the devotion, enthusiasm and professional competence of a keen minority of Russian historians – a refreshing contrast with the untrammelled market principles on which Russian society is now supposed to operate.

This minority has produced valuable monographs and annotated collections of archival materials. Until the early 1990s, most of the significant work on Soviet history was published by Western rather than by Soviet historians. But by the mid-1990s our Russian colleagues had 'overtaken and surpassed' us. In Chapters 10–17 I present some characteristic examples of the new history, all based on recently released archival materials. This is not intended to be a comprehensive survey, but merely to provide a sample of the new research. In particular, I have been able to offer only brief glimpses of the many local investigations which have already been published. The present account reports work on repressions in the Urals (p. 161), the Tambov uprising (pp. 129–37) and the special settlements in West Siberia (pp. 172–3, 247). But an adequate treatment of local research would require a separate study. A great deal of fresh work has also appeared about the Tsarist era.[6] But I have confined myself to internal developments in the post-revolutionary years, partly because this is the period about which most new material is available, partly because it is what I know best.

9 Teaching about the Soviet Past

History teaching collapsed in May 1988: school examinations were cancelled. Pupils entered the 1988/89 session with the old textbooks and with no approved syllabus.[1]

The authorities rushed through a new pamphlet on Soviet history. It reached the press on 12 November 1988, and was issued early in 1989. It covered the years 1921–41, and replaced the chapters dealing with this period in the standard textbook for Grade (Class) IX. The 3 306 000 copies issued were enough for every pupil in Grade IX in the whole Soviet Union to receive a copy.[2]

The pamphlet was written by Yurii Borisov. Borisov was the unfortunate lecturer on Stalinism who had been challenged from the body of the hall in April 1987 by 22-year old Dmitri Yurasov with startling evidence about the repressions. (Borisov admitted that Yurasov 'knows much more than I do' and expressed his gratitude for the information.)[3]

Borisov, from the Institute of the History of the USSR (now the Institute of Russian History), is quite open-minded, and his pamphlet contained information about the destructive consequences of Stalinism which had been almost unknown to the Soviet general public before 1988. A new edition of the whole textbook was also prepared in a great hurry, sent to the press on 16 December 1988, approved for publication on 16 February 1989, and published in 3 110 000 copies well in time for the opening of the new school session on 1 September 1989. It covered the history of the USSR from 1900–1941, and incorporated the chapters on NEP and the 1930s by Borisov, which were unambiguously anti-Stalinist. The concluding section of the textbook was open-minded, but conveyed a Leninist message:

> . . . Why were socialist ideals not only not lost but strengthened, in spite of undergoing such serious trials? This is because the people made their choice firmly in 1917. The first difficult years after the revolution gave the people belief in their own strength, belief in the Communist Party. The transition to NEP showed that the policy of building and developing socialism can and must be flexible and efficient, taking into account the interests of the very broad mass of people.[4]

Although the textbook was far more frank than its predecessors, its critical spirit lagged far behind the public debate. Teachers had to go beyond the new textbook if they were to retain the respect of their pupils.[5] The seventeen-year old pupils who studied the Soviet period of history were well aware of the debate about the October Revolution which raged on TV as well as in the press, and they regarded orthodox history with the utmost scepticism.

The State Committee for Education announced an open competition for future textbooks in July 1988.[6] And later in the year it also insisted that the examinees should have 'the unconditional right to express their own well-grounded opinion, which may not coincide with the opinion of the teacher or of the authors of the present textbooks'.[7]

Until the defeat of the August 1991 coup, however, the view of pluralism taken by the education authorities was strictly circumscribed: 'an account of history from an anti-Marxist viewpoint is impermissible in our country', an official of the Academy of Pedagogical Sciences announced in January 1989.[8]

After August 1991 everything soon changed. By coincidence, at the time of the coup a new two-volume university-level general history of the Russian Empire and the USSR, *Our Fatherland*, came off the press in 50 000 copies. This was a lively pluralistic work, with individual chapters written by historians whose point of view ranged from 'democratic Leninism' to implacable hostility to the Bolshevik Revolution.[9] One of the editors told me that during the three days in which the Emergency Committee was in power the books were distributed in Moscow to intellectuals and officials as a morale-builder against the old regime.

The first post-coup school textbook on twentieth-century Russian history to be approved by the Ministry of Education of the Russian Federation was completed in December 1991 and published in the spring of 1992 in 1 246 000 copies. It was submitted to the Ministry by two teachers from Kherson, Lyudmilla Zharova and Irina Mishina.[10] By a quirk of fate, at the time the textbook came out its authors were no longer citizens of the Russian Federation – Kherson (the old Greek town of Chersonessus) is in Ukraine, which by then had declared its independence.

Zharova and Mishina open the textbook with a thorough exposition of the nature of Tsarist society, and its strengths and weaknesses. They present in an unprejudiced manner the main controversies about the Stolypin reforms and the causes of the 1917 revolutions. Their account of the Civil War brings out both the ideals of the revolutionaries and the human suffering. The chapter on the 1920s is entitled 'NEP – the Path to Democratic Socialism?' It argues that industrialisation was an urgent task, and that the need to accumulate resources for investment made it very difficult to work within the framework of a mixed economy. But the authors also suggest that the Soviet socialist economy was doomed to failure because of its inherent inefficiency.[11]

The chapter on the 1930s, entitled 'Totalitarianism. The Cult of Personality', is the weakest and most biassed in the book. Totalitarianism is defined as 'a regime controlling all sides of life, including the internal world of human beings'; and the system is described as having achieved this goal. The authors condemn our old friends the 'lumpens', with their mass psychology of equalisation, for providing the social basis of totalitarianism: 'the crowd gave birth to tyranny'.[12] Against this bleak background the book explains that the majority of the population 'sincerely and consciously believed in the bright future of their country'.[13] But no attempt is made to describe the social and economic changes of the 1930s in the way that the pre-revolutionary decade is so successfully described at the beginning of the book.

The use of the term 'totalitarianism' to characterise the Stalin regime is an extremely controversial issue. But the Ministry of Education of the Russian Federation elevated the concept into a new orthodoxy. In the list of sample examination topics issued by the Ministry in 1993 the political topic for the 1930s (topic no. 15) was 'The Formation of the Totalitarian System in our Country and the Establishment of the Regime of Personal Power.'[14] Teachers from Russian schools and pedagogical institutes who proposed to Ministry officials that they should discuss the merits and demerits of the 'totalitarianism' concept with their students and pupils were firmly instructed that the children must be told that Stalinism was a totalitarian system.

With this important exception the lists of sample questions and the syllabuses issued by the Ministry in 1992 and 1993 were on the whole remarkably dispassionate. The questions on late Tsarism and the revolution and civil war, for example, were framed without hinting at a 'correct' answer.[15]

The post-1991 syllabuses still suggested periods and topics, and the number of hours to be devoted to each. But the outstanding new feature of school life is the extent to which every region, town and school has acquired the ability to decide its own syllabus and methods of teaching.

Practice varies. In some schools inspired teachers combine openness of mind and profound knowledge. An American visitor to a Novgorod school at the end of 1991 attended a class on the 1905 Revolution in which the teacher read out a translation of an article by Leopold Haimson, and discussed the impact of 1905 in the Novgorod province; the session ended with a pupil's report on the personality and activities of Stolypin. But at other schools, perhaps the majority, 'talk and chalk' prevailed; and teachers worked to a rigid syllabus.[16] A British educationalist reported that in May 1993 in Yaroslavl' there was the occasional class debate, and teachers used their discretion in choosing topics within the syllabus. But in their methods most history lessons were 'similar to those in English schools 30 years ago'.[17]

While schools went their own way to a greater extent than ever before, in the Ministry of Education the reform of the history syllabus was hotly debated. In all Soviet schools, world history and the history of the USSR were taught chronologically in Grades VI–XI as two separate subjects. Each course reached the present day at the end of Grade XI. Some influential educationalists had long advocated the merging of the two courses. After 1991 their case was strengthened by the belief that Russian history was an integral part of the history of world civilisation, and that the Soviet period was a mere temporary lapse. On 11 May 1993, a document issued by the Education Committee of the Russian Federation envisaged that in Grades V–IX a unified course 'Russia and the World' would teach Russian history in the context of world history. Only in Grades X and XI would separate courses be taught on 'The Main Turning Points in the History of Humanity (the History of World Civilisations)' and 'Russia from the Earliest Times to the Present Day'. Many historians strongly protested. According to the deputy Dean of the History Faculty of Moscow University:

> Russian history will be diluted, and general history will be considered only in relation to the history of Russia. The experience of the 1920s, when history as a separate subject was abolished, and vulgar sociology triumphed, convincingly demonstrated that this approach was unacceptable.[18]

After much discussion, in December 1994 the collegium of the Ministry of Education reached a compromise: in Grades V–IX history could be taught 'either in separate coordinated parallel courses of Russian and general history, or in integrated courses on "Russia and the World"'.

The same session of the collegium also solved a problem which had long troubled teachers – and the general public. Many children left the general school after Grade IX at the age of sixteen for work, or to attend a specialised school or college. For these children the syllabus for both Russian and world history only went up to 1900, and they were never taught twentieth-century history. Henceforth, however, the syllabus would reach the present day at the end of Grade IX, and Grades X and XI would study aspects of Russian and world history in greater depth.[19]

The new programme is a recommendation and not an instruction, and is being introduced slowly and unevenly. Even in many Moscow schools the lack of textbooks has made a switch to the new syllabus in Grades VI–IX impossible. In some schools Russian and world history are now taught as a single subject in Grades X and XI. But the number of pupils remaining at school in the last two Grades has been declining. For financial reasons, this reduction is encouraged by the Ministry of Education. Some pupils are barred from continuing into Grade X on the grounds, sometimes spurious, that they are not able enough. Some schools charge fees for the top two Grades which not all parents can afford.[20]

The three new textbooks on twentieth-century Russian history issued in 1994 and 1995 reflected both the flexibility of the new syllabus and the consolidation of a new but fairly mild orthodoxy about the Soviet past. Danilov and Kosulina's textbook is for Grade IX, and covers the period 1900–94.[21] Ostrovskii and Utkin covers the same period, in about the same detail and somewhat less depth, but is for Grade XI, and is presumably intended to serve the more advanced course for 18-year olds.[22] The third book, by Dolutskii, is for Grade X, and deals with 1900–41; a second volume will deal with 1941 to the present day (presumably for Grade XI).[23] This is more sophisticated and detailed than the other two.

Any pupil or teacher who had to work their way through both Danilov–Kosulina in Grade IX and Ostrovskii–Utkin in Grade XI would be overcome by the boredom of repetition long before the end of Grade XI. Even the use of Dolutskii in Grade X would involve a lot of repetition. A new model syllabus for Grades X and XI, published in the history teachers' journal, also suffers from the defect that it works through the whole of history in some detail, rather than concentrating on special problems and issues.[24] These new arrangements will certainly need to be reconsidered in the light of experience.

The three textbooks have quite different approaches. Ostrovskii and Utkin is the most biassed. It claims, for example, that the greatest weakness of Tsarism was that the power of the state limited the rights of property owners. And the Bolsheviks were victorious because they used 'organised force never experienced before in history' and because the army opposition and the popular opposition to Bolshevism were disunited. The lesson is drawn from the experience of 1917–20 that revolution cannot be justified:

It is clear that in the Twentieth Century Russia had already reached its limit where revolution is concerned. Countries which drew conclusions from their revolutions and embarked on the firm path of evolution, gradual changes and the improvement of life achieved far more.[25]

The notion that evolutionary change is always to be preferred is now a very common one. A textbook on nineteenth-century Russian history even argues against the proposal by Pestel', one of the 'Decembrists' who revolted in December 1825, to abolish the castes or estates (*sosloviya*), claiming that it would have resulted in chaos. It also suggests that at the time of the serf reform of 1861 the radical democrat Chernyshevsky was wrong to demand that the peasants should receive maximum land for minimum repayment because this would have bankrupted the landowners.[26]

In Ostrovskii and Utkin, the whole section on 1921–39 is entitled 'The Totalitarian Regime: Formation and Apogee'. Soviet history from the Civil War onwards is treated as a continuous movement towards totalitarianism. NEP was doomed to failure because 'the market, in whatever form it appeared, threatened the domination of the Communist Party'.[27] The questions for discussion on the Stalin period assume that a totalitarian regime existed and that it was the same in principle as the totalitarian regime in Nazi Germany.[28]

Danilov and Kosulina's book is more objective and more thoughtful. Alternative assessments of the collapse of Tsarism and the victory of the Bolsheviks are carefully presented. The Civil War is discussed in separate sub-sections from the point of view of the Whites, the Reds, and the 'Between "Whites" and "Reds"', such as the Antonov movement (see pp. 129–33 below). The economic, social and political factors leading to the rise of Stalinism are discussed, and the viability of NEP is carefully explored. On all these issues pupils are invited to make up their own minds.

The 1930s is discussed within the 'totalitarian' framework. But the authors acknowledge that the term 'totalitarianism' is a 'quite conditional term' and that 'we use the concept of totalitarianism to emphasise more clearly the negative sides and features of this tragic period'. The chapter on 1928–38 is entitled not 'Totalitarianism' but 'The Stalinist Modernisation of Russia', and cultural and economic advances and social changes are acknowledged and described. On the whole a pupil using this textbook would acquire a good knowledge of the main facts and problems of Russian twentieth-century history.

Dolutskii's large and sumptuous book was sponsored by the Soros Foundation and bombards the reader with interesting information and difficult problems. Unlike all other contemporary Russian textbooks, it does not discuss Stalinism in terms of 'totalitarianism'. It rather approaches its subject by building up a complex picture of the achievements and inhumanities of the regime, and their social, political and ideological roots. But its account is so complex, and its questions to the reader so numerous, that it could be successfully used only by an extremely well-informed teacher. I think it would prove too difficult to use as a textbook for a second-year special course on Soviet history in a British university.

All the textbooks have in common an enthusiastic account of Soviet victory in the second world war. The authors also describe the lack of preparedness, the repressions and the unnecessary loss of life in ill-thought-out campaigns. They pay no attention to Suvorov's fashionable books, which claim that Hitler was fighting a 'preventive war' against the Soviet Union (see pp. 56–8 above).

Other books, pamphlets and articles by Russian historians, or translations of Western historians, are also available to teachers. In 1992 the pre-revolutionary textbook by Ilovaiskii was reissued.[29] An American historian points out that Ilovaiskii was regarded by pre-revolutionary liberals and the national minorities as 'the quintessential expositor of autocratic rule, intolerant Orthodoxy, and chauvinist Russification'. The book was used as a text in one of the new Orthodox schools established since 1991.[30] The lectures of the great liberal historian Kluchevsky have also been published.[31] Among the most useful Western publications issued in Russian translation have been E. H. Carr's *The Russian Revolution from Lenin to Stalin* and Nicolas Werth's short history of the Soviet Union.

With the support of the Volkswagen Foundation, a series of ten history textbooks has been published for 'students, researchers and teachers', unfortunately only in a fairly small circulation. A. K. Sokolov's *Lectures in Soviet History, 1917–40*, take the reader near to the frontiers of our knowledge.[32]

The 'Independent Institute of Social and National Problems' is also producing history textbooks. This institute is the reconstituted Institute of Marxism-Leninism (IML), the main research institute of the Communist Party. Its first textbook on Russian history, lavishly illustrated, and presumably intended for Grade XI, deals with the decade since *perestroika*. It was mainly written by V. V. Zhuravlev, formerly deputy director of IML, a respected historian. It naturally gives a much fuller presentation of the case against Yeltsin and his reforms than appears in official publications.[33]

A syllabus for Russian history courses in Orthodox *gimnazii* (grammar schools) examines Soviet history 'through the prism of the history of the Russian Church, because the events of the so-called Soviet period acquire meaning, significance and a true interpretation only when they are seen as a background against which the Church followed the path of the Cross and devotion'. The syllabus, which has strong monarchist leanings, is already taught in over 100 secondary schools, many of them secular.[34] This is pluralism!

Two monthly journals also contain a great deal of material of direct value for teachers. *Prepodavanie istorii v shkole* ('The Teaching of History in School'), after a period of disorientation, now publishes many useful accounts of syllabuses, and discussions of key problems. The most popular general history journal, *Rodina* (Homeland), lavishly illustrated, and published in 90 000 copies, contains many informative and controversial articles and reports of Round Tables – mainly about pre-revolutionary history. The post-1991 teachers' newspaper, *Pervoe sentyabrya* (The First of September, the day on which the school year begins), issues a separate supplement for history teachers.

From 1995, 50 per cent of the Russian history curriculum is supposed to deal with regional or local history.[35] Many local authorities have begun to issue their own materials. But the shortage of every kind of material is *the* chronic problem for history teachers. The textbooks we have been discussing are very scarce – in recent years they have been issued in a few hundred thousand copies, though a couple of million would be needed if every pupil was to have a copy.

Moreover, textbooks such as Dolutskii's and Sokolov's are regarded as unofficial material; their cost has to come from the teachers' own pockets.[36] Teachers – outside prestigious schools in big cities – do not have any facilities for photocopying, and many do not even have typewriters. In one district of St Petersburg, teachers keep a common pool of press cuttings, and typed and handwritten materials for general use.[37] But many teachers have no alternative but 'talk and chalk', using outdated textbooks.

Nevertheless the outlook is not entirely bleak. The textbooks of 1995/ 96, for all their faults, are far more honest and informative than those of 1987/88. In the past, many entrants into higher education studied history because it was an 'ideological' subject which eased their way into comfortable posts in the propaganda machine. Now no one would be likely to study history unless they were enthusiastic about it.

10 Lenin and the Civil War

Russian historians are deeply divided in their assessment of the Bolshevik Revolution and the Civil War.

Some historians offer easy solutions. Volkogonov's *Lenin* unhesitatingly took the point of view that the October Revolution was an arbitrary event inspired by a Utopian ideology, and drove Russia away from the general path of human progress (see p. 54 above). The new documents by and about Lenin have naturally tended to confirm this negative assessment. They were concealed by the Soviet authorities before 1990 precisely because they showed Lenin in an unfavourable light.

Historians have now begun to undertake research on a much wider front than the role of Lenin himself, using sections of the central and local archives which were previously closed. It will be many years before the accumulation of knowledge enables a fundamental reassessment of the Civil War. This chapter does not attempt to be comprehensive. It presents brief accounts of a few of the most illuminating recent publications.

'DECOSSACKISATION'

The Cossacks were a privileged social group, installed by the Tsars as a means of policing and settling the frontier lands. Their history has been the subject of particularly anguished debate in the Russia media. Since 1991 they have been the subject of a series of Presidential decrees. The new draft Law placed before the Duma in 1995, supported by almost 100 Cossack 'atamans', dealt with major issues of their status which were already disputed long before 1917; the draft Law resolved most of them in the Cossacks' favour.[1]

In the provinces near the river Don the Cossacks constituted half the population in 1917, but owned as much as four-fifths of the land. In spite of their élite status, many Don Cossack ex-soldiers supported the Bolsheviks when they returned from the front; a minority remained loyal to the new regime throughout the Civil War. But they were antagonised by the redivision of the land in 1918 in favour of the poorer non-Cossack peasants, and by the requisitioning of food by the state and the Red Army. Most of them rallied round the anti-Communist forces of the ataman, General Krasnov. As early as May 1918, 77 *stanitsy* (rural districts) had already joined the anti-Communist uprising.

The Don Cossacks treated their opponents with characteristic cruelty. The slogan *Don dlya dontsov!* ('The Don for the Don-ites') often meant in practice that the Cossack troops sought to exterminate all non-Cossack fellow-Russians living in the region, characterising them as 'aliens' (*inogorodnye*). One of Krasnov's Orders called for ten deaths for every Cossack killed.[2]

Party and military archives provide evidence that the Soviet authorities were no less cruel.[3] On 25 January 1919, the Orgburo of the party central committee called for 'merciless struggle with all the upper groups of Cossacks by destroying every one of them'; all Cossacks 'participating directly or indirectly in the struggle with Soviet power' were also to be destroyed.[4] In March 1919 the commander on the Southern Front ordered the 'merciless extermination of the whole adult male population and the burning down of dwellings' in all villages which had assisted the anti-Communist uprising. Syrtsov, in charge of civilian administration in the Don region, demanded 'the execution by shooting of a hundred Cossacks for every Red Armyman or member of the revolutionary committee who is killed'.

These savage policies did not go unchallenged. Sokol'nikov, who was a member of the Military Council of the Southern Front, objected to the directive of 25 January on the grounds that it failed to differentiate between social groups within the Cossacks. By March 1919 he had persuaded the party central committee to abandon the policy of terror in relation to the Cossacks of the Northern Don, who were more amenable.

This shift in policy apparently had little practical effect. The Donburo, in charge of the Communist Party in the region, sharply criticised the whole Cossack way of life and its reactionary patriarchal traditions: 'the wealthier and more senior Cossacks, and a tightly-knit group of officers and officials, dominate life and politics'. The Donburo feared the 'permanent danger of a counter-revolutionary uprising', and accordingly declared:

> The Cossacks as a special group with their own economic way of life must be completely, speedily and decisively eliminated; the economic foundations of this group must be destroyed. The caste of officials and officers, and in general all the upper groups of actively counter-revolutionary Cossacks, must be physically eliminated, and rank-and-file Cossacks must be dispersed and rendered harmless.

As part of this process, peasants from Central Russia should be resettled on Cossack lands in substantial numbers.

This was the background of the tragic and strange fate of the revolutionary Cossack leader Filipp Mironov, the circumstances of which still remain unclear. Mironov was sentenced to death three times, once by Krasnov and twice by the Bolsheviks. In 1918 he played a prominent part on the Bolshevik side against Krasnov; but in 1919, enraged by the effects of deCossackisation, he tried to take a neutral position between Reds and Whites. 'As a result of the Order on red terror,' he declared, 'tens of thousands of unarmed people have been executed. . . . The Don is dumb with horror.' He condemned as enemies of the social revolution both the Communists and General Denikin, who was by this time in command of the Whites in the Don area. In October 1919 he was sentenced to death by a Bolshevik court, but pardoned by a Politburo decision. In 1920 he again fought on the Bolshevik side. But in 1921, while visiting his native village, he was arrested by the Soviet secret police, apparently as a result of a false denunciation, carried off to Moscow and executed on 2 April.[5]

THE TAMBOV UPRISING (1919–21)

One of the most important recent collections of archival material concerns the Antonov movement – the *Antonovshchina*. Aleksandr Stepanovich Antonov was the leader of the peasant uprisings in Tambov province, Black-Earth region, during the Civil War and after.[6] The main revolt began in August 1920 and reached its peak in the spring and early summer of 1921. Some 40 000 partisans fought in the uprising. According to the account by the Cheka (the secret police), it embraced 'almost the whole population of Tambov province', numbering 3½ million.[7]

The rebel 'Union of Working Peasantry' explicitly sought 'the overthrow of the power of the Communist Bolsheviks'.[8] Antonov's partisans ruthlessly tortured and executed Communists and Soviet officials. A contemporary Soviet report claimed that 1500 party members and Soviet officials had been executed by June 1921.[9]

According to the compilers of this collection, this uprising, like that of the Cossacks, was suppressed with 'horrifying mercilessness'. This assessment is confirmed by many of the official instructions which are printed from the archives in this volume.[10] The authors particularly draw our attention to two Orders issued in June 1921 when the rebellion was at its height. The first, Order No. 171, dated 11 June, was issued by Antonov-Ovseenko (plenipotentiary of the Soviet government) and Tukhachevsky (Red Army Commander in Tambov), together with the head of the provincial soviet. It aimed at the 'rapid calming-down (*uspokoenie*) of the province'. The word *uspokoenie* is significant: the authors of the document must have known that it was used by Stolypin in his notorious justification of the savage repressions after the 1905 revolution – 'first calming-down, and then reforms'. The Soviet Order was harsher than Stolypin at his most severe. It instructed local authorities:

1. Citizens who refuse to state their names shall be executed on the spot without trial.
2. In village settlements in which arms are concealed, hostages shall be taken, and shall be executed by shooting if the arms are not surrendered.
3. If concealed arms are found, the senior working person in the family shall be executed by shooting on the spot without trial.
4. A family in whose dwelling a bandit is hidden shall be arrested and exiled from the province; its property shall be confiscated; the senior working person in the family shall be executed by shooting without trial . . .
6. In the event of the flight of the family of a bandit, its property shall be distributed among peasants faithful to Soviet power, and the dwellings shall be burnt down or dismantled.
7. The present Order shall be carried out strictly and mercilessly.

The laconic second Order, issued by Tukhachevsky on the following day, 12 June, is even more chilling:

1. Forests in which bandits are concealed shall be cleansed by poison gas, carefully arranging that the cloud of poison gas shall be spread completely through the whole forest, exterminating everything concealed in it.
2. The inspector of artillery shall immediately transfer the necessary quantity of poison-gas cylinders and specialists as required.
3. The commanders of military units shall carry out the present Order firmly and energetically.
4. Report measures taken.[11]

These Orders were obviously intended to frighten the population into submission. They were not published in Moscow, and were concealed afterwards; but at the time the local population was made well aware of them. Thus Order No. 171 was issued in 30 000 copies, and local authorities were instructed to arrange for it to be read out at village assemblies.

But the Orders were not just propaganda. The taking of hostages was already a common practice during the Civil War.[12] Many Bolshevik officials were utterly ruthless in their attitude to the rebels. In August 1920, at the beginning of the uprising, the head of the local Cheka insisted that when the whole population of villages supported the rebels, 'these villages must be wiped off the face of the earth.'[13]

In the case of Order No. 171, a report sent to the Politburo five weeks after its promulgation described *'the intensification of the terror in relation to the bandits and their families, and their protectors'*. In one rural district (*volost'*) '152 bandit hostages were executed, 227 bandit families were seized, 17 dwellings were burnt down, 24 dismantled and 22 handed over to poor peasants'. In another district 80 hostages were 'publicly executed in batches until the arms and the active participants in the gangs were handed over'.[14] In one case women hostages were executed; the report complacently explained that 'this method gave favourable results'.[15] Simultaneously a large number of peasants were expelled from their villages. By the end of June 1921, 50 000 rebels and members of their families were confined in concentration camps.[16]

The evidence about the practical application of the poison-gas order is somewhat less clear. But one army document specifically refers to the release in one rural district of 59 chemical weapons.[17]

The Orders did not remain unchallenged in high places. The compilers have discovered a document which reveals that the majority of the members of VTsIK (the All-Russian Central Executive Committee of Soviets, at that time the supreme government body) objected to Order No. 171, albeit belatedly. According to a letter by Rykov:

> The presidium of VTsIK proposes, with the support of the majority of its members, 1) to annul the Order; 2) to recall Antonov-Ovseenko and Tukhachevsky.[18]

The date on which the VTsIK proposal was made is not known. It must have been before 16 July 1921, because on that day the Politburo, in which ultimate authority was vested, decided to refer the matter to the Commission on Banditry, headed by Trotsky, and to accept their decision as final.[19] Within three days Trotsky's Commission had nominally annulled the Order and Tukhachevsky had been recalled. But the minutes of the Commission refrained from making even the slightest criticism of Tukhachevsky and were careful to claim that it was because the emergency had passed that the Order had been annulled.[20] And a further memorandum ruled that the Order was to be annulled only in those places where the attitude of the peasants had fundamentally changed.[21]

The conflict behind the scenes briefly mentioned in these documents was evidently very intense. Bukharin was apparently one of the principal critics of the severity of the military action. Lenin, who knew about Order No. 171 and certainly did not oppose it, sent Bukharin a report about the repression of the uprising which claimed that the measures adopted by Tukhachevsky were 'entirely expedient and correct'. Lenin scribbled a note to Bukharin on the report:

> *Bukharin – secret.* Return this, after *reading it through* line by line as a punishment for panicking. 17/viii [1921]. Lenin.[22]

For the Russian historians who edited this collection, the politics of the suppression of the Tambov uprising, though significant, are a secondary feature of the story. According to Viktor Danilov, the principal compiler, the Tambov revolt should be seen as one major link in the chain of peasant revolution in Russia, which was 'more or less continuous from 1902 to 1922'. Peasant uprisings under both Tsar and Bolshevik were characterised by resistance to arbitrary state power. The Tambov peasants at first sympathised with the Bolsheviks, but 'the peasants' spontaneous revolutionary drive and the Bolsheviks' effort to achieve revolutionary transformation had different aims, and began to bifurcate sharply, especially after the introduction of the food dictatorship and food requisitioning'.

Danilov concludes that both sides in the Tambov conflict were peasants, and that their activities were 'identical in their social content':

> They were largely organised in the same way, including the establishment of commissars and political departments, themselves manned by former peasants. The Antonovites and the army led by Tukhachevsky both carried red flags, and addressed their colleagues as 'comrade' – the only possible mode of address in both cases. Even the main slogan was the same: Victory to the True Revolution![23]

The Soviet authorities, even in their secret internal communications, attributed responsibility for the revolt to the machinations of the Socialist Revolutionaries. The leaders, including Antonov, certainly had close past associations with the SRs.[24] But this volume provides strong evidence that this was an autonomous movement, in which the SR organisations played little part. The remnant of the SR party which still existed in 1920–1 opposed the revolt.[25] And Danilov points out that 'there is no correlation between the tiny SR and other revolutionary cells in the countryside and the peasant uprisings'.[26] The uprising spread because grain requisitioning reduced the villages to near-starvation after the bad harvest of 1920. The arbitrariness of the marauding food detachments exacerbated peasant fury. A delegate from Tambov declared at the X party Conference in May 1921 that 'the strong hand of the food agents to a huge extent fostered Antonovshchina in our localities.'[27]

While the rebels were not directly inspired by SR organisations, the rebel programme was strongly influenced by Socialist-Revolutionary ideas. It called for free elections to a Constituent Assembly, freedom of the press, and socialisation of the land. Food and other necessities would be supplied via cooperatives; prices of goods produced by state-owned factories would be regulated; 'factories will be partly denationalised – large-scale industry, coal and metallurgy must be in the hands of the state'.[28]

The economic proposals had much in common with NEP. Paradoxically, however, owing to the desperate shortages, requisitioning and other controls similar to those of War Communism were soon introduced by the rebels on their own territory. In the words of two of the Tambov historians, '"Antonov's NEP" hardly came into being'.

These historians argue persuasively, however, that 'the struggle of the Tambov peasants nudged forward the introduction of "Lenin's" NEP'.[29] As early as October 1920 a Bolshevik plenipotentiary in the Tambov province proposed that requisitioning should be replaced by a kind of tax in kind; soon afterwards a 'non-party conference' at a Red Army garrison took a similar line.[30]

Nevertheless, these documents also show that even after the adoption of the tax in kind in March 1921, in practice the food policy pursued by Soviet agencies in the province did not substantially change; and the Red Army continued to supply itself with clothes and food by commandeering them from the local peasants.[31] The delay in implementing the March decisions was certainly a major factor in protracting the uprising, which was not finally defeated until the end of July.

*　　*　　*

The events in the Don and Tambov regions are revealing in several respects. They show that Lenin and the Bolsheviks were imposing civil peace by the most ruthless methods not only during the Civil War, as in the case of 'DeCossackisation', but also in repressing the Antonovshchina several months after the moderate *economic* policies of NEP had been introduced. As far as I am aware, the public execution of hostages did not take place under Stalin even in the most tense period of collectivisation. The treatment of the Cossacks in 1919 and the notorious Orders of June 1921 in Tambov embody British experience in the Boer War and foreshadow Nazi terrorisation by hostage-taking, and American destruction of whole villages by napalm during the Vietnam war. The use of the term 'bandit' in dealing with the Tambov rebels to describe what in other circumstances would be called 'resistance fighters', partisans or guerrillas is characteristic of the jargon of oppressive ruling powers. Yet these measures were adopted in time of peace. Their use against large numbers of peasants less than four years after the Bolsheviks had supported them in liberating themselves from the landowners is strong evidence of the early degeneration of the revolution. But it would be wrong to conclude that Soviet Russia was already an autocratic dictatorship of the Stalin type. The repudiation of official policies by an important section of the leadership indicates that a flexible and more moderate approach was also a significant tendency within Bolshevism.

These events also demonstrate rather starkly the dangers of identifying particular individuals as 'heroes' and 'villains' in drawing lessons from Soviet history – a favourite activity during the great historical debates of the Gorbachev era. In all the literature of *perestroika*, Syrtsov, Antonov-Ovseenko and Tukhachevsky are presented as heroes. Syrtsov opposed Stalin's industrialisation and collectivisation policies as too extreme in the autumn of 1930, after Bukharin and his associates had already capitulated to Stalin. Antonov-Ovseenko was a strong supporter of the Left oppositions in the 1920s, dismissed from his post as head of the Political Administration of the Red Army, and executed in 1939. He was one of the group of ex-Trotskyists sensationally referred to by Mikoyan as 'comrade' for the first time since the late 1930s in his published speech to the XX party Congress in 1956. And Tukhachevsky was the great military strategist who built up modern armaments in the 1930s. The replacement of Tukhachevsky and his associates by nonentities after their execution in 1937 was one of the important factors leading to the humiliating failure of the Red Army after the German invasion in 1941.

The present studies show another face of these anti-Stalinist heroes. Syrtsov was one of the fiercest advocates of deCossackisation in 1919, and in 1921 during the Tambov uprising Antonov-Ovseenko and Tukhachevsky were the principal villains – the ruthless commanders whose cruelty had to be overruled by the politicians in Moscow.

11 Lenin, Stalin and the New Economic Policy, 1921–5

The key events of these years are more or less common ground among historians. In 1921 Lenin persuaded the party to adopt NEP (the New Economic Policy). Compulsory food requisitioning was replaced by a market relation between the state and the peasants. Small-scale industry was denationalised, state industry was required to be profitable, and private trade was legalised. But simultaneously Lenin insisted on consolidating and even strengthening the one-party system. In his famous letter to the dissident Myasnikov in August 1921 he argued that the world bourgeoisie was vastly stronger than Bolshevik Russia. Without strict control of the state, and of the press, the first workers' state would inevitably be defeated.

Then in the winter of 1922–3, during his fatal illness, Lenin reconsidered important aspects of Bolshevik policy, and in 'Lenin's Last Struggle' he sought to push through a more flexible policy in state administration, party organisation and towards the nationalities, against Stalin's opposition. He insisted in his articles on cooperation that 'we must recognise a fundamental change in our whole point of view about socialism'.

Much continues to be disputed about these events. Was NEP a purely temporary retreat – or should it be seen, as Soviet reformers argued in 1988, as an alternative and much more fruitful road to a socialist economy than the one followed in the 1930s? Did Lenin's further reform proposals in 1922–3 outline the way to a humane political and social order? Or were they the vague inconclusive ramblings of a sick man, which would have made little difference if put into effect?

The new evidence provides no conclusive answers to these questions. But on several important issues it offers significant new information – often dramatic in character.

LENIN'S PENULTIMATE STRUGGLE

The verbatim reports of most party Conferences and Congresses have long since been published. But the report of the X Party Conference, held in

135

May 1921, has not been published, and until 1991 it was not even made available to researchers.

We now know why. The Conference was held at a crucial time, two months after the X Party *Congress* of March 1921 had replaced requisitioning by the tax in kind. The report confirms that in practice requisitioning still continued, even though the spring sowing was almost completed. Meshcheryakov, then a *Pravda* editor, claimed at the Conference that in the countryside 'everything remains the same and the former policy of the People's Commissariat for Food has been continued in practice: squeeze, press, and take'.[1] The resistance, both mute and open, of local party and food officials had so far prevailed over the decisions of the party Congress.

So much could also have been deduced from the press of the time. But the Conference proceedings also reveal that even at this late date Lenin still had to push through his new policies against the opposition of many senior party officials and ordinary members. Speakers at the Conference accepted the necessity of the tax in kind, but objected to the extension of NEP. I. M. Vareikis from Belorussia criticised Lenin for abandoning support for the poor and middle peasants in favour of the peasantry as a whole. Chubar' supported him, arguing that the kulaks were stronger in Ukraine than in Russia. Larin, an independent-minded economist, and Kiselev, former member of the Workers' Opposition, condemned the lack of attention to large-scale industry and the working class. Another delegate condemned the centre for introducing 'chaos', blaming 'the accursed denationalisation of medium, near-medium and part of large-scale industry'. One delegate even condemned the use of the word 'trade'.[2]

The proceedings of the Conference thus show Lenin exercising all his considerable authority in what might be described as 'Lenin's Penultimate Struggle' to achieve the abandonment of War Communism in favour of the mixed economy of NEP.

In presenting this material, I have cheated slightly. Elsewhere in Part III of this book I have confined myself to the works of Russian and other historians from the former Soviet Union. However, while Russian historians have written at length about Lenin's ruthless enforcement of political dictatorship, only one historian – Sergei Tsakunov – has presented material from the X Conference showing Lenin as a doughty fighter for the New Economic Policy. Before August 1991 party officials prevented the publication of this information because they were unwilling to admit that the party as a whole was so inflexible. And since August 1991 it has been unfashionable to present Lenin's NEP as a genuine economic reform, rushed through against severe obstacles. Characteristically, Volkogonov's *Lenin* does not mention the X Party Conference – and says almost nothing about NEP. Part of my account in this section has therefore been based on the biography of Lenin by Robert Service, the first Western historian to use the verbatim report of the X Conference.

THE LENIN–STALIN ALLIANCE

Accounts of Lenin's last years have had much to say about his disputes with Stalin during his last months of active life in the winter of 1922–3. Much less was known before the archives were opened about Lenin's very close relationship with Stalin in the spring and summer of 1922, after Stalin had been appointed party General Secretary.

The records show that Stalin visited Lenin in his Gorki retreat on twelve occasions between the end of May and the end of September 1922, more frequently than any other politician.[3] Even as late as December 1922, when they were supposed to be at daggers drawn, Lenin consulted him about exiling prominent intellectuals.[4]

A recently-published memoir by Lenin's sister M. I. Ul'yanova records that after Lenin's stroke in the spring of 1922:

> Stalin was V. I. [Lenin]'s first visitor. Il'ich [Lenin] met him in a friendly fashion, joked and laughed, got me to provide him with refreshments, bring in wine, and so on. They spoke about Trotsky during this and later visits, spoke in my presence, and it was clear that at this point Il'ich was with Stalin against Trotsky.[5]

Ul'yanova's memoir also provides a consistent – though unverifiable – account of the famous 'Lenin and poison' controversy. In his biography of Stalin, Trotsky reports that at the end of February *1923* Stalin informed Politburo members, including Trotsky, that Lenin had asked him for poison. Trotsky expresses bewilderment. How could Lenin have turned to Stalin with such a request, which 'presupposed the highest degree of personal confidence'? Only a month before this, according to Trotsky, Lenin had written the pitiless postscript to his Testament, calling for Stalin's removal from the post of General Secretary. Trotsky concludes that Lenin's sudden death in January 1924 occurred because Stalin either poisoned him, or supplied him with poison.[6]

Trotsky's theory about Lenin's death was rejected by nearly all the Western biographers of Lenin and Stalin. Ul'yanova's memoir now makes it clear that Trotsky, who wrote his account in 1939, many years after these events, got the year wrong. According to Ul'yanova, Lenin asked Stalin for poison on two occasions – during his first serious illness in 1920 or 1921, when Stalin promised to supply poison when the time came, and in May *1922*, after his stroke – not *1923* as Trotsky mistakenly recalled:

> Why did V. I. turn to St[alin] with this request? [wrote Ul'yanova]. Because he knew him to be a firm, steely person, alien to any kind of sentimentality. There was no-one else to whom he could put a request of this kind.
>
> . . . . [In May 1922] V. I. decided that it was all up with him, and requested that St should come in to him for a very short time. This request was so insistent, that it wasn't refused. St was with V. I. only about 5 minutes, no more. And when he came out from I-ch he told Bukharin and myself that V. I. had asked him to get hold of poison, as the time to carry out the promise he had given earlier had arrived. Stalin promised. V. I. and Stalin kissed and St left. When we discussed it together afterwards we decided that V. I. must be reassured, and Stalin went back to V. I. He told him that after talking to the doctors he was convinced that all was not lost and the time to carry out his request had not come. V. I. noticeably cheered up, and agreed, although he said to Stalin 'Are you being cunning?' Stalin answered 'When have you seen me being cunning'.[7]

The poison incident serves to emphasise how close Lenin and Stalin were at that time.

LENIN'S LAST STRUGGLE

No new Lenin documents have appeared which shed light on his rethinking at the end of his life. We have to form our opinion on the basis of his last writings, which were all available forty years ago.

But we now know much more about his relationship with Stalin. It has long been known that the dispute initially turned on Stalin's attitude to the nationalities. Stalin wanted to incorporate the Soviet republics into the Russian Republic, rather than establish a federal Union of Soviet Socialist Republics; and he supported the high-handed attitude of Ordzhonikidze to the Georgian Communists. On both these issues he was overruled as a result of Lenin's intervention.[8] The Politburo documents for this time now enable us to trace Lenin's growing disquiet fairly precisely.[9]

The tension between Lenin and Stalin in these months is displayed much more starkly than in previous accounts. On a famous occasion Lenin's wife Krupskaya wrote a note to Trotsky on Lenin's behalf, dated 21 December 1922, asking him to take on the job of supporting the monopoly of foreign trade. Stalin was furious. In view of the state of Lenin's health, the plenum of the party central committee had resolved three days previously that 'cde. Stalin shall be personally responsible for the isolation of Vladimir Il'ich in respect of both personal contact with staff, and correspondence'. The despatch of Lenin's note by Krupskaya violated this decision. Stalin was obviously also alarmed that Lenin had turned to Trotsky rather than Stalin as his main political support. On 22 December he telephoned Krupskaya and vigorously reproved her, threatening to raise the matter with the party control commission.[10] We have long known that the telephone call upset Krupskaya. Ul'yanova's memoir tells us that Krupskaya was *very* upset. 'She was completely beside herself, burst into tears, rolled on the floor, and so on'.[11]

Lenin by this time was coldly indifferent to Stalin. 'Shall I pass on your greetings to Stalin?', Ul'yanova asked Lenin:

'Yes,' Il'ich replied fairly coldly.
'But, Volodya,' I continued, 'after all Stalin is intelligent (*umnyi*).'
'He is not at all intelligent,' Lenin replied decisively, and frowned.[12]

On 5 March 1923, six weeks after the incident with Krupskaya, Lenin wrote Stalin an angry letter threatening to break off relations with him if he did not 'take back what you said [to Krupskaya] and apologise'.

Little was known until recently about Stalin's own reaction to the breach with Lenin. Ul'yanova's memoir reports that he was also very upset. On one occasion he told her that he had not slept all night – Lenin 'treats me as some kind of traitor; I love him with all my heart'.[13]

Although on this occasion Stalin tried to win the sympathy of Lenin's sister and through her to restore himself to Lenin's confidence, on other occasions he spoke of Lenin slightingly and even with contempt. Stalin replied on the day he received Lenin's letter about Krupskaya, 7 March 1923, with a cool formal apology:

I did not follow any other objectives but your speedy recovery . . .
Nevertheless, if you consider that in order to maintain 'relations' I must 'take back' the words I said as above, I can take them back, but I refuse to understand what this is about, where my 'guilt' lies, and what is really wanted of me.

I. Stalin.[14]

Lenin's further illness prevented the delivery of this letter, which would no doubt have deepened the breach between them.

To his colleagues Stalin spoke quite sharply about Lenin at this time. In a letter to the Politburo he accused Lenin of 'national liberalism' (27 September 1922); in a note to Kamenev on the following day he wrote: 'in my opinion we must be firm against Il'ich. If a couple of Georgian Mensheviks influence the Georgian communists, and they influence Il'ich, where does "independence" come into it?'[15] A few months later, in a note to Ordzhonikidze on the same subject, he grumbled that Lenin 'solidarises with the deviationists' (7 March 1923, the day on which he wrote his letter to Lenin about Krupskaya).[16]

At the XII Party Congress in April 1923, in Lenin's absence, Stalin in a speech to the section on nationalities strongly criticised Lenin's national policy, accusing him of muddle and lack of practical sense. Rakovsky from Ukraine claimed to have Lenin's support for the view the republics should continue to have their own commissariats of foreign affairs, held jointly with that of the USSR. Stalin replied:

> We will have no Union [of Soviet republics] if every republic has its own People's Commissariat of Foreign Affairs. Cde. Lenin has forgotten, he has forgotten a lot recently. He has forgotten that we agreed the principles of the Union jointly with him.

These callous remarks were made at a time when Lenin was extremely ill following a series of strokes.

At the same session Stalin was also strongly critical of Lenin's view that foreign countries could be persuaded to join the USSR as constituent republics:

> I want to tell you the history of this. I was on the Southern front, and before the II Congress of Comintern [July 1920] cde. Lenin sent his draft on the national question and asked me, like others, to comment. It said that Comintern would achieve a federation of nationalities and states. I said at that time – this is all in the central committee archives – that this would not work. If you intend to remain within the framework of the federation of nationalities in old Russia, that's understandable, but you are mistaken if you think that Germany will some time join you in a federation with the same rights as Ukraine. Cde. Lenin sent me a threatening letter, saying that this was chauvinism and nationalism, and that we need a centralised world economy, administered from a single agency.[17]

This is a confident Stalin, and other archival publications confirm that Stalin's position in 1923 was considerably stronger than we previously realised. During Lenin's last illness the party was in effect controlled by the triumvirate Zinoviev, Kamenev, Stalin. To the outside world it seemed as if Stalin was the weakest member of the triumvirate. But this is not how it appeared to Zinoviev. Writing to Kamenev on 30 July 1923, he complained bitterly of Stalin's power:

> You are simply letting Stalin mock us.
>
> Facts? Examples?
>
> Allow me.
>
> 1) *The nat[ional] question.*
>
> ... Stalin appoints the plenipotentiaries (instructors) of the central committee ...
>
> 2) The Gulf Convention. Why not ask us and Trotsky about this important question. *There was enough time.* By the way, I am supposed to be responsible for the People's Commissariat of Foreign Affairs ...
>
> 3) Comintern ...
>
> V. I. devoted a good 10 per cent of his time to Comintern ... And Stalin arrives, looks and decides. And Bukh[arin] and I are 'dead bodies' – we are not asked anything ...
>
> 4) *Pravda.* This morning (this was the last straw) Bukharin learned from Dubrovsky's personal telegram that without informing him or asking Bukh[arin] the ed[itorial] board had been replaced ...
>
> We will not tolerate this any longer.
>
> If the party is condemned to go through a period (prob. *very* brief) of Stalin's personal power (*edinoderzhavie*) – so be it. But I at least do not intend to cover up all this swinishness. All the platforms refer to the 'triumvirate', believing that I am not the least important person in it. In practice there is no 'triumvirate', there is Stalin's dictatorship.[18]

Zinoviev was rather inclined to engage in hysterical outbursts, but his assessment is partly confirmed by other accounts of top-level decision-making at this time. By the time of Lenin's death in January 1924 Stalin had acquired a great deal of authority within the party leadership.

This does not mean that he had already become a personal dictator. E. H. Carr, writing about this period, said that 'few great men have been so conspicuously as Stalin the product of the time and place in which they lived'.[19] In the light of the new evidence, this view seems one-sided. But it is certainly true that in 1924 Stalin was not yet himself an independent actor on the historical stage, committed to a distinctive set of policies for the transformation of society. And at this time the powers of the Politburo – and hence of Stalin as General Secretary – were relatively limited. Within the Soviet regime, there was more than one centre of authority. And the regime as a whole was able to impose its will on society only in quite restricted ways.

THE EXTENSION OF NEP?

Other recent publications from the archives confirm that attempts to extend NEP met with strong resistance in party circles. In October 1924, nine months after Lenin's death, Strumilin presented a report to the presidium of Gosplan 'On the Method of Planning in the USSR'. Strumilin later in the 1920s was one of the leaders in the campaign for purposive planning and rapid industrialisation, and persistently advocated the domination of planning over the market. But in 1924 he argued that the proletariat, and state industry, 'do not need the path of revolutionary compulsion'; instead, they should compete with the private sector on the market. State enterprises should seek to establish mastery over their private competitors 'by the methods used by any financial concern, production or trade syndicate of a capitalist country'. Optimum results would be obtained 'not with a cudgel, but with the ruble' (*ne dub'em, a rublem*).

Strumilin was supported by the non-party specialists Groman and Bazarov, but almost all the other speakers opposed him, insisting that the private sector would not be defeated without class struggle, and some use of compulsion. Strumilin later submitted a second version of his report, significantly renamed 'On the Method of Overcoming NEP'. This new version refrained from advocating the use of capitalistic methods by the state sector.[20]

In his study of the apparently recondite subject of Soviet foreign exchange controls during NEP Yurii Goland provides a further example of the strength of the resistance of the party to the extension of NEP. Goland uses a variety of archives, including the Presidential Archive, to piece together the story of the decision to remove the ruble from the international exchange in 1926.[21]

In 1923–6 the State Bank and Narkomfin (the People's Commissariat of Finance) sought to maintain the exchange rate of the ruble by discreetly selling gold coins within the country. In addition, Narkomfin sold state loans on the private market at home and abroad through secret intermediaries, using both the official and the black exchanges. The Narkomfin official in charge of what was known as 'currency intervention' was Lev Volin, non-party specialist who was head of the Special (or Secret) Department of its Foreign Currency Administration. These activities were carried out in close contact with the OGPU (the secret police), and all the agents of the Special Department were registered with the OGPU.

From the summer of 1925 inflationary pressures resulting from the increased pace of industrialisation imperilled the stability of the ruble – and the policy of currency intervention. Goland has discovered records of the discussion and voting in the higher party and state agencies – these are very rarely available.

On 8 January 1926, at a session of STO (the Council of Labour and Defence, a government committee concerned with economic and defence matters) Smilga and Pyatakov, representatives of Gosplan and of industry, both strong supporters of industrialisation, criticised the attempt to maintain the parity of the ruble. Yurovsky, head of the Foreign Currency Administration, insisted that currency intervention to support the ruble was essential. The issue was remitted to a special commission of the Politburo. This met on 18 January, equipped with rival memoranda from Narkomfin and Gosplan economists. Rykov, the influential head of Soviet government as chair of SNK (the Council of People's Commissars), defended 'some' intervention. He was in principle supported by Stalin, who warned, however, that 'we could become a toy in the hands of speculators'. Trotsky and Dzerzhinsky, both strong supporters of industry (Dzerzhinsky was head of both industry and the OGPU) were sceptical. The Politburo commission adopted a vague resolution, and referred the question back to STO.

On 3 February 1926, STO considered a compromise resolution which proposed that currency intervention should be continued, but that expenditure on it should be reduced. Six people voted in favour of continued intervention – Rykov (in charge of both STO and of SNK of which it was a sub-committee), Rudzutak (one of his deputies), Bryukhanov (head of Narkomfin), Sheinman (head of the State Bank), Frumkin (representing the trade commissariat) and Vladimirov (representing the trade unions). Four voted against – Krzhizhanovsky (head of Gosplan), Pyatakov (long-term associate of Trotsky, representing industry), Unshlikht (representing the commissariat for war) and Kuibyshev (another deputy of Rykov, and close to Stalin). This was the line-up of government departments which might be expected – with Gosplan and industry concerned with economic expansion rather than financial stability, opposed by Narkomfin and the State Bank. But the heads of the government were divided: the more moderate Rykov and Rudzutak versus the economic expansionist Kuibyshev.

The issue was discussed at several subsequent meetings of STO during February. But by this time the OGPU had intervened. On 23 January, five days after Stalin's remark about 'speculators' at STO, the head of the OGPU economic administration presented a memorandum to Dzerzhinsky proposing that certain currency intermediaries should be arrested. According to the memorandum, they had carried out dealings with the black exchange without Narkomfin permission, and had made enormous personal profits. On 4 February, the Politburo approved the STO decision of

3 February recommending the continuation of currency intervention. But it also resolved delphically 'no objection to the agreement between comrades Rykov, Sheinman and Dzerzhinsky about the black exchange'. The 'agreement' was evidently that the dealers should be arrested; the arrests began three days later.

The stage was now set for the destruction of the system of currency intervention established three years earlier. On 1 March Volin himself was arrested by the OGPU. On 4 May, with Politburo permission, he was executed. The removal of the ruble from the international exchange followed a month later, and it did not again become an international currency until 1992.

The transformation of the ruble into a purely internal currency may have been a necessary consequence of rapid industrialisation; if so, currency intervention was obviously no longer required. But even on this assumption the use of the OGPU to eliminate Volin and his officially-approved currency experiment meant that the issue was discussed not in terms of the economic problems involved but of the fight against capitalist enemies. And the case against the 'enemies' was supported by doubtful evidence obtained by the OGPU. In the same month in which Volin was executed the Moscow provincial procurator and the president of the Moscow provincial court complained to the OGPU:

> A considerable number of the cases sent forward by [your] Economic Administration do not contain an objective examination of the circumstances and a critical check of the evidence. The officials use the most backward means of disclosing the truth, restricted to the confession of the accused.

Thus OGPU methods were already those familiar from later years, though imposed less harshly.

Rykov was himself persuaded to change sides by the dubious information provided by the OGPU, at a time when he was still able to form and express an independent opinion. In April he told the central committee plenum about Volin that 'the Secret [i.e. the Special] Department of the Foreign Currency Administration of Narkomfin was headed by a man who was not only completely alien to us, but also vitally connected through his relatives and others with the black exchange'.

*   *   *

On the whole the new material about the Civil War and the early years of NEP provides little comfort to dinosaurs like myself who would like to see the world resume its movement towards 'socialism with a human face'.

There were attempts within the ruling party to move towards a more flexible and more humane regime. Sokol'nikov challenged deCossackisation. The majority of the Central Executive Committee objected to the shooting of hostages during the Tambov rising. Strumilin sought to widen the boundaries of NEP. Some flexibility remained in the system. Serious discussions on major questions of economic policy took place in economic agencies such as Gosplan and Narkomfin, and the arguments of the contending viewpoints appeared in articles in the press. Decision making was not confined to the Politburo; STO and other agencies retained some autonomy.

But on present evidence such trends were weak and easily overcome. And Lenin himself – while struggling for a new approach to socialism – retained his commitment to a one-party system in which all other political groups were ruthlessly suppressed. Above all, 'evidence' supplied by the OGPU influenced the policy of the party leaders; and the political role of the secret police continuously expanded.

12 Stalin and his Entourage

Since 1989 our knowledge of the political activities of Stalin and his closest associates has vastly increased. The minutes of the meetings of the highest party and state authorities, and their decisions, are available for the pre-war years. They record the role played by Stalin in many crucial matters. The files also contain hundreds of memoranda written by Stalin, and thousands of memoranda addressed to him, many from members of the Politburo.

The evidence is still far from complete. Several important archives remain partly or completely closed (see Chapter 8): the Presidential Archive contains many documents which would shed more light on decision-making under Stalin. But we possess perhaps twenty or thirty times more hard evidence about Stalin as political actor now than in 1988. The compilers of the most important collection of documents from the party archives, entitled *Stalinskoe Politbyuro* (*Stalin's Politburo*), correctly if cautiously conclude that in spite of gaps the information already available 'to a considerable extent' enables us to resolve the problems which have long puzzled historians about how the Politburo worked in the 1930s.[1]

From the early 1920s until the collapse of the Soviet system in 1991 the Politburo was the supreme agency of state power. It approved all important and many minor decisions by party, state and other bodies. Ever since its foundation in 1919 it had operated in secrecy, and the degree of secrecy increased relentlessly. A decision of 5 May 1927 insisted on 'the old tested principle that secret matters must be known only to those who absolutely *need* to know'. Accordingly the minutes (protocols) of Politburo meetings should be sent only to members of the party central committee, and should be returned by them within three days. Other officials merely received 'extracts' (*vypiski*) from the minutes – copies of those decisions which affected them directly. Particularly secret decisions were recorded separately and classified as 'special file' (*osobaya papka*). These included foreign affairs, defence, so-called 'counter-revolutionary activities' and many other matters. The 'special file' was not sent even to members of the central committee. Instead, 'extracts' containing individual decisions were communicated only to those few persons who 'needed to know'. With rare exceptions, recipients were required to return the 'extracts' within a few days.[2]

In the 1920s the Politburo, and the much larger central committee to which it was formally subordinated, were the scene of intense debate among party leaders. It was in the Politburo that Lenin successfully advanced the New Economic Policy. Members of the Politburo who supported successive Oppositions attempted to use it (usually unsuccessfully) to bring about further changes in party policy.

The main arguments advanced by both the Oppositions and the party leadership in the 1920s have long been well-known. But the new material reveals much more clearly the stages by which Stalin secured a unified political command of which he was the unchallenged head.

One of the most important files is a collection of letters written by Stalin to Molotov between 1925 and 1936, presented to the party archives by Molotov. They have now been published in both English and Russian.[3] Most were written during the couple of months in each year when Stalin was on vacation in the South. They were conveyed to Moscow by the courier service of the OGPU.

When the correspondence begins Stalin, supported by Bukharin, Rykov and the majority of the Politburo, was engaged in a bitter struggle against Trotsky and the Left Opposition, and against his former allies Zinoviev and Kamenev. Stalin's letters show how he masterminded the campaign against his opponents with careful and relentless persistence. Thus a typical letter, dated 25 June 1926, discusses the tactics to be pursued in the 'Lashevich affair'. Lashevich, a leading military figure who supported Zinoviev, addressed a clandestine meeting of oppositionists in a forest on the outskirts of Moscow. The meeting was reported to the party by one of the participants, and the party control commission recommended that Lashevich should be dismissed from his military post and from the central committee.

These measures did not satisfy Stalin. In his letter to 'Molotov, Rykov, Bukharin and other friends' he proposed to use this incident in the general struggle against his principal opponents. 'I thought for a long time about the "Lashevich affair", and I hesitated', he wrote. After much thought he now proposed that as the Zinoviev group was the most harmful the Lashevich affair should be used to remove Zinoviev from the Politburo:

> I assure you that this will be approved in the party and the country without the least complications – people won't be sorry for Zinoviev, because they know him well.

He explained to his colleagues that he originally thought that the central committee plenum should pass a broadly-worded statement in favour of party unity, but he had now decided that it would be better to approve a short resolution specifically tying the issue of party unity to the Lashevich affair. The resolution would explain that Zinoviev was being deprived of his post not because of his disagreements but because of disloyalty. In a remarkable passage, he set out the reasons for this in characteristic Stalin fashion:

> With a *broad* resolution of the plenum (the former plan) we would have to *officially unite* Zinov[iev] and Tr[otsky] in a single camp, which is perhaps premature and strategically irrational at the moment. It is better to defeat them one by one. Let Tr[otsky] and Pyatakov defend Lashevich, and we shall listen to them.[4]

Stalin's tactics proved successful. As he anticipated, Trotsky and his supporters came to Zinoviev's defence; they were indignant about the lack of any evidence that Zinoviev knew about the clandestine meeting. Trotsky's intervention made it look as if party unity was being violated not by Stalin but by Trotsky and Zinoviev.

Similar methods were employed in 1929 and 1930 against Stalin's former allies, the 'Rightwingers' Rykov and Bukharin. They opposed rapid industrialisation and the forcible collectivisation of agriculture, and were supported in their opposition by most of the non-party specialist advisers to the government.

Stalin had always been suspicious of the 'bourgeois specialists'. In 1925, in the midst of the struggle with Zinoviev, he complained to Molotov that on economic questions it was not the Politburo but Gosplan which was effectively in charge – and 'even worse, not even Gosplan, but the sections of Gosplan which are controlled by specialists'.[5]

In 1929 and 1930, most of the top specialists advising the government were arrested, including Groman, a senior member of Gosplan, and Kondratiev, the economist world-famous for his 'long cycles'. The OGPU forced them to confess that they had engaged in sabotage and planned to set up an anti-Communist government with the support of foreign powers. There was no substance in these charges, but many specialists were found guilty in major trials in 1930 and 1931.

Stalin's letters provide fascinating details about his control of these events from his Southern vacation resort. Six letters written in the summer of 1930 set out the tactics to be used. His comments ranged from broad hints to virtual instructions about the nature of the confessions to be obtained. 'It is essential to arrest Sukhanov, Bazarov, Ramzin', he insisted in August 1930, 'and Sukhanov's wife should be probed (she is a communist!)'. 'By the way', he remarked on 2 September, 'how about Messrs. the defendants admitting their *mistakes* and disgracing themselves politically, while simultaneously acknowledging the stability of Soviet power and the correctness of the method of collectivisation? That would be rather good.'

In the same letter he referred with approval, in a classic and almost untranslatable phrase, to the 'work of inspecting and bashing' (*proverochno-mordoboinaya rabota*) being carried out in the State Bank and the Commissariat of Finance by the OGPU and the Workers' and Peasants' Inspectorate.[6]

A month later, in a letter to the head of the OGPU discovered by the Russian editors, Stalin commented on the preliminary testimonies from the accused which he had been sent. He made quite detailed suggestions about further confessions which might be obtained:

> In any new (future) testimonies . . . pay particular attention to the question of foreign intervention and its timing . . .
>
> Run Messrs. Kondratiev, Yurovskii, Chayanov etc. through the mill; they have cleverly tried to evade [the charge of having] a 'tendency to intervention' but they are (indisputably) interventionists . . .
>
> If Ramzin's testimonies are confirmed and corroborated in the depositions of other persons accused (Groman, Larichev, Kondratiev and Company, etc.) that will be a serious success for the OGPU . . .
>
> > Understood?
> >
> > > Greetings!   J. Stalin.[7]

The curbs on the specialists made it much easier to overturn the more moderate economic policies of the 1920s.

Simultaneously Stalin sought to increase control by the Politburo over the central machinery of government. Between 1926 and 1930, Rykov was in charge of the governmental apparatus through his posts as chair both of the Council of People's Commissars (SNK) and its main sub-committee the Council of Labour and Defence (STO). These influential posts were previously held by Lenin. A small committee of Rykov's deputies (*soveshchanie zamov*) was responsible for many of the more detailed decisions of the Soviet government. Rykov, a moderate politician strongly committed to NEP, clashed with Stalin in 1929. Though Rykov soon capitulated, Stalin seized the opportunity to limit greatly the relative autonomy of the government apparatus.

On 2 September 1930, he wrote to Molotov arguing that Rykov '*undoubtedly helped*' the Gromans and the Kondratievs. Eleven days later a further letter fiercely criticised the whole machinery of government:

> Our central Soviet top level (STO, SNK, the committee of deputies [*soveshchanie zamov*]) is suffering from a fatal illness. STO has been transformed from a businesslike militant agency into an empty parliament. SNK is paralysed by Rykov's insipid and essentially anti-party

speeches. The committee of deputies ... is *opposing itself* to the C[entral] Committee of the party. It is obvious that this cannot continue.[8]

Stalin now had the bit between his teeth, and on 22 September he wrote to Molotov proposing that Rykov should be dismissed together with the 'bureaucratic machinery of secretaries and consultants'. He suggested that Molotov, who was extremely loyal to Stalin, should take over:

This will achieve the full unity of the top Soviet and party level, which will undoubtedly double our strength.[9]

In December 1930, Stalin's scheme was put into effect; some details about how this was done are now available in the archives. At the plenum of the central committee Rykov was intemperately criticised by a number of speakers, and shouted at from the body of the hall. At the end of the session Stanislas Kosior, Ukrainian party secretary, proposed that Rykov should be replaced by Molotov; he had obviously been put up to this by Stalin. The proposal met with the 'prolonged applause of the entire hall'.[10] Rykov was thus subjected to the treatment meted out to Trotsky at the October 1927 plenum of the central committee, and which would be used against Stalin's former allies at central committee plenums held during the Great Purge of 1937–8.

SNK was thoroughly reorganised. The committee of deputies was abolished. Decisions about defence had previously often been taken by a subcommittee of STO. They were now concentrated at the top, in a new Commission of Defence, responsible to both the Politburo and SNK. The five members of the Commission were all members of the Politburo (Molotov, Stalin, Voroshilov – commissar for war, Kuibyshev – head of Gosplan, and Ordzhonikidze – in charge of industry).[11]

The Politburo now consisted entirely of the triumphant group around Stalin. It continued for a time to be a forum at which some discussion took place. But during the 1930s its powers greatly declined. It met less frequently. There were about 60 regular sessions in 1931, 46 in 1932, and only 14 in 1933. The 1933 pattern continued until 1936, but all Politburo procedures were disrupted during the Great Purge, when one full member of the Politburo and three candidate members were arrested and executed.[12]

The compilers of *Stalinskoe Politbyuro* conclude:

As the Politburo became politically weaker as a collective body, and the power of Stalin increased, the practice of delegating the powers of the Politburo to various kinds of 'narrow groups' became more widespread.[13]

On 14 April 1937, at the climax of this process, the Politburo established a permanent commission of five persons 'to prepare for the Politburo, and in the case of special urgency, to take decisions on, questions of a secret character, including questions of foreign policy'.[14] The Politburo did not recover the powers it had possessed in the 1920s until after Stalin's death. Even then the successive party General Secretaries sometimes by-passed it on important questions of defence and foreign policy.

In the 1930s Stalin thus established himself as the almost unchallengeable authority within the party – the position that Zinoviev had feared he was acquiring back in 1923. In August 1933 a fairly minor incident provided a striking example of his power. Vyshinsky, flexing his muscles as deputy prosecutor, brought a case against industrial officials for delivering incomplete combine-harvesters. In his speech at their trial, he provocatively declared that the trial 'provides a basis for raising general questions about the work of the People's Commissariat of Heavy Industry and the People's Commissariat of Agriculture'.[15] Ordzhonikidze, commissar for heavy industry, was extremely indignant about this intervention in his affairs by an official who was not even a member of the Politburo. Two days after the speech appeared in the press the Politburo at Ordzhonikidze's suggestion reproved Vyshinsky for 'providing a pretext for incorrect accusations' against the two commissariats.[16]

Stalin, who was on vacation, received the papers about the Politburo decision and was equally indignant. He wrote to Molotov accusing Ordzhonikidze of 'hooliganism'.[17] On the same day the Politburo hastened to rescind its decision.[18] Stalin was so angry about this incident that he wrote again both to Molotov and Kaganovich insisting that Ordzhonikidze and those who sided with him were 'in the camp of the reactionary elements'.[19]

Powerful heads of state in more democratic countries were at times capable of exercising similar powers. During the second world war Churchill could invariably push a policy through when he was determined to do so, and Margaret Thatcher was in a similar position after the Falklands war. But Churchill and Thatcher were both eventually ejected from office – a fate which Stalin did not need to fear.

And unlike Churchill and Thatcher Stalin could personally decide whether Soviet citizens of whom he disapproved should live or die. His grim powers are starkly illustrated by documents in the archives. He had confidence in what he was doing, and did not bother to conceal from future generations that he held the smoking gun. Thus on 27 August 1937 he despatched a coded message to the Smolensk party in reply to a telegram about alleged 'counter-revolutionary wreckers' who were on trial in an agricultural district:

I advise you to sentence the wreckers of Andreev district to execution by shooting, and publish information about the executions in the local press.

Secretary C[entral] C[ommittee] Stalin.

This message was sent at 5 p.m. Ten minutes later, at 5.10 p.m., he responded to a similar coded telegram from Krasnoyarsk:

The arson at the grain mill must have been organised by enemies. Take every measure to find the arsonists. Accelerate trial of guilty. Sentence – execution by shooting. Report execution in local press.[20]

Other decisions by Stalin about executions and imprisonments were far more sweeping. In the course of the Great Purge, on 2 July 1937, a Politburo minute signed by Stalin 'On Anti-Soviet Elements' resolved that 'hostile' former kulaks and criminals should be sentenced to death or exile by triumvirates set up in every region. On 31 July the Politburo approved a detailed instruction prepared by the People's Commissariat for Internal Affairs which set out the number of people to be 'subject to repression' in each of sixty regions. Although the instruction did not yet include all regions and republics, the number to be executed amounted to 73 000, the number to be deported to camps for 8–10 years to 187 000, a quarter of a million in all.[21] Many more such decisions lurk in the 'special file' of the Politburo.

Such evidence convincingly demonstrates the vast scope of Stalin's ruthless personal power. But it does not of course provide the whole story of the nature of his rule. The archives also show that Stalin's close associates attempted to modify his policies, sometimes successfully. Some historians have argued that until the Great Purge of 1937–8 there was a fairly consistent 'moderate' group in the Politburo, including Kirov, Kuibyshev and Ordzhonikidze. Kirov's murder in December 1934 is often interpreted as Stalin's attempt to break the power of this group. This attractive hypothesis is not confirmed by the evidence available so far. The Russian compilers of *Stalinskoe Politbyuro* conclude:

The relationships between individual members of the Politburo (and the conflicts between them) were determined not by different political positions but rather by departmental interests. (However, these group interests could of course objectively reflect a definite political position.)

The files of personal correspondence between Politburo members show that Kaganovich and Ordzhonikidze were particularly close, as were Molotov and Kuibyshev. This runs counter to the notion of the 'moderate'

Ordzhonikidze and Kuibyshev versus the 'hard-line' or 'radical' Molotov and Kaganovich. But it does fit the hypothesis that Kaganovich and Ordzhonikidze, being responsible for particular government departments (transport and heavy industry), tended to be in a distinct group from Molotov and Kuibyshev, who as the Politburo members in charge of the Council of People's Commissars and Gosplan were responsible for state policy as a whole.[22]

Although they were not divided into definite political groups, some Politburo members did attempt to change Stalin's policies on important issues – and sometimes succeeded. Oleg Khlevnyuk, in his meticulous study of Stalin and Ordzhonikidze, has shown that while Ordzhonikidze was not prepared to enter into a serious struggle against Stalin, 'he may have supported a "softer" strategy'.[23] Ordzhonikidze certainly sought to resist the extreme forms of repression. Until the last few months of 1936 he more or less successfully protected industrial managers and officials, and other associates.[24] In the end he failed to stem the advance of the purges, and on 18 February 1937 he shot himself or was murdered. Two weeks later, Stalin revealed his conflict with Ordzhonikidze and his own anger about Ordzhonikidze's softness towards 'enemies' in a speech to the members of the central committee at the February–March 1937 plenum:

> Cde. Sergo [Ordzhonikidze] was one of the first, one of the best members of the Politburo, a leader of the economy of a higher type. But I would say that he also suffered from the disease that he would get attached to someone, declare people personally devoted to him, and then get too close to them, in spite of warnings from the party, in spite of warnings from the CC[central committee]. How much trouble he caused himself in order to back up Lominadze. How much trouble he caused himself, hoping and hoping that he would put Lominadze right, and Lominadze duped him and deceived him every step of the way. How much trouble he caused himself to defend against everyone else such people as Vardanyan, Gogoberidze, Meliksetov, and Okudzhava – who are now obvious scoundrels, exposed in the Urals. How much trouble he caused himself, and how much trouble he caused us.

Stalin removed this passage from the published version, and it was not published until 1991.[25] Lominadze was an independent-minded Bolshevik who took a critical line towards Stalin's policies in the autumn of 1930, but was later – like many other oppositionists, including Bukharin – given posts in the industrial commissariat. In January 1935, following Kirov's murder, he committed suicide after being accused of participating in a terrorist organisation. Ordzhonikidze provided support for Lominadze's family until his own death in 1937.

Stalin naturally consulted others, inside and outside the Politburo, before adopting a particular course of action. He was also prepared to consider seriously unsolicited appeals from scientists and other public figures for whom he had respect. Sholokhov, the outstanding author of novels about the Don Cossacks during Civil War and collectivisation, approached Stalin successfully on several occasions. During the famine of 1933, he wrote him a long letter describing the terrible conditions of the villagers and the depredations of the local officials in Veshenskii district in the North Caucasus, where he lived, and in the neighbouring district. He appealed to Stalin to allocate grain to these districts to save lives.

Stalin was unwilling or unable to change his general policy towards the famine, and large numbers of peasants in other districts died of starvation. In justification of his general line Stalin wrote to Sholokhov chiding him for his one-sided failure to realise that 'the respected grain growers of your district (and not only your district) have carried out a "go-slow" (sabotage!), and would have been willing to leave the workers and the Red Army without bread'. Nevertheless he provided the grain requested by Sholokhov for his own districts in full, and sent out a high-level commission, which found that Sholokhov's charges were justified.[26]

The story of Sholokhov and Stalin provides an instructive example of the need for caution about new revelations from the archives. None of the events we have described were reported at the time. The Soviet press in 1933 was not allowed to mention the existence of famine. It merely published an anodyne telegram from Sholokhov which complained that transport was not available to move seed from Veshenskii district to another district; this telegram said nothing about the prevalent hunger.[27] Then thirty years later in 1963, during the campaign to discredit Stalin, Khrushchev cited Sholokhov's letter and Stalin's critical reply. But he was so anxious to blacken Stalin's reputation that he did not reveal either that Stalin had allocated extra grain in response to Sholokhov's appeal or that a high-level Politburo commission had investigated Sholokhov's charges.[28] The correspondence was published only in 1994, after a further lapse of thirty years. And the full story may not yet have been told. The documents are in the Presidential Archive, and historians do not yet have free access to them.

Stalin was also influenced by his opponents as well as by his associates and supporters – usually adopting the policies of his critics without any acknowledgment that he had changed his line. Thus in July 1930 Pyatakov, head of the State Bank, and a former supporter of Trotsky, came to the conclusion that inflation was getting out of hand, and sent a memorandum to Stalin arguing that the state budget for the following year must be in surplus, and that no further currency should be issued.[29] Stalin's indignation knew no bounds. In successive letters to Molotov he claimed that both Pyatakov and the People's Commissar for Finance were being manipulated by supporters of Kondratiev and Groman, and called for Pyatakov's dismissal. He described him as 'a truly Right-wing Trotskyist'(!).[30] In October both Pyatakov and the Commissar for Finance were duly replaced.[31]

Thus Stalin had apparently established a political framework for further inflation. But at this point he initiated or acquiesced in an abrupt change in policy. Even before the new appointments the Politburo decided to tighten the financial screw.[32] And in December 1930 the economic plan for 1931 proposed that the state budget should be in surplus and no further currency should be issued.[33] Pyatakov had been removed; but his proposals had been adopted. This is a striking example of Stalin's well-known ability to 'wear other people's clothes'.

We now also know that Stalin was a voracious reader of Menshevik and Trotskyist émigré literature. His personal library contained many books by Trotsky, heavily annotated by Stalin.[34] There is strong circumstantial evidence that he sometimes modified his policies in response to émigré criticisms.

This consideration is relevant not only to our knowledge of Soviet society in the Stalin years but also to our assessment of the operation of the Politburo. The most secret OGPU reports were received not by the whole party central committee, or even by the whole Politburo, but by those who 'needed to know'. The reports received by Stalin informed him not only about disaffection in the country at large but also about the private conversations of his opponents, and of prominent citizens. From January 1928 the secret political department of the OGPU opened the correspondence of the Right-wing politicians Rykov, Bukharin, Tomsky and Uglanov and bugged their conversations.[35] Zinoviev and Kamenev 'were actively observed by agents from October 1932, their correspondence was opened and their telephone conversations were bugged'.[36] No evidence was found of conspiracy or contact with foreign agents, but we may reasonably guess that the OGPU reports revealed the hostility and near-contempt with which the former Bolshevik leaders regarded Stalin, while praising him to the skies in public. The stream of information which Stalin was receiving about unrest throughout society must also have helped to form his outlook. On the other hand his unscrupulous willingness to seek out evidence to demonstrate the treachery of his opponents encouraged the OGPU to intensify the one-sidedness of its reports. Even the most secret information must be scrutinised for bias.

The opening of the archives has failed to shed much light on the most tantalising political mystery of the Stalin period: the death of Kirov, member of the Politburo and Leningrad party secretary since the ejection of Zinoviev from that post in February 1926. Kirov, who was popular both nationally and in Leningrad, was killed at party headquarters by a revolver fired by a disaffected party member – Leonid Nikolaev.

The murder of Kirov formed the pretext for the launching of a reign of terror. The first to suffer were Zinoviev and his supporters, for whom the Kirov murder played a similar role to the Lashevich affair of 1926. It then spread to the Trotskyists and to the NKVD itself. The murder figured prominently in the trial of Yagoda in March 1938. At the time of Kirov's murder Yagoda was People's Commissar for Internal Affairs.

The view that Stalin was responsible for Kirov's murder has long been advanced by prominent Western historians. Khrushchev referred to the murder in his secret speech at the XX party Congress in February 1956 as 'concealing much that is incomprehensible and dubious, and requiring the most careful investigation'. Then five years later at the XXII party Congress he strongly hinted that Stalin was responsible for the murder.

We now know that two Commissions investigated the murder in Khrushchev's time. A party Commission established on 31 December 1955 investigated 'materials on the mass repressions of full and candidate members of the central committee elected at the XVII party Congress' of 1934. The Commission was headed by P. N. Pospelov, who prepared Khrushchev's secret speech (a draft of it in Pospelov's handwriting is in RTsKhIDNI).[37]

The Commission did not reach any conclusions about the Kirov murder, and in 1960 another Commission was established specifically to deal with this crucial issue. Shvernik, a Politburo member, was in the chair. Its proceedings have never been published.[38] Pospelov, who was a member, at one point prepared a memorandum which seemed to favour Stalin's guilt – evidently influenced by the wishes of the top leadership at that time.[39] But the Commission apparently concluded that 'Nikolaev was a lone terrorist and Stalin used the murder of Kirov for the physical isolation and extermination both of the leaders of the Zinoviev opposition and of their former supporters'.[40]

The Kirov murder was considered again by the Politburo Commission on the Repressions established during *perestroika*. It delegated the question to a working group containing officials from the KGB, the Procuracy, the Supreme Court and the archives. They produced in 1990 a long report which unambiguously declared that, with the exception of Nikolaev, all those found guilty in 1935–8 of conspiring to murder Kirov were innocent. There were no conspiracies. The working group also found Stalin innocent. It concluded that the murder was conceived and carried out by Nikolaev acting alone.[41]

This report, like the others, was not published. In a long article in *Pravda* the chair of the Commission on Repressions, Aleksandr Yakovlev, conceded that there was no 'deliberate bias' in the report, but argued that it had considered the issues too narrowly. 'Almost nothing was done to study the relationship between Kirov and Stalin'; instead the whole matter was 'reduced to a superficial evaluation of particular facts'.[42]

In reply to those who are convinced of Stalin's guilt Alla Kirilina, formerly on the staff of the Institute of Party History for the Leningrad region, has produced a pamphlet defending the working group's point of view in detail.[43]

A newly-available memoir which discusses Stalin's attitude at the time seems to support the case for his innocence. Mariya Svanidze, sister-in-law of Stalin's first wife, frequently visited him, and kept a fascinating diary. The entries for the weeks before Kirov's murder frequently refer to his friendship with Stalin. Thus she wrote on 4 November 1934:

> After dinner I. [Stalin] was in a very good mood. He went to the inter-urban government phone [*vertushka*] and called Kirov, and began to joke with him about the abolition of the rationing of bread and the increase in its price. He advised Kirov to come to Moscow at once to defend the interests of Leningrad region from a greater increase in prices than in other regions. Evidently Kirov tried to get out of it, and I. gave the phone to Kag[anovich], who persuaded Kir[ov] to come for one day. I. loves Kirov and, as he had just got back from Sochi, evidently wanted to meet him, steam in a Russian bath and clown around while talking shop – the increased bread prices were a pretext.[44]

On 5 December, the day of Kirov's funeral, she called uninvited on Stalin in the evening together with her husband and Evgeniya Allilueva (the wife of Pavel Allilueva, brother of Nadezhda, Stalin's second wife, who committed suicide two years previously):

> We found him just sitting at the table for his modest supper. The children were in the corridor and hurried to their father. We took off our coats . . .
> I., as usual, was kind. He had become more drawn and pale, there was a hidden suffering in his eyes. He smiled, laughed and joked, but my heart ached to look at him. He is suffering very much.

According to Mariya Svanidze, after Nadezhda's suicide Kirov was 'the person closest to him, who was able to approach him simply and from the heart and give him the warmth and comfort he lacked'.[45]

Those who are persuaded that Stalin organised Kirov's murder will argue that Stalin was a consummate actor and Mariya Svanidze was a very naïve woman. In spite of her affection both she and her husband were executed in 1941–2. A prudent Russian historian has concluded:

> the supporters of the two extreme points of view . . . do not possess facts with the aid of which the question could be finally cleared up. Most likely such facts do not exist. Obviously political assassinations are planned in the strictest secrecy and instructions about them are not given on an official form with a rubber stamp.[46]

While the new Politburo and Stalin files have not solved the Kirov murder, they have illuminated aspects of Stalin's personality. In the Foreword to the English-language edition of *Stalin's Letters to Molotov*, Robert Tucker, the distinguished biographer of Stalin, argues that they demonstrate Stalin's exclusive preoccupation with politics, that 'he was a thinking, reacting, plotting politician during every waking hour'.[47] A volume of documents in Russian issued by the Presidential Archive, *Iosif Stalin v ob''yatiyakh sem'i* (*Joseph Stalin in the Embraces of His Family*), contains Stalin's correspondence in 1928–1931 with his wife Nadezhda Allilueva, and letters from Allilueva and Stalin to his mother. In my opinion this correspondence does not entirely fit in with Tucker's portrait.

Stalin's letters to his mother were certainly brief and almost entirely formal – 'Greetings to my mother! Live ten thousand years! My greetings to old friends and comrades. Kisses. Your Soso'.[48] But he did get round to sending her money ('One hundred and fifty rubles – I can't manage any more'), photographs of himself and the children, and medicine.[49] And after Allilueva's suicide, on one occasion he dropped his guard and wrote to his mother in a postscript 'After Nadya's death, my personal life is naturally difficult. But a steadfast person must remain steadfast.'[50]

His letters to Allilueva reveal even more clearly that he devoted some waking hours to matters other than politics. He grumbled about his mother-in-law and, in conformity with rumour, was contemptuous of his son Jacob by his first marriage ('a hooligan and blackmailer', presumably a reference to his attempted suicide).[51] But he also displayed much affection for Allilueva. He asked for news of the children, and urged her to find time to visit him ('It's very boring here, Tatochka. I sit at home alone, like a gloomy owl').[52] He sent her lemons and 'peaches from our tree', and rose to her defence when she reported that the Molotovs had complained that she was neglecting him.[53]

Both sets of letters also reveal that Stalin spent many waking hours worrying about his health. During these years he complained of fish poisoning, an injured arm, an attack of quinsy, overstrain, 'near-inflammation of the lungs', and influenza.[54] He also sought sympathy from Allilueva because he was undergoing a lengthy course of dental treatment – a tooth had been removed and others had been filled.[55]

But Tucker is certainly right that Stalin was not deflected for a moment by his bodily troubles, or by any compassionate feeling, from inflicting politically necessary suffering on others. In the midst of his complaints about his health, he told Molotov that in the State Bank and Commissariat of Finance 'two or three dozen wreckers from the administration must be executed, including a dozen cashiers of various kinds' and that 'Kondratiev, Groman and another couple of scoundrels must certainly be executed'.[56] In September 1930, while Stalin was undergoing his dental treatment in Sochi, 48 'food wreckers' were shot on his instructions, scapegoats for the shortages resulting from his policies.[57]

13 The Secret Police and the Camps

The forced labour system developed on a mass scale in the early 1930s, and expanded remorselessly until Stalin's death in 1953. At first the Soviet press gave it a certain amount of publicity – albeit very selective. In 1931–3 the construction of the White Sea canal by prison labour was extolled as a practical demonstration of the way in which a socialist system of justice would re-educate and rehabilitate criminals. But the dark side of the camps – the hunger and the brutality – was concealed. Later in the 1930s the press fell silent.

In 1956–64, as part of Khrushchev's de-Stalinisation campaign, many articles and fictionalised documentaries exposed the camp system to public scrutiny. This new openness culminated in the publication – on Khrushchev's personal authority – of Solzhenitsyn's *One Day in the Life of Ivan Denisovich* in the literary monthly *Novyi Mir* in November 1962. *One Day* describes the grim conditions in a typical Siberian camp, engaged in constructing a power station during the second world war. But in Khrushchev's time nothing was published in the Soviet press about the total number of prisoners at any date since 1929, or about the amount of production for which they were responsible. And the authorities banned the publication of any generalised information about death rates or sickness rates in the camps.

The censorship which still operated under Khrushchev is indicated by a remarkable memorandum addressed to the party central committee by the head of the KGB on 26 December 1962. The memorandum drew attention to an anomaly in the procedures for rehabilitation of those unjustly executed. When relatives were informed that someone condemned by special tribunal had been rehabilitated, they were not told that he had been executed. Instead:

> State security agencies inform members of the families of the condemned that their relatives were sentenced to 10 years' corrective labour and died in their place of confinement. In necessary cases . . . the death of those executed is registered, and a certificate is issued on request in

which the date of death is given within the limit of 10 years from the
date of arrest; the cause of death is invented.

This procedure was obviously adopted to conceal the scale of the executions and the high levels of death in custody during the Great Purge of
1937–8. In his memorandum of 1962 the head of the KGB proposed that
this falsification, introduced when rehabilitation began in 1955, was no
longer necessary. But the move towards honesty which he proposed was
very limited. In future relatives would be told *by word of mouth* the true
circumstances of the death, and the death certificate would show the true
date of death. However, on the certificate the cause of death would be left
blank. Moreover, the truth would not be told to relatives of those who had
been rehabilitated before this new procedure; and the old system of falsi-
fying the date and cause of death would continue when information about
rehabilitation was sent abroad.[1]

The full truth about these concealed executions was revealed only quite
recently. A practical example of this tangled web of deception is provided
in a recent monograph about the repressions in the Urals. It includes
facsimiles of two death certificates issued for Anton Antonovich Fridrikhovich. Fridrikhovich was a former exile who had been restored to civil
rights in 1935 owing to his good work as a 20-year old Stakhanovite, but
was then arrested in 1937. His fate was completely concealed for 21 years.

Then, on 11 April 1958, the first death certificate, issued following his
rehabilitation, stated that he had died on 12 January 1946, at the age of 31.
Cause of death: tuberculosis of the lungs.

A second death certificate was issued thirty four years later, on 11
February 1992, six months after the failure of the August coup. It revealed
that Fridrikhovich had in fact died on 10 October 1938, at the age of 23.
Cause of death: execution by shooting.[2]

After the fall of Khrushchev in October 1964, even the modest openness
of the Khrushchev years attenuated, and then disappeared until 1987. The
only exception was the continued publication, in a somewhat rosy glow,
of accounts of the deportation of kulaks in the early 1930s and their
'labour re-education' in special settlements.[3] Virtually nothing else appeared in the press or other media about the labour camp system, or about
political repression under Stalin. When biographies appeared of prominent
figures executed during the Great Purge of 1937–8, the cause of their
death was ignored. A 1970 biography of the revolutionary leader and great
industrial administrator Sergo Ordzhonikidze, who committed suicide (or
may have been murdered) in February 1937, described his last hours as
follows:

21.30. Sergo went out to the People's Commissariat, where he remained until 0.20 a.m., and then returned home . . . On the next day he ceased to exist (*ego ne stalo*).[4]

The author went on to ask dramatically 'But did Sergo really die?' No anti-Stalinist revelations followed. Instead the author answered his own question in the words of the novelist Aleksei Tolstoy: 'Great warriors and heroes do not die'. In the case of lesser figures the problem of the date of their death was dealt with in publications by a simple device. It was not mentioned at all.

This does not mean that in the 1970s and 1980s Soviet citizens were ignorant of the existence of the Gulag system under Stalin. Every family had a relative, or at least an acquaintance, who had served a sentence, or died, in a camp or 'special settlement' in the Stalin years. Russians would refer in conversation to the rumours that 'millions' had been incarcerated or executed by Stalin. Several hundred thousand peasant families were deported in the early 1930s, and millions of peasants died in the 1933 famine. Large numbers of people with professional training, from writers to engineers and army officers, were arrested in 1937–8; many were executed. Several million people from the national minorities were deported during the second world war. Even the most favoured social class – the industrial working class – was hit by the severe labour legislation of the 1940s, which imposed fines or prison sentences for violating the laws on absenteeism and on leaving an occupation without permission. Every class of society was affected.

But knowledge of the camp system was vague. Many families found it too painful – or too dangerous – to talk about relatives who had been sent to camps. And those who returned in the years after Stalin's death often remained silent about their experiences.

Meanwhile, in the West, ever since the early 1930s Sovietologists had sought to find out how many people had been imprisoned in the camps, and how important they had been for the Soviet economic and military effort. All kinds of patchy Soviet data, together with émigré accounts, were used to try to reach the truth. Estimates varied wildly, as the following examples illustrate:[5]

	Camp population (*millions*)	Year
Timasheff (1948)	2.3	End-1937
Jasny (1952)	3.5	1940–1
Wheatcroft (1981)	4–5 maximum[a]	1939
Swaniewicz (1965)	6.9	1940–1
Conquest (1968)	9[b]	End-1938

[a] Labour camps (and colonies) only
[b] *Excludes* criminals

Such estimates were accompanied by equally contradictory figures, both for the total number arrested and exiled in the Stalin period, and for the number of 'excess deaths' (deaths above the normal level) due to famine, abnormal levels of disease, and executions. Conquest claimed that there were at least seven million excess deaths in 1930–5 as a result of the repressions, partly during collectivisation itself, and partly in the camps; a further three million died in 1937–8. In addition, seven million people died in the 1933 famine. This resulted in a minimum figure for excess deaths in 1930–8 of seventeen million.[6] He claimed that these were conservative figures. But Wheatcroft, Cooper and I with various reservations accepted Lorimer's estimate that excess deaths in 1927–38 amounted to about 5½ million.[7]

The Western discussions about camps and excess deaths were pursued with particular ferocity in the early 1980s, on the eve of *glasnost'* and *perestroika*, and spread over into general publications about Soviet affairs. Extreme (and untenable) figures often prevailed. Stephen Cohen stated that 'prisons and remote concentration camps swelled to 9 million inmates by late 1939 (compared to 30 000 in 1928 and 5 million in 1933–5)'; he cited Conquest as his authority.[8] He also claimed that 'twenty million is a conservative estimate' for the 'deaths that resulted from collectivisation and police terror, particularly from 1929 to 1939'.[9] More recently, Martin Malia (with far less excuse in view of the information now available) has also cited Conquest's very high figures for deaths from political causes under Stalin, claiming that 'it is the largest single harvest of terror in history'.[10] The normally sober Alan Bullock cited approvingly Conquest's figure for excess deaths in 1930–8.[11]

On the other hand, in a notorious passage, Jerry Hough claimed of deaths in the purge of 1937–8 that 'a figure in the low hundreds of thousands seems much more probable than one in the high hundreds of thousands'.[12]

He later stated more precisely 'I do put the purge deaths 1937–1939 in the 75 000–200 000 range'.[13] As we shall see, the archives reveal that Conquest's figures for the 1930s as a whole are far too high, and Hough's for 1937–9 are far too low.

There was certainly a political dimension to these disputes about imprisonment and death under Stalin. Some of those who advocated high figures were anxious to demonstrate that Stalin's Communism was at least as murderous and brutal as Hitler's fascism. Thus the veteran historian Leonard Schapiro stated shortly before his death that posterity would presumably record that Stalin killed many more people than did his near rival, Hitler.[14] Some of those who defended low figures were concerned to demonstrate that a demonic image of the Soviet Union – including Stalin's Soviet Union – was being presented by hawkish American propagandists in the interests of the Cold War.

The most bitter controversy was waged not about the camps themselves but about the terrible famine of 1933. The United States Congress, with strong backing from American Ukrainian organisations, established a Commission on the Ukraine Famine. In 1988, the Commission found that the famine was 'man-made', and that 'Joseph Stalin and those around him committed genocide against Ukrainians in 1932–1933.'[15] In the publicity surrounding the Commission, the famine in Ukraine was often referred to as a 'holocaust', the term usually used to characterise Hitler's extermination of the Jews.

It would be wrong, however, to assume a straightforward link between Cold War hardliners and high figures for the Stalinist repressions. Thus Stephen Cohen, whose high figures have just been cited, was a consistent opponent of American policy in the Cold War, and insisted that Stalin and Stalinism rather than Communism and the October Revolution were responsible for the repressions of the 1930s. Roy Medvedev, dissident Soviet historian who regarded himself as a Leninist, also made extremely high estimates of the number of persons repressed under Stalin.[16]

THE NEW DATA ON FORCED LABOUR

The data in the Soviet archives have at last provided a solid statistical foundation for the discussion of these issues, and have resolved several of the major controversies – though this is not yet recognised by some of the participants. The Soviet authorities released new information about forced labour slowly and intermittently. From early 1987 onwards many accounts were published about conditions in the camps and about the repressions generally.[17] Some critical Soviet intellectuals cited very high figures for repressions as if they were proven fact. Thus Academician Tikhonov claimed that some thirteen million peasants had been exiled or sent to camps during the collectivisation of agriculture[18] (this was four times the true figure). Such figures were sometimes taken straight from Robert Conquest's *Great Terror* without acknowledgement.[19]

It was not until 1989, over four years after Gorbachev took office, that a few privileged historians were permitted to cite official statistics from the NKVD archives in the Soviet press. In accordance with the bizarre arrangements for consulting confidential material which prevailed before the August coup, and to some extent still continue, these historians were not permitted to cite the archival reference numbers of these documents. Other Soviet historians, and all Western historians, were not at this time permitted to see these documents at all. This cast a cloud of suspicion over the new data. The cloud became thicker because one or two of the privileged historians, in seeking to use the archives to refute the high estimates, presented incomplete data as if it covered the whole story. For example, figures were published for the number of persons in camps and colonies as if they referred to the total number in confinement; this excluded those in prisons and special settlements. And the number of persons imprisoned in camps and colonies during 1937–8 was treated as if this was the total figure for repressions, *omitting executions.*[20]

Since the defeat of the August 1991 coup, both Russian and Western historians have been given access to the large collection of NKVD files in the State Archives of the Russian Federation, and most restrictions on the citation of archival references have been lifted. The archives on population in the 1930s have also been released. These include the population censuses for 1937 and 1939. The 1937 census was banned by Stalin and its organisers were executed, and many historians believed that it had been completely destroyed. Only a few tables from the 1939 census were published before 1990. The new materials, together with the Ukrainian and local Russian archives, make it possible to present a reasonably comprehensive account of the scale of the Stalinist forced labour system. The best English-language sources which survey this complex mass of material are Alec Nove's commendably short and incisive article 'Victims of Stalinism: How Many?' in *Stalinist Terror*; an article by Getty, Rittersporn and Zemskov; and Edwin Bacon's *Gulag at War.*[21] Zemskov, a Russian historian, has published more material from the archives on this subject than any other scholar.

The paragraphs which follow summarise the data on forced labour so far available from the archives. I should first explain that, while the system underwent many administrative changes between 1929 and 1953, it contained four main divisions throughout this period:

1. prisons;
2. labour camps (originally known as concentration camps);
3. labour colonies, mainly for those receiving lower sentences (three years or less);
4. special settlements (sometimes known as labour settlements), containing exiles.

In addition to these four categories, some citizens, known as *ssyl'nye*, were exiled without being confined in a settlement (they were required to live in a certain town or area, or in one of a list of towns and areas). Others who had completed their term were no longer confined to a camp, colony or settlement but were not permitted to return to their home town or village. The numbers in these last two categories are not precisely known. The *ssyl'nye* were apparently not very numerous, but the number of people who had completed their sentence but were not permitted to return home may have been very large.

In addition, legislation about lateness at work without due cause introduced immediately before the war imposed judicial fines on citizens which infringed the legislation; they continued to work as before but for a period of up to six months a percentage (usually 25 per cent) was deducted from their pay. This category, entitled 'corrective labour without deprivation of liberty', has been omitted here; it included 1 770 000 people in 1940 and a total of 10 904 000 people in the whole period, 1940–52, in which it was in force.[22]

With these important reservations, the total number of prisoners in the forced labour system was approximately as follows on 1 January of each year (thousands):[23]

	1933	1937	1939	1941	1953
Prisons	800[a]	545[e]	351[c]	488[c]	276[c,f]
Camps	334[b]	821[e]	1317[c]	1501[c]	1728[c]
Colonies	240[c]	375[e]	355[c]	420[c]	741[c]
Special settlements[d]	1142	917	939	930	2754
TOTAL	2516	2658	2962	3348	5499

The different modes of imprisonment are carefully explained in the article by Getty *et al.* Most of those arrested, both criminals and those charged with political offenses, were first sent to prison for investigation;

after sentence, they were transferred to a labour camp or, for shorter sentences, to colonies. Those exiled by administrative order, however, were normally sent direct to special settlements. An important distinction between these places of confinement is that camps and colonies contained individual prisoners who had received sentences, while whole families were sent to the special settlements. On the eve of the war, for example, women comprised only 8 per cent of the camp population, and minors under 18 only about 1 per cent.[24] But in the special settlements 30 per cent were adult women and 40 per cent were minors under 17; adult men were only 30 per cent of the total.[25]

Special Settlers

Russian historians have so far examined the special settlers in much more detail than the prisoners in camps and colonies. The first major wave of deportations to special settlements was in 1930–3; the vast majority of these were 'kulaks'. Russian historians now generally agree that 2.1–2.2 million persons were deported to special settlements in these four years; this excludes peasants resettled or exiled within their own region.[26]

National groups comprised the vast majority of the second major wave of deportations. The deportation of nationalities began as early as 1936–7, with the exile of 36 000 Poles from the Western regions, and of 175 000 Koreans from the Far East to Central Asia.[27] The deportations of Poles, Balts and Germans in 1940–1 and of numerous Caucasian peoples in 1944–5 are well-known.[28] Russian historians have now published large collections of archival documents tracing these deportations in great detail. According to the official records, between 3 226 000 and 3 442 000 persons were exiled in the 1940s.[29] For most of the nationalities, Robert Conquest's estimates of the number deported, made on the basis of population figures before the archives were opened, are quite accurate (in contrast to his considerable overestimate of kulak deportations).

Prisoners of War

The archives have also provided patchy information about the post-war fate of returning Soviet prisoners of war and other 'repatriates'. Many Western and Soviet reports have claimed that the overwhelming majority of former prisoners were sent to labour camps. Thus Martin Malia writes of the 'two million plus Soviet prisoners' transferred to the USSR from the West that they 'were either executed or sent to the Gulag'.[30] According to the data cited by Russian historians from the archives, however, of the 4.2

million civilian and military repatriates who had been checked by 1 March 1946:

- only 6.5 per cent were transferred to the 'special contingent' of the NKVD;
- 58 per cent were sent home (6 per cent of these were members of deported national minorities and required to join their compatriots in Central Asia and elsewhere);
- 14 per cent were sent to military 'working battalions';
- 19 per cent were called up for the army.[31]

Officers received much more unfavourable treatment than other ranks. Of the 50 400 officers freed from captivity by 1 October 1944, nearly 20 000 were sent to 'storm battalions';[32] in these formations the risk of death was exceptionally high. For all officers, according to Zemskov, 'return to military service or transfer to the reserve was an exception, transfer to the NKVD was the rule'.[33] But all repatriates were treated with suspicion:

> The suspicious attitude to repatriates [Zemskov writes] as a category of citizen who had lived in a foreign environment came from the higher echelons of power, and primarily from Stalin personally . . .
> It cannot be said that repatriates were morally and psychologically treated as outside society, but in the first post-war decade they were at least as it were put on its outer rim.[34]

Deaths in the Gulag

Information about the number of deaths in the Gulag system is patchy and incomplete. So far neither Western nor Russian historians have found files which report the number of deaths in prisons, or in the course of the journey to camps and special settlements. In the camps, the average annual death rate in 1936–50 was reported as 61 per 1000. This was substantially higher than the death rate for the population as a whole, even though the camp population contained only a small percentage of the very young and the old, among whom death rates were higher. Stephen Wheatcroft estimates that, age for age, the death rate in the camps in 1934–40 was between $5\frac{1}{2}$ and nine times as high as the normal civilian death rate.[35]

The death rate fluctuated greatly. In 1938, the peak of the Great Purge, it increased to 91 per 1000, and in the war years 1942–3 it reached the very high figure of over 170 per 1000. By 1952 it had fallen, according to the official record, to 6 per 1000.[36] Death rates among special settlers were extremely high in the famine years, reaching 133 per 1 000 in 1933, but declined to 16 per 1000 by 1940.[37] The death-rate was also extremely high among the nationalities deported in 1944–5. According to NKVD records, 24 per cent, or 145 000 persons, of the deported Chechens, Ingushi, Balkars and Karachai died between 1944 and 1948.[38] This does not include the large number who died on the journey from the Caucasus to their place of exile.[39]

Completely contradictory figures have been published for the number of people executed in the Stalin period, which are not included in the reported deaths in camps and settlements. The figure of seven million executions has frequently been cited, sometimes referring to the whole period 1929–53, sometimes to 1935–45, sometimes only to 1935–41.[40] This figure is completely inconsistent with the data so far traced in the archives, and difficult if not impossible to reconcile with the population censuses of 1926, 1937 and 1939. According to a formerly secret report in the archives, prepared for Malenkov and Khrushchev, in 1921–52 inclusive 799 257 persons were executed by the decision of various agencies and tribunals of the OGPU and its successors and by the Military Collegium;[41] these figures, if correct, seem to comprise the vast majority of all those executed. The number of executions was much higher than normal in six of the 32 years:

1921:   9701
1930:   20 201
1931:   10 651
1937: 353 074
1938: 328 618
1942:   23 278

1921 was the first year of NEP, and these figures reflect the political repression which accompanied the economic relaxation.

1930 and 1931 were the decisive years of collectivisation and dekulakisation. Presumably most of these 31 000 victims were 'kulaks', executed on the basis of the OGPU order of 2 February 1930, which directed that the 'most malicious and stubborn activists' should be executed by shooting.[42]

1937 and 1938 were the years of the Great Purge. The 681 692 executed in these two years were as many as 85 per cent of all those reported as executed.

1942 was the most dramatic and stressful year of the second world war, in which many defeats were followed by the triumphant Battle of Stalingrad. In a letter written from jail to other members of the Politburo in 1953, Beria, pleading for his life, reminded them of one of his achievements: at the beginning of the war 'several tens of thousands of deserters' were executed by firing squad by the special department of the NKVD in order to stop the flight of the armies.[43] It is not known whether such summary executions are included in the above figures.

One important puzzle about a key section of the population has been partly solved by the opening up of the archives: the fate of Red Army officers during the Great Purge of 1937–8. Before the archives were opened, it was generally believed that between 25 and 50 per cent of all officers had been arrested, and an unknown but large number of these executed. Conquest suggested that 35 000 out of a total corps of 70 000 were arrested; the foremost Western historian of the Red Army, John Erickson, estimated 20–30 000 out of 80 000.[44] A report in the former party archives dated 5 May 1940, summarised by Roger Reese in *Stalinist Terror*, records that 35 020 officers were arrested or discharged from the army in 1937 and 1938. But 10 994 of these were reinstated, so that the net number arrested or discharged was 24 026. Much more important: the total number of army officers turns out to have been not 70–80 000, as was previously believed, but 142 000 in 1937 and 178 000 in 1938. It was not 50 or even 25 per cent of the total number of officers which were removed from the army, but about 15 per cent; about 11 per cent of the total number of officers may have been arrested.[45] A very high proportion of senior officers was arrested and executed, so the officer corps of 1940 was much less experienced than the officer corps of 1936. But the new figures make it much easier to understand how the army managed to recover from the purges, and then sweep to victory during the war.

EXCESS DEATHS IN THE POPULATION AS A WHOLE

There were many excess deaths in the Stalin period in addition to executions and premature deaths in camps and colonies. Many of those deported to remote areas died of hunger, cold or disease in the course of being transferred. The greatest single cause of premature death in the 1930s was the famine of 1933. There is no agreement about the number of people who died in the famine. On the basis of the newly released Soviet data on birth and death registrations, Stephen Wheatcroft estimates deaths at four to five million.[46] But other historians believe that in addition many babies died soon after birth, and that neither their births nor their deaths were registered. The highest figure so far is by three Russian statisticians – Andreev, Darskii and Khar'kova – who estimate that excess deaths in 1932–3 alone amounted to eight million.[47] At an international conference in Toronto in January 1995 it emerged – perhaps not surprisingly – that the authors regarded this not as an absolute figure but as a possible or probable estimate within a range. A French demographer comments delicately on their estimate that 'these authors have chosen to concentrate the population deficit of the 1930s substantially on the single year 1933, which may seem a little extreme'.[48]

The new statistics have not provided a firm figure for the number of excess deaths under Stalin, but they considerably narrowed the range of feasible estimates. In his article in *Stalinist Terror*, Alec Nove accurately sums up our present knowledge: 'the evidence seems consistent with the view that 10–11 million perished in the thirties, with the peasants numerically the main victims'.[49] Conquest's estimate of seventeen million or more was too high; Lorimer's estimate, of $5^1/_2$ million, accepted by Wheatcroft and myself, was too low.

No firm figures are yet available for the years after 1939. The best estimate of the number of excess Soviet deaths during the second world war is 25–26 million.[50] It can be roughly estimated from the archives that there were some one million excess deaths in camps, colonies and settlements (excluding the deportation of nationalities) during the war. The archives also report 42 000 executions;[51] but this may not include all summary military executions of deserters and others. Only rough estimates can be made of how many of the three million or so citizens deported to remote areas died during the war. And no agreement will ever be reached on how many of the wartime military and civilian deaths should be attributed to the incompetence and poor judgement of Stalin, and of the Stalinist system.

Russian historians who have worked in the formerly secret archives peremptorily reject the high estimates of Conquest and others. On the number of prisoners in camps, colonies and prisons in 1939–40 Viktor Zemskov, described by Conquest as 'a thoroughly reliable researcher',[52] claims that 'the statistical data adduced by R. Conquest and S. Cohen are exaggerated by almost 500 per cent'.[53] And he also insists that the figure of seven million executions in 1935–41 is 'overestimated by a factor of ten.' But since the first burst of public interest in these statistics in 1989 and 1990, articles by the Russian historians have appeared only in small-circulation historical and social-science journals. They must be much less prominent in the minds of Russian citizens than the enormous figures for deaths from repressions frequently reported in popular newspapers and on television. Solzhenitsyn produced one of the highest figures, basing himself on estimates by the émigré Kurganov: between 1917 and 1959, excluding all deaths during the war, '66 million people perished from

extermination by hunger, collectivisation, the exile of peasants to extermination, prisons, camps and simple shootings, including our civil war'.[54]
    We do not yet know with any precision the true figure of deaths from
executions, harsh camp conditions and famine during the Stalin years. But
the archival data are entirely incompatible with such very high figures,
which continue to be cited as firm fact in both the Russian and the Western
media.

FORCED LABOUR AND THE ECONOMY

In their publications based on the archives, Russian historians have so far
paid much more attention to the numbers involved and the terrible conditions
under which the prisoners lived than to the role of forced labour in the
economy. The findings reported here must therefore be seen as preliminary.
    The decision to use prisoners extensively for economic purposes was
made in 1929. In 1928 the People's Commissar for Justice of the Russian
Republic, the old Bolshevik Yanson, wrote to Stalin proposing that criminals should be used on large building sites and in the timber industry.[55]
And Yagoda, deputy head of the OGPU, urged that the camps should
gradually be transformed into 'colonising settlements', in which prisoners
were joined by their families.[56] On 27 June 1929, the 'concentration camps'
of the OGPU were renamed 'labour camps', and were set the official
objective of developing national resources 'by the use of the labour of
those deprived of freedom'.[57] The special settlements to which kulaks
were deported soon acquired similar functions.
    The abundant material now available about dekulakisation clearly shows,
however, that the economic motive was not the main reason for the
deportations of the early 1930s. The Politburo did not established a Commission on the settlement of kulaks until April 1930, months after mass
dekulakisation had begun. Danilov and Krasil'nikov comment:

> This kind of 'delayed reaction' was a reflection of the general situation
> in administrative circles at that time. The political leadership at the top
> and middle (or regional) levels had not acquired the ability to foresee
> the consequences of their decisions.[58]

According to Danilov and Krasil'nikov, during the further wave of
dekulakisation in 1931, 'the requirements of the economy and the claims
for labour of government departments began to exercise a considerable
and perhaps decisive influence both on the territorial location of the special
settlers and on the timing and scale of the campaign to exile peasant

households in 1931–1932'.[59] But even then the belief that the power of the kulaks must be broken by mass exile was stronger than the pressure of economic necessity. For example, the Politburo ruled that 150 000 of the 230 000 families to be exiled in 1931 should be settled in Kazakhstan and used for industrial and agricultural purposes. This may appear to demonstrate that economic necessity was responsible for the decision to exile so many peasants. But this poorly thought-out decision was evidently not motivated by pressure for labour from the economic authorities concerned with Kazakhstan. A couple of months later the Politburo reduced the number of families to be exiled to Kazakhstan to 56 000 on the grounds that it was 'technically impossible' to resettle as many as 150 000.[60]

The next main wave of repressions after the dekulakisation campaigns of 1930–2 was the Great Purge of 1937–8. These dreadful events were evidently not primarily motivated by the need for labour. According to the official record, in these two years 1 345 000 persons were sentenced by OGPU special agencies and the Military Collegium. Of these, as we have seen, 682 000 were executed. So at most half of those arrested were available for forced labour.[61]

In *Stalinist Terror* Roberta Manning argues that the Great Purge was economically motivated in the sense that the Soviet economy entered a period of stagnation or decline in 1936, and that 'these economic difficulties contributed substantially to the expansion of political terror'.[62] The Russian historian Oleg Khlevnyuk finds this hypothesis unconvincing:

> There are many reasons for doubting the view that the mass repressions of 1937–1938 were brought about to any substantial extent by economic problems. For example, the socio-economic crisis of 1932–1933 was much sharper and more dangerous for the regime. But then Stalin did not embark on mass actions like the 'Ezhovshchina'. Moreover, that crisis compelled the search for methods of relative liberalisation . . .
>
> It should also be remembered that in the 1920s and the first half of the 1930s the Stalinist leadership frequently had to cope with the destructive effect of political repressions on the economy . . . Stalin must have understood that a political purge would involve substantial economic costs. In view of this it seems more probable that it was the relatively stable position of the economy in the previous few years which was the reason . . . for beginning the terrorist campaign in 1936. It was in 1937 that the considerable reduction of the rate of growth of industrial production began.[63]

While economic necessity was not the main factor which brought about the Great Purge, there is no doubt that the economic significance of forced labour steadily increased throughout the 1930s. From the mid-1930s the Politburo treated forced labour as an indispensable factor in the economy. But the extent to which new waves of arrests were dictated by the labour shortage in remote areas has not yet been seriously investigated.

The archival data confirm the assessment of the economic significance of forced labour made by both Jasny and Baykov on the basis of the Soviet plan for 1941 captured by the Germans during the second world war. According to the plan, in 1941 NKVD industry would produce 1.2 per cent of all gross industrial output and the NKVD would be responsible for 18 per cent of all capital construction.[64] The data now released from NKVD archives for 1938–40 are the same order of magnitude.[65]

Such global data underestimate, however, the significance of forced labour in crucial sectors of the economy. The capital investment figure includes the value of building materials and newly-installed machinery as well as direct building costs. It implies that on the eve of the second world war the NKVD was responsible for something like a quarter of all direct building work, and for an even higher proportion of new buildings. Over the vast areas of the Urals, Siberia and the Far East it was the NKVD and its prisoners which were primarily responsible for the construction of mines, factories, railways and roads.

Although the NKVD was responsible for only a very small proportion of total industrial production, forced labour was very important in certain industries located in remote areas. Forced labour was responsible for the production of a substantial percentage of all Soviet tin, nickel and other non-ferrous metals, and of gold, which the Soviet Union produced in large quantities for export.[66] Throughout the 1930s and 1940s the NKVD was also responsible for the felling and transporting of timber from the Northern Urals and elsewhere – according to the 1941 plan, 12 per cent of all Soviet timber and firewood was to be produced by the NKVD.[67] During the war the NKVD produced 10–15 per cent of all Soviet shells and other ammunition.[68]

In Russia important local monographs are now appearing, based on both archival data and personal reminiscences, which describe some of these major NKVD projects in harrowing detail. The archival documents are written in a dry laconic tone. In contrast, articles and reminiscences prepared by former prisoners or their relatives are understandably bitter, and often denounce Bolshevism, Leninism and the October Revolution in ringing tones. But both archives and memoirs, whatever their tone, contain a wealth of material. For example, a volume on the repressions in Nizhnii Tagil, a historic metal town in the Urals, describes the construction during the war of the second phase of the modern iron and steel works, using both

NKVD documents and memoirs. After the site was taken over by the NKVD at the end of 1941, the number of building workers increased from 3500 to 43 000 within a year, largely by the transfer of prisoners from the Volga hydro-electric project. They lived in overcrowded barracks, usually sleeping on bare boards, with inadequate food and clothing in spite of the severe climate. Scurvy, pellagra, dysentery and typhus were widespread. In 1943 as many as 21 per cent of the prisoners died, and many others were not fit to work. The central hospital, built in spring 1942, was known by the initials OPP (*ozdorovitel'no-profilakticheskii punkt*), but the prisoners joked grimly that this stood for 'department for preparation of the deceased' (*otdel podgotovki pokoinikov*). The prisoners were replenished from Central Asia by conscripts and Polish exiles, but death and disease were endemic among the Central Asians, and many of those who survived were sent home again. In the following year, 1944, however, food and sanitation greatly improved, and the death rate fell to 3–4 per cent.[69]

SIDELIGHTS ON THE GULAG

Official NKVD documents in the archives record in bureaucratic detail the inhuman practices of the Gulag world with which we are familiar from personal memoirs. A top-secret memorandum to Stalin from the Minister of State Security (MGB), dated 17 July 1947, sets out 'the practice which has been established for conducting investigations into cases relating to spies, diversionists, terrorists and participants in the anti-Soviet underground'. Some sample paragraphs from this elaborate document:

4. . . . When the arrested person does not provide frank statements and avoids direct and truthful answers to the questions put, the investigator, in order to put pressure on the arrested person, makes use of compromising data which the NKVD has at its disposal, which the latter is concealing. Sometimes, in order to outwit the arrested person and give him the impression that the agencies of the MGB know everything about him, the investigator draws the arrested person's attention to particular intimate personal details from his personal life, vices which he conceals from his associates, etc . . .

7. In relation to arrested persons who stubbornly oppose the demands of the investigator, and conduct themselves in a provocative manner and seek in all ways to drag out the investigation or to deflect it from the right path, a strict regime under guard is to be introduced.

This includes the following measures:

a)	transfer to a prison with a more strict regime, where hours of sleep are restricted and the maintenance of the arrested person in regard to food and other domestic needs is worsened;
b)	solitary confinement;
c)	forbidding walks, food parcels and the right to read books;
d)	placing in a punishment cell for a period up to 20 days.

Note. In a punishment cell there is no other furniture but a stool screwed to the floor and a bed without bedclothes; the bed is available for sleep for 6 hours a day; the prisoner in a punishment cell is issued with only 300 grams of bread and boiling water each day, and hot food once in three days; smoking is forbidden.

8.	In relation to spies, diversionists, terrorists and other active enemies of the Soviet people, who insolently refuse to give away their accomplices and do not give evidence about their criminal activity, the agencies of the MVD, on the basis of the directive of the CC CPSU (b) [Central Committee of the Communist Party of the Soviet Union (Bolsheviks)] dated 10 January 1939, apply measures of physical pressure [i.e. torture].

The document also sanctions the regular use in the case of recalcitrant arrestees of bugging devices, and of informers in the cells and among acquaintances of the accused who are at liberty.[70]

One of the darkest episodes in the history of the Soviet secret police was the establishment of the 'special laboratory of the NKVD'. This was perhaps the moment at which a Soviet organisation most closely resembled a Nazi extermination camp. The purpose of the laboratory, headed by Professor Grigorii Mairanovskii, who held a higher doctorate in medical science, was to produce undetectable poisons, and with this objective experiments were carried out on prisoners who had been sentenced to death, as well as on animals. The most successful preparation was said to be 'K-2'; after taking it the victim appeared to shrink and became quiet, and died within fifteen minutes. On the proposal of the first department of the NKVD, the laboratory designed the notorious pointed walking sticks, umbrellas and fountain pens through which poison was administered, as well as poisoned bullets. Even under Stalin someone in high places decided that this experiment had gone too far. In 1951 Mairanovskii was arrested and before Stalin's death he was sentenced to ten years' imprisonment for the illegal possession of poisonous substances.[71]

The NKVD exercised a great deal of ingenuity in its efforts to expose spies. In 1941 it established a series of fake frontier posts in the Far East, about 50 km from Khabarovsk. A person suspected of spying or some other anti-Soviet activity was asked to carry out a task for the NKVD on foreign territory. The unsuspecting agent was then sent through a fake Soviet frontier post to a fake Japanese police post, apparently on Manchurian territory but in fact within Soviet territory. The agent was then seized by Soviet secret policemen disguised as 'Japanese', and transferred to a third fake installation – the 'Japanese military mission', where he was interrogated for days and even weeks by 'Japanese' intelligence officers and 'Russian émigrés' – all members of NKVD staff. This bizarre set-up was known officially by the NKVD as the LZ (*lozhnyi zakordon* – 'false abroad') and unofficially as 'the mill'.

According to the report on these activities prepared some years later under Khrushchev, many of the victims of this exercise, tortured and fearing death, confessed to the fake Japanese that they were in what they believed to be Manchuria on a spying mission. After this, the 'Japanese' recruited the victim as a 'spy for the Japanese'. He was then 'returned', as he believed, to Soviet territory. The NKVD then arrested him and sentenced him to long periods of confinement or to the death penalty. In one case, a victim informed the NKVD when he 'returned' (so he thought) to the USSR that the Japanese had attempted to recruit him, but he was nevertheless sentenced to death on the basis of forged documents submitted to the Soviet procurator by the NKVD. In another case, a Soviet citizen of Chinese nationality who worked in the 'false abroad' was so incensed by the deception that he smashed the Japanese crockery with which it was equipped; he was promptly shot. One victim who guessed that the set-up was a fake was executed for fear that he would reveal the secret to others. The 'false abroad' continued until 1949, and is estimated to have cost more than a million old rubles; during the ten years 150 people passed through it.[72]

PRISONER RESISTANCE

Many formerly secret reports of disturbances and uprisings in camps and special settlements lurk in the archives. Only a few have so far been published. I will summarise one from the beginning and one from the end of the Stalin period.

The largest disturbance among 'kulak' exiles took place in Siberia in the summer of 1931. At that time NKVD policy was to despatch peasants from neighbouring villages together, in the belief that clusters of neighbours from similar backgrounds would be better able to organise themselves in exile. 33 000 peasants from a few districts in the Altai and the Kuzbass were settled together in Narym, some 400km north of Novosibirsk, under the 'Parbig administration' of the NKVD. The disturbances lasted a week, and are described by the Russian historians who published the declassified NKVD and party reports about the disturbances as 'rather a mass organised attempt to flee than an uprising in the full sense of the word'.

According to these reports the exiles complained of lack of food and clean water, medical help, tools and horses, and that those in charge treated them badly. The reports claimed that 1500–2000 men took part, armed with weapons seized from the NKVD or with rifles obtained from local huntsmen. OGPU troops were brought in to suppress the uprising. Five officials were killed in the course of the disturbances. How many peasants were killed is not stated. An OGPU report dated 24 September complained that one armed group of party activists had executed 'up to 15 people', and that these may have included innocent people as well as kulaks. According to the OGPU, the armed group stole the clothes of those they had executed, and celebrated the executions with a drunken orgy. Peasants who survived were transferred to a punishment settlement still further North.[73]

Over twenty years later, after Stalin's death, the camp system was shaken by a series of disturbances. One of the longest and most bitter uprisings took place at the Kengir camp, a division of 'the Steppe Camp' (*Steplag*) – Special Camp No. 4 of the NKVD – in May and June 1954.

The special camps – successors to the 'hard labour' (*katorga*) camps introduced in 1943 – were established by a decree of the Council of Ministers dated February 21, 1948. This ruled that those who had committed 'particularly dangerous' state crimes were to be transferred from normal to special camps. The list of categories to be transferred included those condemned for spying, terrorism and diversions, and also members of Right-wing, Trotskyist, Menshevik, Socialist-Revolutionary, anarchist, nationalist, Whiteguard and other anti-Soviet organisations. A 'strict regime' was to be established: the prisoners were mainly to be employed in heavy physical labour; the working day was to be ten hours; no remission of sentences or other privileges was to be permitted. A further decree on the same date ruled that on completion of their sentence those guilty of particularly dangerous state crimes were to be settled in exile (*ssylka*) in remote areas of the USSR.[74]

In Stalin's last years the system of Special Camps remorselessly expanded. By the beginning of 1953 there were ten Special Camps (actually clusters of camps) containing 210 000 persons.[75] According to the official record, Steplag contained 20 698 prisoners in June 1954. Nearly half of these were Ukrainians, many of whom were nationalists who had fought the Soviet government. 5597 persons were located in the Kengir group of camps – Division 3 of Steplag – including 2407 women. Division 1 of Steplag, containing 5114 prisoners (all male) also went on strike for a few days during the weeks of the Kengir uprising.[76]

Solzhenitsyn devotes a fifty-page chapter of *Gulag Archipelago* to the 'forty days of Kengir'.[77] The fifty pages of official documents published from the archives in 1994[78] provide a unique opportunity to compare the two accounts of these events: Solzhenitsyn's version based on prisoner reminiscences, and the version in the formerly top-secret archival documents prepared by officials for internal use at the time.[79]

On the whole the two accounts complement rather than contradict each other. The archival records so far published have little to say about the background to the uprising. Solzhenitsyn, on the other hand, describes in some detail the arbitrary shootings in the previous winter. These led to a strike in February 1954, after which the camp commandant retired. In April ordinary criminals were brought into the camp, with the object of disrupting the prisoners' resistance – but, in an unprecedented development, the thieves and the 'politicals' made common cause. This alliance continued throughout the uprising. (These events are obscurely hinted at in the official documents.)

Following the arrival of the 'thieves', on 17 May disturbances broke out at the camp, in the course of which a large group of men broke through into the women's zone. The guards opened fire – according to the official record, eighteen people were killed. A few days following this bloody incident, on 25 May the whole camp was taken over by the enraged prisoners, including the food stores. All camp officials and guards were excluded. This state of affairs continued until 26 June.

Solzhenitsyn's account of living and working conditions in the camps is naturally far more vivid and detailed than that in the official documents. But there is a close similarity between the two records of the prisoners' demands, of the Commission set up by the prisoners to negotiate with the authorities, and of the authorities' response. According to a telegram sent to the Minister of Internal Affairs by a delegation of high Gulag officials, who hastily flew from Moscow to the camp, the prisoners' demands included: punish those guilty of the shootings on 17 May; grant immunity to members of the prisoners' commission; reduce the length of all 25-year sentences; do not exile prisoners after they are released; increase wages to the level of those of free workers and introduce an eight-hour day; permit men and women to meet freely in the camp; send a member of the party Presidium [i.e. Politburo] or central committee to negotiate.

On 28 May, according to the archives, the authorities made a number of concessions. They dismissed four senior camp officials as responsible for the shootings, and sent their cases to court; and they agreed to some improvement in wages and working conditions, and to release prisoners under 18 and sick prisoners from the camps. But most other issues, including the crucial question of the length of sentences, were passed to the higher authorities, who took no action. The strike continued.

Both Solzhenitsyn and the archives agree that there were divided opinions among the prisoners and in their commission, and that Ukrainian nationalists were leading members of the resistance. But on other matters Solzhenitsyn and the archives part company. Solzhenitsyn describes the chair of the commission, Colonel Kapitan Kuznetsov, as a loyal officer, who was imprisoned because, while he was commanding a regiment in Germany after the war, one of his men had escaped to the West. According to a memorandum in the archives, however, Kuznetsov was captured by the Germans in 1942 and appointed as commandant of a German camp for Russian prisoners-of-war. The archives also give the MVD's version of the biographies of eight other members of the prisoners' commission: two had collaborated with the Germans, three had belonged to Ukrainian nationalist organisations, two were Trotskyists, and one had been imprisoned for 'anti-Soviet agitation'.

The archives throw a great deal of light on the behaviour of the authorities in dealing with the uprising. Solzhenitsyn asks 'Why did it drag on so long? What can the bosses have been waiting for? . . . There is no knowing on what date and on what level the decision was taken.' We now know part of the answer. From as early as 18 May S. N. Kruglov, Minister of Internal Affairs of the USSR, was actively involved in decisions about the strike (no doubt he in turn received instructions from the Politburo). On several occasions he insisted on caution. In telegrams on 3 and 4 June he instructed his deputy on the spot not to attempt to introduce armed force into the camp 'in order to avoid the need to use firearms', and to open fire on prisoners only if they attacked the guards. In a further telegram on 16 June Kruglov told his deputy that a platoon of five T-34 tanks was being sent to Kengir, but five days later, in a further telegram of 21 June, he stated that 'it seems to us that the tanks must be used more as a moral factor and as battering rams, avoiding the use of artillery fire'.

Meanwhile a dramatic development put a stop to this leniency; nothing was known about this until the 1994 publication from the archives. On 20 June the Minister for the Construction of Metallurgical and Chemical Industry Enterprises, D. Ya. Raizer, and the Minister of Non-Ferrous Metallurgy, P. F. Lomako, sternly warned the Council of Ministers that the failure of the prisoners to work had placed the 1954 plans in jeopardy. Both copper-ore production and the construction of copper industry enterprises were lagging badly behind the plan. Insisting that this situation was 'completely intolerable', they called upon the Council of Ministers 'to oblige the MVD of the USSR (cde. Kruglov) to establish good order in the Dzhezkazgan [i.e. Kengir] camp within ten days, and to ensure prisoners turn up at work in the numbers required to fulfil the 1954 plan'. Three days later, on 23 June, Malenkov wrote on this letter 'The Minister of Internal Affairs (cde. Kruglov) is to take the necessary measures and report on their fulfilment'.

Drastic action swiftly followed. On the following day, 24 June, Kruglov sent two telegrams to his deputy. The first, at 11am, approved the use of tanks, dogs, fire engines and arms to restore order, but still instructed the deputy Minister: 'endeavour by every possible means not to permit human sacrifices'. The second telegram, despatched at 13.40pm, was much more severe. It called for the use of all resources simultaneously with the object of seizing key points in the camp. During the night of 25–26 June, at 3.30am, this frontal assault was carried out. According to the MVD report, most of the camp was seized immediately. A group of 500 men and women in six barracks resisted with home-made grenades, pistols, picks, iron bars and stones, but were overcome in 1½ hours by armed soldiers, and by tanks firing rockets and blank shells. 35 prisoners were killed and four soldiers were wounded, no soldiers died. Solzhenitsyn claims that prisoner losses were far higher: according to him, there were 700 casualties including at least 300 killed.

Solzhenitsyn reported that the rebel leaders were tried in autumn 1955, but 'we do not know what sentences were passed'. The laconic notes to the published documents report that Kuznetsov was sentenced to death on 8 August 1955, but the sentence was commuted to 25 years in a camp; on 12 March 1960 he was fully rehabilitated and released. According to these notes, another member of the prisoners' commission was also sentenced to death on 8 August 1955, and the sentence was carried out on 18 September 1956. Nothing is said about other sentences in the published documents, though these must be recorded in the secret police archives.[80]

The relative leniency shown to Kuznetsov is explained by a document in the archives which I found particularly chilling: his confession. This 43-page handwritten statement, dated 29 June, three days after the suppression of the uprising, justifies his actions as chair of the rebel leaders by his desire to mitigate the role of the 'conspiratorial centre' of Ukrainian nationalists and criminals. He denounces by name those prisoners who were particularly recalcitrant.

The authorities drew two kinds of lesson from the experience. An MVD report of 16 September 1954 called for considerable improvement in the treatment of prisoners. But it also proposed measures to limit such outbreaks in future. Prisoners were to be dispersed into smaller units, ranging from 300 to 1500 persons; food and fuel stores and workshops were to be situated entirely separately from the living quarters; women's quarters were to be located at least 3–5 km away from the men's quarters; the network of informers in the camps was to be strengthened.

These archival documents illustrate several striking aspects of the ambiguous attitude of the central Soviet authorities to the camp system in the period after Stalin's death. On the one hand, they sought somewhat halfheartedly to improve the treatment of prisoners and their living and working conditions. They also made some attempt to avoid bloodshed. In Stalin's day it would have been unthinkable that prisoners would take over a camp for more than five weeks without armed force being used against them. On the other hand, the economy could not yet manage without the camps. Following pressure from the industrial ministries, the MVD troops eventually suppressed the revolt with great brutality. And the secret police had not yet abandoned the most vicious instrument of misrule: the uncorroborated confession.

DISMANTLING THE FORCED LABOUR SYSTEM

'Kulaks' and their families exiled in the early 1930s began to be released from the special settlements from the end of the 1930s. On 22 October 1938, a government decree ruled that children of special settlers should be freed when they reached the age of sixteen. During the war many ex-kulaks were called up for military service; they and their wives and children were simultaneously freed from special settlement. Between 1938 and 1945 the number of ex-kulaks in special settlements declined by over one-third.[81]

In the immediate post-war period, the number of ex-kulaks in special settlements steadily declined. Most releases were undertaken on the basis of proposals submitted by regional party committees to the Soviet government, supported by Beria and the secret police authorities, and presumably on the authority of or with the acquiescence of Stalin. The top-secret documents making these proposals for release usually argued that special settlers had conducted themselves patriotically during the war, that most of them had fundamentally changed their attitude to the Soviet system, and also worked well and conscientiously. By the time of Stalin's death in

1953 only 27 000 ex-kulaks remained in special settlements. The following table shows the number of ex-kulaks, including members of their families, in special settlements (thousands; on 1 January of each year unless otherwise stated):[82]

1939	939
1945	607 (1 October)
1946	599
1947	481 (1 April)
1948	211
1950	108
1952	42
1953	27
1954	17

As we have seen, simultaneously with the liberation of the ex-kulaks, Germans, Chechens and other nationalities were exiled to existing and new settlements, and the total number of special settlers greatly increased. The new exiles included many thousands of kulaks deported from the Baltic republics after their post-war re-incorporation into the Soviet Union.

The dismantling of the system of camps, colonies and special settlements began immediately after Stalin's death; as the following table shows (thousands; on 1 January of each year unless otherwise stated):[83]

	1953	*1954*	*1957*	*1959*
Camps and colonies	2469	1360[a]	?	948
Of which 'counter-revolutionaries'	580[b]	480[c]	114[d]	11
Special settlements	2754	2720	211	49
Total in camps, colonies and settlements	5223	4080	?	997

[a] 1 April
[b] 1950–1
[c] Autumn 1953
[d] 1956

On 27 March 1953, a decree of the presidium of the Supreme Soviet, proposed by Beria, released 1 202 000 prisoners from camps and colonies.[84] These were primarily criminals. Of the 580 000 prisoners condemned for 'counter-revolutionary' crimes – these may broadly be described as 'political prisoners' – only those sentenced to five years or less were released, and 480 000 'counter-revolutionaries' remained in camps and colonies in the autumn of 1953.

During the next few years, primarily on Khrushchev's initiative, nearly all the 'counter-revolutionaries' were released; the number declined from 480 000 in the autumn of 1953 to a mere 11 000 on 1 January 1959.

Following the failure of Beria's attempt to release special settlers in 1953 (see p. 208 below), the process was resumed under Khrushchev in the following year. On 5 July 1954, all the children of special settlers ceased to be recorded as special settlers. This was about one-third of all special settlers. Then in 1955 and 1956 most of the deported nationalities were removed from special settlement. By the beginning of 1957 the total number of special settlers had fallen to less than one-tenth of the number at the time of Stalin's death.[85]

This was only a partial liberation. Many former camp inmates were forbidden to live in specified major towns; the banned towns were specified in their internal passports. Chechens and Ingushi were permitted to return to their homelands; but the lands of the Volga Germans and the Crimean Tatars had been occupied by Russians and other citizens and more than half the total number of former special settlers had to remain in their places of exile. Moreover, although large numbers of 'counter-revolutionaries' were rehabilitated and released, the rehabilitation of Bukharin, Preobrazhensky and the other revolutionaries executed on Stalin's orders did not take place until over thirty years later. But the post-Stalin reforms dismantled much of the Gulag system, with its watchtowers, barbed wire and inhuman conditions. This was the beginning of the end of Stalinism.

14 Opposition to Stalinism

Opposition to Stalin and his policies in party circles was at its maximum in 1932–4 – the years of famine and its aftermath. The anti-Stalinist Ryutin platform, produced by a small group of dissident Communists in the autumn of 1932, was widely known among the Moscow and Leningrad élite.[1] New evidence has confirmed the rumours that a substantial number of delegates to the XVII Party Congress in January–February 1934 failed to cast their votes for Stalin as a member of the central committee. Even the extremely cautious official party account issued in 1989 concluded that 166 delegates had failed to vote in the elections for the central committee, a most unusual event at a party congress.[2]

So far no serious evidence has been found of organised political opposition to Stalin after 1933. But it seems probable that a critical view of Stalin was widespread among old Bolsheviks at this time – in contrast to the unrestrained enthusiasm of many who joined the party after the October Revolution. Numerous accounts have appeared of individual party members who, in spite of the dangers, boldly or quietly criticised Stalin's policies.

Throughout the Stalin years, nearly all dissidents, party and non-party, criticised the regime not because it failed to emulate Western capitalism, but because it failed to live up to socialist ideals. Nikolaev, who fired the shot which killed Kirov, left a letter entitled 'My Answer to the Party and the Fatherland', written to the Politburo two months before the assassination:

> For us working people there is no free access to life, work and education . . . War is inevitable, but it will be destructive and salutary [sic]. The people have never suffered as much as in our revolution 17–30–50 million people – with all its consequences.

In his diary he wrote about the need to revenge himself on 'heartless officials', and asserted that 'Thousands of generations will pass, but the idea of Communism will still not be put into effect'.[3] He may not have been part of a conspiracy, but he was certainly disillusioned with his party.

In high party circles Mariya Svanidze, although utterly devoted to Stalin personally (see pp. 157–8 above), wrote bitterly in her diary at the end of 1936:

> In the course of 19 years they have not been able to dress the people properly . . . And what about the construction of big houses and villas,

the frantic money thrown at maintaining luxurious rest homes and sana-
toria, a waste of state resources not necessary to anyone . . . I hate people who don't care as long as they have got everything, unfortunately
we have many people who speak and act like Louis IV [*sic*] – 'after us
the deluge'.[4]

Many non-party intellectuals of the older generation held fast to their
hostility to Bolshevism, or the Stalinist version of it, even when working
within and even honoured by the system. Academician Ivan Pavlov (1849–
1936), the internationally famous physiologist, awarded a Nobel Prize in
1904, was presented in Soviet propaganda as a former opponent of Communism who had been won over to the system. His published statements
led this to be widely believed in the West.[5] But we now know that behind
the scenes he remained intransigent. On 21 December 1934, under the
influence of the arrests and executions in Leningrad following the murder
of Kirov, he wrote a bitter letter to Molotov as chair of the Council of
People's Commissars:

Your belief in the world proletarian revolution is futile . . . You are not
sowing the seeds of revolution in the cultured world, but of fascism –
with great success. Fascism did not exist before your revolution. Only
our political babies in the Provisional Government tolerated even two
dress rehearsals from you before the October triumph. All the other
governments have no desire to experience what happened and is still
happening here, and of course they realised in time that to avoid this
they should introduce what you used and still use – terror and
violence . . . Under your direct influence fascism is gradually embracing
the whole cultured world, except the powerful Anglo-Saxon section . . .
which, after all, is bringing the nucleus of socialism into existence:
i.e. the slogan that labour is the first obligation and the main virtue of
a human being, and is the foundation of human relations, ensuring the
corresponding existence of each person.
   But what I find hard to take is not that world fascism will hold up the
rate of natural human progress for a time, but what is happening here
– which in my opinion threatens our country with a serious danger.
   We have been living and are still living under an unremitting regime
of terror and violence. If our ordinary reality were to be depicted in full,
without omissions, with all the everyday details – this would be a ter-
rifying picture. The shocking impression which this made on *real people* would hardly be significantly muted if the other picture of our reality
was placed beside it – with our towns miraculously growing as if from
scratch, our Dnieper dams, giant factories and innumerable scientists

and educational establishments. When the first picture occupies my attention, I see most of all the similarities between our life and the life of ancient Asiatic despotisms . . . Perhaps this is temporary. But it must be remembered that it is easy for human beings, descended from the animals, to fall, and difficult for them to rise. Those who maliciously condemn to death masses of people similar to themselves and those who carry this out with satisfaction, and those who learn by force to participate in it – it is hardly possible for them to remain beings which feel and think *like human beings*.

Spare our country and its people.

Academician Ivan PAVLOV

Molotov sent a copy of the letter to Stalin, scathingly describing it as 'another stupid letter from Academician Pavlov'. On 2 January 1935, he sent Pavlov a firm but quite polite reply, insisting that Pavlov was entirely ignorant of the scientific foundation of politics, and remarking that 'the Soviet political leaders would not dream of allowing themselves to display a similar zeal in questions of physiology.'[6] (Ironically, fifteen years later the Soviet leaders used their authority to back the Pavlov school against its more modern successors.)

Pavlov was not tamed. In the year before his death in 1936 he sent at least five further letters to Molotov appealing to him to intercede for persons under arrest, interspersed with critical political comments.[7]

Another Nobel prizewinner, from a much younger generation, Lev Landau (1908–68, awarded the Nobel Prize for Physics in 1962), was arrested in April 1938, at the climax of the Great Purge. He was accused of preparing a leaflet jointly with another physicist which boldly opposed the regime from a more radical socialist standpoint than Pavlov's:

Proletarians of all lands, unite!

Comrades!

The great cause of the October Revolution has been ignobly betrayed. The country is drowned in an sea of blood and filth. Millions of innocent people have been thrown into prison, and no-one can know when their turn will come. The economy is breaking down. Famine is threatened.

Comrades, surely you see that the Stalinist clique has carried out a fascist coup d'état. Socialism cannot be found anywhere except on the pages of the newspapers, which are absolute liars. In his frenzied hatred of true socialism Stalin has rivalled Hitler and Mussolini . . .

The only way out for the working class and all working people of our country is a decisive struggle against Stalinist and Hitlerite fascism, the struggle for socialism . . .

The proletariat of our country, which overthrew the power of the Tsar and the capitalists, can overthrow the fascist dictator and his clique. Long live the First of May – the day of struggle for socialism!
MOSCOW COMMITTEE OF THE
ANTI-FASCIST WORKERS' PARTY.

The leaflet is available only in a typewritten copy in the files of the KGB.[8] As with other such secret police documents, its authenticity is not certain. Physicists who knew Landau after the war doubt whether it is genuine; they thought he was a completely unpolitical person. But Gennadii Gorelik, the principal Russian authority on the history of Soviet physics, believes that it is genuine, and reflects the beliefs and enthusiasms of young physicists in the 1930s.[9] This issue must remain open; but from other evidence there is no doubt that Landau was very critical of the regime.

On the day of Landau's arrest, Peter Kapitsa, his boss, and himself a Nobel Prizewinner in 1978, appealed to Stalin to release him. Landau was eventually released a year later in April 1939 after Kapitsa had somewhat ambiguously promised Beria that he would make sure that Landau did not 'pursue any counter-revolutionary activity against Soviet power in my institute'. 'If I notice any statements on Landau's part aimed at harming Soviet power I will immediately inform the agencies of the NKVD.'[10]

Landau continued to be closely scrutinised by the secret police. A KGB report written as late as December 1957 reveals that one or more of his close colleagues were informers, and that his laboratory, apartment and car were bugged. The KGB claimed that Landau still expressed radical views to his close colleagues, arguing that the Bolshevik Revolution had put a class of bureaucrats and officials into power. Landau insisted that the system was not socialist, because 'the means of production do not belong to the people but to the bureaucrats'.[11]

A striking example of quiet dissidence is provided by Solomon Lur'e (1890–1961), a classical historian educated before the revolution. According to his son, he was an enthusiastic supporter of the February–March Revolution; and never wavered in his hostility to the October Revolution. In the early 1930s he was strongly criticised for his deviant interpretation of ancient history, and lucky to escape arrest. He was not as rash as Pavlov or Landau (in his non-priority field any such rashness would have been summarily dealt with). But after his death a yellowing notebook without a cover was found among his papers in which the text was written partly in Latin script, and partly in 'Cyprian syllabary', the script used in Cyprus in the V and IV centuries BC. When transliterated, the manuscript proved to be an extensive commentary on the Soviet system, written in 1947. His caustic comments include the following:

> The characteristic feature of the Soviet regime is its distinctive duality, which has not occurred elsewhere in history. The lives of citizens of the USSR are difficult and bleak. But they are also obliged throughout their whole lives to appear continuously as actors in a jolly festival performance about an earthly paradise . . .
>
> I have sometimes had occasion to argue with supporters of the old Leninist Communism (I have not met supporters of Stalinist Communism – those who claim to be such are either complete fools or – much more frequently – careerists and scoundrels). Their point of view is as follows: success is possible in political and state activity only when guided by the principle 'the end justifies the means' . . .
>
> This is a fundamental delusion, and the personality of the leader has no decisive significance.

Lur'e went on to argue that both Lenin and Stalin's idea of creating a communist oasis in the USSR had led to vast military expenditure to guard against capitalist encirclement. In consequence a society had been established which he variously described as 'state capitalism' or 'slavery':

> The values created by the flesh and blood of the producers do not go to them for consumption – this should be the main feature of a socialist society. At best they retain a minute minimum sufficient in order not to die from hunger (death from hunger of fully employed people has recently become a normal occurrence in the USSR). All the remainder goes to the 'needs of defence', and also to a vast army of parasites – the military, the rulers, the officials, and their families. And of course within this class of exploiters there is no social equality, the ratio of the actual size of the highest pay to the lowest (including rations, special allocations, unlimited bank accounts etc.) is 1:100 [*sic* – should be 100:1], if not more.[12]

In his clandestine notes Lur'e castigated professional soldiers as 'a gang of parasites and bandits, maintained at the expense of the people'. But Colonel-General Vasilii Gordov (1896–1950) and Major-General Filipp Rybal'chenko (1898–1950), respectively the former commander and the chief of staff of the Volga Military District, were professional soldiers of his own generation who shared many of his views.

Their views became known to Stalin because from 1943 onwards he arranged that the quarters of his Marshals and Generals should be bugged. Two transcripts of Gordov's conversations, 'obtained by operational technology', were sent to Stalin. The first, on 28 December 1946, at Gordov's Moscow flat, was between Rybal'chenko and Gordov, who had recently been compulsorily retired, ostensibly on grounds of illness. The record read in part:

> *R. [Rybal'chenko]* . . . Everyone is dissatisfied with life, everyone says this openly in the trains, they say this straight out everywhere.
> *G. [Gordov]* Yes, everything is based on bribes and grovelling. They sacked me in a couple of seconds because I don't grovel.
> *R.* Yes, everything is based on bribes. And look what's happening around us – unbelievable hunger, everyone is dissatisfied. 'The newspapers are deceiving us from start to finish' – that's what they're all saying. They've imposed so many Ministries, administration is distended. Nowadays it is just like it used to be – the priest, the local official, the elder – 77 people sat on every peasant . . .
> *G.* It would have been all right if things had been done on time. We needed to have real democracy.

The second conversation took place on 31 December 1946, between Gordov and his wife Tatyana Vladimirovna:

> *G.* . . . You know what really upsets me – I'm no longer a high-up.
> *T. V.* I know. You should spit on that whole business. It's a pity Stalin hasn't received you . . .
> *G.* And why should I go to Stalin and abase myself before that (there followed insulting and obscene expressions addressed to comrade Stalin).
> *T. V.* I'm convinced he will last only another year . . .
> In the past people could go underground with their convictions, and do something . . . They worked, and collected people together. They were persecuted for it, sent to prison. And nowadays nothing can be done. Look how they broke a fine spirit like Zhukov's . . .
> *G.* . . . What did for me was being elected as a deputy [to the Supreme Soviet]. That was my downfall. I travelled round the districts, and when I saw everything, all that terrible situation, I completely changed . . . It gave me attitudes and opinions, and I started to tell them to you, and someone else, and it seemed like a platform. I do say, this is my conviction, that if the collective farms are removed today, tomorrow there will be order, there will be a market – everything . . .
> *T. V.* Nowadays no-one tries to do anything useful for society . . .
> *G.* There is no society.

Generals Gordov and Rybal'chenko were arrested in 1947 and executed on 24 and 25 August 1950.[13]

The post-war opposition group about which most is known is the Communist Party of Youth, organised in the provincial town of Voronezh by 17-year old school pupils. They also objected most strongly to the existence in the name of socialism of a powerful well-fed ruling group, side by side with the abject poverty and powerlessness of the mass of the people.[14]

MASS UNREST

The archives also contain valuable material on mass unrest in the Stalin years. During the Khrushchev thaw in the early 1960s some information was published about the widespread opposition to collectivisation in the countryside in 1930.[15] Much more is now known.[16] Resistance continued during the second collectivisation drive in the first few months of 1931. In the Nizhnii-Novgorod region posters were torn down and peasants demonstratively left meetings summoned to support collectivisation. In some districts of the Moscow region the meetings voted against collectivisation. In the USSR as a whole, according to official reports, as many as 15 per cent of all collective farms were subjected to 'attacks' (*napadeniya*) in the first six months of 1931 – the principal forms being arson, assaults on activists and damage to machines.[17]

In industry, textile strikes inspired by food shortages in the Ivanovo–Voznesensk region were reported in the émigré Menshevik journal *Sotsialisticheskii vestnik* soon after they occurred in the spring of 1932. The documents in the archives show that the upheaval was more widespread and more political in character than the Menshevik journal indicated. According to top-secret party reports, in one district workers beat up the chief of police and broke into the OGPU building, while another group raided party headquarters. A leaflet left at the special shop for the élite in Ivanovo–Voznesensk complained that 'while they shoot at the hungry workers of Vichuga and Teikovo for demanding bread, here the senior communists and the red gendarmes of the GPU fatten themselves, concealed behind curtains'.[18]

These were not isolated incidents. In the Donbass coal region at this time shops were smashed up, bread was seized from bakeries, and children demonstrated.[19] This widespread discontent contributed to the decision to launch sweeping economic reforms in May 1932.[20]

Unrest broke out again in the Ivanovo–Voznesensk textile factories in the autumn of 1941, when the Germans were approaching Moscow. During the first three months of the war, the conversion of factories to military orders, the call-up of skilled mechanics and the lack of materials all resulted in a decline in output, and nominal wages fell by 30–40 per cent or more. Only bread, sugar and confectionery were available on the ration; meat and dairy products, and fruit and vegetables, had to be purchased on the market at rapidly increasing prices. So real wages fell drastically.

In August and September 1941, several Ivanovo–Voznesensk factories went on strike, and a party commission sent from Moscow reported that 'an inclination to strike, inflamed by hostile elements, is spreading among a large section of the workers'. Then in October the authorities decided in strict secrecy to evacuate a large part of the machinery. In one combine, preparation for evacuation began on a rest day (Friday 17 October), and when the workers, who were nearly all women, turned up on 18 October they found a large part of the equipment already packed. Crowds gathered and protested that they were being left without work while the officials had already evacuated their families. On the following day, 19 October, 150 workers broke into the director's office in one factory and he and his assistants fled in panic. At a further mass meeting the party secretary of the region announced that the equipment would not be evacuated after all; but the angry workers beat up the director of the combine.

Similar disturbances took place at three other Ivanovo–Voznesensk factories and at a factory in Privolzhsk, a nearby town. Many rank-and-file communists participated. By 21 October the disturbances had quietened down. The Moscow front stabilised, so the plan to evacuate the factories was dropped. The authorities blamed the trouble on 'the disruptive provocations of spies, agents of German fascism and hostile individuals who infiltrated the factories', but also criticised managers, trade-union and party officials and the NKVD staff for incompetence and for neglecting the needs of the workers.[21]

The first scrutiny of previously closed archives has also revealed occasional reports of small-scale worker unrest in the 1930s and 1940s. Thus in November 1935 leaflets attacking Stakhanovism were distributed in the Donbass at a higher education institute for chemical engineering. They called for 'a new policy directed towards real improvement of the material well-being of working people'. Five of the eight students placed under arrest were former miners or industrial workers.[22]

Other examples of worker resistance to bad conditions and high-handed treatment await their turn to be discovered in central and local files.

15 Science and Stalinism: The Example of Physics

We are only just beginning to draw aside the veil which conceals many mysteries of the mutual relation of scientists and the structures of power. Solving these mysteries is important to us in order to understand one of the most interesting paradoxes of the XX Century: how, in conditions of a totalitarian state, of absence of freedom, was such a high level of scientific development achieved in many directions, particularly in physics, together with the formation of such outstanding scientists as Sakharov and Landau?[1]

Yu. N. Krivonosov, 1993

In seeking to explain the successful development of Soviet physics, the historian of science A. V. Andreev rejects the 'widespread notion that a definite period of Soviet history (roughly from 1917 to the end of the 1950s) is primarily characterised by the total politicisation of all sides of social life, including the natural sciences'.

Using the archives of Moscow University, Andreev shows that in the early 1930s, when 'politicisation' of science is usually assumed to have been total, a party philosopher, A. A. Maksimov (1891–1976), played a positive role in protecting the progressive school of physics led by L. I. Mandel'shtam. The school included I. E. Tamm (Nobel prizewinner, 1958), and played a major role in later developments. Maksimov wrote a memorandum at the end of 1929 which criticised the near-monopoly position of the dominant Romanov–Timiryazev group in the Physics Research Institute of Moscow university. He pointed out that one professor had been appointed to a leading position in spite of his reactionary political views simply because he opposed the theory of relativity.

Following Maksimov's memorandum, a working group of Rabkrin (the Workers' and Peasants' Inspectorate) investigated the institute. Rabkrin was a party agency, and its intervention in economic matters at this time had usually been disastrous. But in this instance Rabkrin supported Maksimov's criticism of the Romanov group. According to Rabkrin, the group had disguised its crude struggle for resources by claiming that it was engaged in 'a struggle between the pro-Soviet professoriate (i.e. the Romanov group) and the anti-Soviet professoriate (i.e. the anti-Romanov group)'. The reorganisation proposed by Rabkrin resulted in the strengthening of the Mandel'shtam school.[2]

Gorelik discusses Soviet physics in a wider context. He finds that before the revolution Russian physics was 'provincial'. The crucial development took place between 1913 and the 1930s, when Soviet physics reached the peak of its world importance. Gorelik accepts that this success occurred partly because the potential importance of physics for industry and defence protected it from the fate of genetics and the humanities. Its practical importance also ensured, of course, that the authorities would supply adequate resources. But he argues that this was not the whole story, citing the example of Landau, whose role as a dissident we have already discussed (see pp. 187–8 above):

> The conditions in which a physicist works and the atmosphere surrounding him influence the character and results of his work. The influence is not simple or 'directly proportionate', but it cannot be doubted. Creative boldness and civil boldness are psychologically similar. But another matter is even more important. Landau passionately desired to create a great Soviet physics and devoted a large part of his creative energy to this. But this desire is possible only if one believes that the Soviet Union is fundamentally healthy, and in its future . . . The predisposition of the physicists of that time to socialism is a fact which deserves further discussion. But Landau and his comrades, as we have seen, called the social system which had triumphed by 1938 by an entirely different name.

These considerations led Gorelik to argue that 'atomic and space successes are essentially by-products of the 1930s, the years when the authors of these successes entered science' – and the years before their disillusionment. By the end of the 1930s the 'centralised bureaucratic system' of science administration had been established. This system 'subsequently evolved by its own bureaucratic laws and increasingly crushed the life out of science in spite of the abundant provision of finance'.[3] Soviet post-war triumphs were a lagged result of the first twenty years of Soviet power.

Krivonosov uses his preliminary survey of the files of the central committee department for science and educational establishments to confirm that the administration of science tended to ossify after the second world war. The department was primarily concerned not with the content and quality of scientific research but with appointments and promotions, and the views and personal life of leading scientists:

Total control was established over appointments to posts on the *nomenklatura*, elections to the Academy of Sciences, foreign visits, scientific events, decisions on membership of international scientific organisations, etc. Our scientists needed the agreement of the higher party structures before they could accept foreign awards.[4]

Military research by-passed the central committee department. Recent Soviet accounts have shown how the atomic bomb programme was organised by high-level committees under the general control of Beria, and received top priority in machinery, materials, food and personnel. The secret atomic city 'Arzamas-16' was built by prison labour, which continued to work there after the town was completed.[5] The Soviet atom programme is fully described in David Holloway's outstanding book, written in close contact with Russian historians and participating scientists. Much of Holloway's material became available only in the past few years.[6]

In the post-war years, as in the 1930s, physics was protected from ideological attack. In 1948, Maksimov, who supported good physics in his youth, headed an obscurantist campaign against 'idealist' interpretations of quantum physics, and against the theory of relativity in general.[7] (While Syrtsov's and Tukhachevsky's role changed from bad to good – see pp. 128–31, 134 above, Maksimov's changed from good to terrible.) The campaign reached its climax in 1952. The last straw for the physicists was his article in the newspaper of the Soviet Navy (!) entitled 'Against Reactionary Einsteinism in Physics'.[8] An 'All-Union Conference on Physics' was intended to play a similar role to that of the pro-Lysenko session of the Agricultural Academy in August 1948.[9]

In December 1952 Kurchatov, scientific head of the atom project, forwarded to Beria a strong criticism of Maksimov by Academician V. A. Fock, 'Against Ignorant Criticism of Contemporary Physical Theories'. Kurchatov endorsed the article and sent Beria a letter of support from eleven prominent physicists, including Tamm, Landau and Sakharov. Beria passed all this correspondence to Malenkov at the party central committee. He attached a note which was sympathetic to the physicists, though he did not explicitly identify himself with Fock's views. After further correspondence, the central committee authorised the publication of Fock's article, and it appeared, together with a reply from Maksimov, in the journal *Voprosy filosofii*, no. 1, 1953 – a couple of months before Stalin's death.[10] From this point onwards physicists no longer had much worry about ideological interference in their research.

In other sciences, Stalinist ideology played a more sharply negative role: physiology (the Pavlovian monopoly); biology and biochemistry (the influence of Lysenko and his school); cybernetics; and even chemistry (the attack on the 'resonance theory'). In all these fields, the ideological incubus was not lifted until the death of Stalin – and in some cases much later. It is an irony of history that many of the sciences which began to flourish after Stalin's death have now been crushed by the weight of the economic reforms.

* * *

The thrust of the new investigations of Soviet science of which these are a few examples is to demonstrate that, as in other aspects of Soviet life, outstanding progress was often achieved in spite of the repressive system. Sometimes, as in the case of nuclear physics, central planning and state power themselves enforced the priority of scientific development.

The Russian historians of science – all of them natural scientists by training – have thus made a significant contribution towards the understanding in present-day Russia of the Soviet past. Social and political historians have focussed their attention on repressions and failures – quite naturally, as they had not been allowed to investigate them before. But historians must also explain the transformation of the USSR into a great industrial power, and the emergence in the Stalin and post-Stalin years of an educated public – the tens of millions whose rejection of the old system was crucial to its overthrow. In the West – and even in Russia itself, the significance of the work of the historians of Soviet science, and their journal *Questions of the History of Science and Technology*, has generally been underestimated.

16 Soviet Society in the Stalin Era

Many hundreds of Russian books and articles in recent years have discussed the general nature of Stalinist society. But social analysis based on new information is in its infancy.

This is quite natural. In Britain and the United States an historical monograph based on original research will often take ten years from conception to publication – and rarely less than five. Russian scholarship in the few years since the archives opened and the censorship was abolished is impressive, as the following examples illustrate.

SOCIETY BEFORE THE WAR

Historians and demographers have undertaken immense labours in recovering, annotating and publishing the population censuses of 1937 and 1939.[1] But this rich raw material, indispensable for an examination of the social structure, awaits systematic study.

A valuable monograph by Elena Osokina uses previously secret instructions and materials of the People's Commissariat for Supply. It deals with what might seem a highly specialised topic – food supply during the rationing period (1928–35).[2] But its title is *The Hierarchy of Consumption*, and it shows how the state distribution machinery was used to enforce the privileges of the élite. Special shops provided them with reliable food supplies at a time when ordinary workers did not receive their bare rations.[3] In addition, those attending major state and party occasions were lavishly regaled with food. In September–October 1932, during the harshest food shortage, the 500 delegates and guests at the plenum of the party central committee were allocated per person, for a period of 15 days, 20 kilograms of meat, 8 kilograms of fish, 1.2 kilograms of cheese and even 600 grams of caviare.[4] At this time the highest individual meat ration, when available, was only 3 kilograms *per month*. This orgy confirmed the strictures on the Stalin regime in Ryutin's platform, which was condemned by the party immediately after the plenum. (By this time Ryutin was receiving a much smaller food allocation – in jail.)

A small top élite, including the members of the Politburo and the People's Commissars of the USSR, and their families, enjoyed even greater privileges. They received food and consumer goods from special funds. They had instant access to the best doctors, to the well-equipped Kremlin hospital, and to the special rest-homes described by Maria Svanidze (see p. 186 above). They used special coaches on the railways; abundant food was of course supplied.[5]

Osokina's study confirms the criticisms of the class-divided society which were a common thread in the platforms, leaflets, diaries and conversations of Stalin's opponents, and a major source of social unrest.

THE SECOND WORLD WAR

In the searchlight of new data exposing the deficiencies, injustices and horrors of the Stalin regime, what has become of the newly-educated Soviet workers, delighted with their promotion from the depths of society, enjoying their new cultural opportunities and toiling enthusiastically for a better future?

They appear, albeit in a muted form, in an impressive study of the second world war, *Moskva Voennaya, 1941–5*, published on the occasion of the 50th anniversary of the Soviet and allied victory.[6] This coffee-table volume was prepared by Mikhail Gorinov and his colleagues in Mosgorarkhiv, the Moscow Union of Archives. It includes documents from the various Moscow repositories and from many national archives, including those of the security services, the Ministry of Defence and the Ministry of Foreign Affairs. Reports from the postal censors provide tantalising glimpses of popular attitudes. The censors claimed to have inspected *all* the letters in and out of Moscow – 2 626 507 in the first fifteen days of November 1941 alone.[7]

The volume concentrates on the first stages of the war: the rapid German advance which drew close to the capital in October 1941 and continued to creep forward until the beginning of December, and the first Soviet counter-offensive from December 1941 to April 1942. Substantial chapters deal with the role of the Air Force and the volunteer armies in defending the capital; the evacuation of industry; women; children; and 'the muses against the guns'.

The authors seek to show, against the background of wartime upheaval, the Moscow population's changing outlook and mood (the Russian word is *nastroeniya* – something like mentalités). The upheaval was immense. By the end of 1941 evacuation and call-up had reduced the population by over two million, nearly half the total.[8] The proportion of women and older people greatly increased. A large number of Communists joined the armed services or were evacuated with their factories. The number of party members in Moscow fell by nearly four-fifths, from 236 000 in June to only 51 000 in December.[9] Thus the war removed from Moscow a high proportion of the active supporters of the regime.

The changing mood of the population is presented in all its complexity. A woman worker grumbled that 'we live worse now than under the Tsar . . . The Germans aren't attacking us, they're attacking Bolshevism.' But a woman in a queue said 'that cannibal Hitler won't lead his lousy armies through the Moscow streets', while another kissed a newspaper which reported the German retreat.[10] Anti-semitism raised its head. The postal censors reported such sentiments as 'You don't see any Jews in Moscow, they all fled, headed by the big bosses . . . Up to 75 per cent of the Moscow population were Jews . . . Our government will make a big mistake if it lets them back into Moscow.'[11]

A large number of the privileged élite fled from the city during the 'great panic' of October 1941. This desertion met with great indignation. According to an NKVD report, the personnel director of one factory loaded a vehicle with a large quantity of food, and tried to leave the grounds, but the workers stopped him and beat him up. In several factories workers who had not been paid gathered in threatening crowds.[12] Three months after the panic, party members who had not flinched complained at a meeting of their cell in 'Trekhgornaya manufaktura', a large rubber goods factory:

Belov. . . . Many Communists ran away at the difficult moment, while we worked unceasingly and untiringly . . .
Antonova. The party *aktiv* [active members] in most cases destroyed their party cards. What kind of *aktiv* is this? – it is already deciding on its own behalf that it can remain in the party . . .
There are slogans pasted up all over Moscow, 'Everything for the Defence of Moscow!' – and with us it was the opposite – everyone ran away from Moscow.
Bedova. We party members should be the vanguard of the working class, and we are in the rear . . . Our leaders are useless, concerned with their personal affairs and arranging things for their families . . . As a result 107 people destroyed their party cards.

Other documents display quiet heroism. The Proletarii factory made its own spades to dig defence fortifications, and worker volunteers laboured from 8 a.m. till nightfall; the factory director and the senior managers joined in.[13] Workers in the third branch of the Metro refurbished it at breakneck speed so that it could be used as a bomb-shelter by 200 000 people.[14] The diary of a courageous woman doctor describes her everyday life and suffering during these difficult months.[15]

Mikhail Gorinov has used the material in this volume to analyse popular mentalités.[16] He distinguishes as many as six sub-stages:

1. *June 1941*. Patriotic altruism for a couple of days – successful mobilisation, with many volunteers; but followed by egoistic attempts to avoid the call-up and to stock-pile food.
2. *July to September*. Society is divided into three parts: patriots unto death; 'the marsh', a prey to every kind of rumour; defeatists, who want the Germans to overthrow a hated regime.
3. *October*. Evacuation. Patriotic altruism of the ordinary Muscovites; egoism and panic of lower and middle party and state officials. But little defeatism and anti-Communism. Was it the courage of the ordinary Muscovite which persuaded Stalin to abandon his plans to blow up the city (15 October) in favour of defence in siege conditions?
4. *November to mid-December*. Almost no defeatism; but growing despair at the appalling food shortage.
5. *Mid-December 1941 to March 1942*. Dissatisfaction at worsening daily life; some lack of confidence in victory, but less than at the beginning of the war.
6. *April to May 1942*. Normalisation of attitudes: population sees food situation as tolerable, and is ready for sacrifice.

Gorinov notes that patriotic resistance was increasingly stimulated throughout the first year of war by popular stories and rumours about the appalling conduct of the German occupiers. Most people regarded these accounts as more trustworthy than official information.

He concludes that there is no simple relation between the mood of the people and their material situation. In November–December 1941, when the military and food situation was particularly bad, optimism and patriotism were high.

*   *   *

The most favourable assessment of the Stalin regime before and during the second world war has unexpectedly been provided by the hated German occupiers. An enterprising Russian historian, Anatolii Yakushevskii, found secret wartime reports from the head of the German security police, preserved in the Bundesarchiv in Koblenz. These are not a serious historical analysis, and they have long been available. Together with other such materials they were published in German in 1984 in 17 volumes.[17] But they are most informative, they have not been used by British or North American specialists on Soviet history, and they have played a significant part in modifying the views of present-day Russian historians. I will therefore not refrain from summarising them here.

The first report was written on 17 August 1942, fourteen months after the German invasion of the USSR. The section entitled 'The Views of the [German] Population about Russia' argues that the Nazi propaganda images of the Communist regime are fundamentally mistaken. It recalls the 'impressive propaganda over many years about disorganisation in agriculture, for example, and in transport, and that the industrial five-year plans were not fulfilled':

In the first months of war against the Soviet Union . . . the feeling has emerged that we were the victims of a definite *misconception* [*Täuschung*]. The huge mass of armaments, its technical quality, and the gigantic industrialisation of the country led us to our first striking impressions . . . Soldiers on the basis of their own experience also stated that although the mass of the people were primitive and poor, they saw huge installations, gigantic industrial enterprises of an American type, power stations, etc. They ask themselves the question: how did Bolshevism achieve all this? 'Some positive influences must also have been operating?'

The *Ostarbeiter* – the Soviet workers in Germany – were unexpectedly 'intelligent, deft, quick in comprehension of even complex processes in the work of machines.' Moreover, 'many of them learned German quite quickly, and did not at all seem as if they had merely received a poor primary education'.[18]

A further report, dated 15 April 1943, also rejected existing German preconceptions. It emphasised that many people were well-educated; the *Ostarbeiter* did not need any more training than German citizens. It also claimed that Russians in large numbers, in spite of Soviet propaganda, retained their faith in religion; this was one aspect of the high moral quality of Russian citizens. The report even concluded that the great emphasis by German propaganda on the importance of terror and the GPU in controlling the population was exaggerated. 'Part of our population has become sceptical and thinks . . . that the activities of the GPU do not determine life in the Soviet Union to the extent which one previously believed.'[19]

Soviet industrialisation has been unexpectedly rehabilitated on the dubious authority of the *Reichsicherheithauptamt*.

SOVIET SOCIETY AFTER THE WAR

Elena Zubkova has made the first systematic attempt to use newly-available information to analyse post-war Stalinist society in motion.[20] Writing in the tradition of the French Annales school, and with a touch of post-modernism, she has sought to examine the 'social-psychological atmosphere' and social consciousness.

She draws on a wide range of sources – memoirs (including her own interviews), newspapers, magazines, films and archives. Her main archival source, the files of the propaganda department of the central committee, contains extensive reports of popular attitudes. Unlike the secret-police reports, which emphasise disaffection, the reports to the propaganda department sought to show that campaigns met with 'universal popular support', and that 'unhealthy tendencies' were relatively insignificant. In the absence of public opinion surveys, Zubkova, like Gorinov, relies on her own judgment to evaluate this evidence.

Her wider objective is to assess how far Soviet society before the fall of Khrushchev was capable of reform. This leads her (mistakenly in my view) to be primarily concerned with 'the politically and intellectually active section of society' – as are most of her sources. The silent majority not yet been given its voice. Although her approach is more sophisticated than Gorinov's, it focuses on a narrower range of urban society.

She distinguishes two overlapping periods before the death of Stalin: 'Hopes (1945–7)' and 'Repressions (1948–52)'. Her 'Hopes' are mainly those of the men and women who grew up in the 1930s and then fought at the front (the *frontoviki*). She rejects the fashionable image of pre-war urban society as a 'barracks regime'. In spite of the repressions many young people in pre-war years were 'pure, romantic, clear and public-spirited'. Society was more like an army in action than a barracks. The citizen carried out stipulated tasks. Nevertheless, 'within the limits of his authority he was all-powerful'.

During the war the *frontoviki* saw themselves as free human beings willingly fighting a hated enemy; but they also acquired the practice of obedience. The conquest of Europe opened their eyes to a different world. In this they resembled the 'Decembrists', the officers who mutinied against the Tsar in December 1825. But unlike the Decembrists they still believed in the unity of society, and in the need to mend the wounds of war. They lacked even a sketchy programme for curing the ills of society.

Immediately after the war the *frontoviki* retained a considerable degree of solidarity. Zubkova describes a little-known social institution:

[They met] as a rule outside their home, either in student hostels . . . or, much more frequently and more typically, in small cafés, snack-bars and pubs which opened after the war (they were popularly known as 'Blue Danubes').

The *frontoviki* – and many other Soviet citizens – were full of hope for the future. Zubkova argues that this explains why the most popular post-war Soviet film was *Kuban Cossacks* . In presenting hungry battered Russia as already a socialist paradise it reflected the spirit of the time. According to a participant in its production:

The well-dressed lads and lasses on the screen were very hungry. But they were gaily looking at stacks of fruit – abundance made of papier-maché . . . We believed that it would be like that, and there would be a lot of everything – bicycles, saddles, whatever you wanted. We really needed that universal glamour, and the singing of those songs.

Most people continued to trust Stalin and the party. But a sense of disillusionment set in. The monetary reform at the end of 1947, like all government decisions, was presented as highly beneficial to the people. But it deprived many citizens of their savings. The simultaneous abolition of rationing involved huge increases in prices. Reality and propaganda were in stark contrast.

The state's own propaganda emphasised the gap between the ordinary people and the party leadership by failing to treat the defeat of fascism as a victory of the people. In May 1945 the victory was presented as a joint achievement of Stalin and the people. But on 25 June Stalin's speech describing the ordinary people as 'little screws' (*vintiki*) treated society as a hierarchy in which he was the supreme arbiter.[21] Then three days later a *Pravda* editorial even presented Stalin personally as the supreme victor, 'who embodied in himself the heroism of the Soviet people'.

There were strong tendencies among the élite as well as the people to favour a 'softer' regime. In 1946 and 1947 a new draft Constitution and party programme were discussed in secret. Many proposals – though worded cautiously – favoured such measures as the abolition of military and other special courts, and greater democracy within the party. But in August 1946 the central committee approved the notorious resolution on literature proposed by Andrei Zhdanov. As a result, 'the rainbow which illuminated these hopes noticeably faded'.[22]

Before 1948 some 'freedom of manoeuvre' and 'commonsense' nevertheless remained. In the Academy of Sciences the respected physicist S.

I. Vavilov, a member of the Mandel'shtam school (see pp. 193–4 above), was elected President in 1945. Vavilov was the brother of Nikolai Vavilov, the geneticist who was persecuted by Lysenko, and died in exile. In 1947 Lysenko was under a cloud because his brother had collaborated with the Germans; influential officials in the central committee, including Zhdanov's son Yurii, regarded him with misgiving or hostility.[23] But in 1948 Stalin took Lysenko's side and obscurantism triumphed.

In 1948–52, the last five years of Stalin's rule, oppression predominated. By the time of Stalin's death the number of prisoners in the Gulag reached its peak (see p. 166 above). Zubkova describes how social tension increased in society at large. Repressive measures against the intelligentsia reached a critical limit. The campaigns for the party line in biology, physiology and linguistics actively sought the support of the entire population against the deviant specialists.

In the wider society, the neglected countryside was 'on the edge of collapse'. By 1952:

> The position of the powers-that-be began to be like sitting on a volcano, inside which energy with a huge destructive power was growing and accumulating . . .
>
> The only way to overcome the manifestations of crisis . . . was reform from above.

Like others who have grappled with the problem of Stalinism, Zubkova is impelled to turn her attention to the personality of Stalin, and concludes that in 1952 the 'only barrier' to reform was 'the figure of the Leader'.

The death of Stalin in March 1953 provides a unique opportunity to examine Soviet politics both with and without the leader.

17 Stalin's Entourage at the End

During the war Stalin unremittingly wielded the tyrannical powers which he had acquired in the previous decade. But he partly relinquished them: in the first eighteen months of war he learned that the Soviet Army would win more battles if Zhukov took the military decisions.

After the war he retained both the post of Secretary of the central committee, which he had held since 1922, and the chair of the Council of People's Commissars (Council of Ministers from 1946) which he had taken on in 1941. He continued as head of both party and government until his death on 5 March 1953.

This was the old Stalin, but with some new ingredients. He was as shrewd as ever, suspicious, vengeful and self-regarding.[1] But now he was a great world leader as well as the head of the international Communist movement. To an even greater extent than before the war he tried to take the long view, in the sense that he sought to fit current policies into his vision of the future Soviet Union and the future Communist world. He also paid more attention to his role in advancing Marxist theory – which he tackled with greater dexterity than any of his successors.

But he was tired and getting old. 'In my opinion he began to feel his age a little in the last years,' Molotov cautiously admitted.[2] From 1950 he spent four or five months a year on his 'working vacation' rather than the traditional couple of months.[3] His deputies often took the chair at the Council of Ministers.[4] Many issues were simply not resolved – Stalin himself spoke of the *tsentrostop* – the 'hold-up at the centre'.[5] And his decisions were often capricious. A Russian historian working on the post-war Politburo papers in 1989, when he, like most historians, was still basically loyal to the regime, said to me 'I can't write about some of the foolish things that were done; it would disorient our people'.

Stalin realised that things were going wrong. Another Russian historian, after inspecting Stalin's private papers, recently commented with some hyperbole that 'when alone with himself, almost to his death he remained honest and self-critical in relation to himself, at times to the point of irony'.[6] His venture into linguistics in 1950 and the protracted discussions which led to the publication of his *Economic Problems of Socialism in the USSR* a few months before his death were both searching for a way forward. In the last period of his life he tended to favour Malenkov,

Khrushchev and (intermittently) Beria rather than Molotov, Kaganovich and Voroshilov.[7] They were more obedient, perhaps – but they were also younger, more feasible as successors.

He suggested to his nervous cronies during those grim jolly nights in his dacha near Moscow that it was time for him to go on a pension.[8] And at the plenum of the central committee in October 1952 he proposed on grounds of old age to give up the General Secretaryship of the party while retaining his other posts. Malenkov, in the chair, took this as a 'test' – his face and gestures, according to an eye-witness, 'were a direct plea to all present to refuse Stalin's request immediately and decisively'.[9]

Stalin's policies in his last few months were particularly bizarre and harsh. At the October 1952 plenum he turned savagely on Molotov and Mikoyan, and expelled them from the inner leadership. Then he authorised the announcement of the Doctors' Plot, which unleashed a wave of anti-semitism throughout the country.[10] A month before his death he apparently insisted that rural taxes should be increased from 15 to 40 milliard rubles a year – an unsupportable sum.[11]

After Stalin's death quite sweeping policy changes were launched immediately. Many of them were announced in the Soviet press: the amnesty (27 March); the release of those doctors who survived their interrogation (4 April); the concentration of investment in the more profitable central regions – an implied criticism of Stalin's favourite 'construction schemes of communism' (10 June); the reduction of the mass loan levied on the population (25 June). Significantly, on 10 June *Pravda* publicly criticised the 'cult of personality', long before Khrushchev's denunciation of Stalin in 1956. In connection with the arrest and trial of Beria, the press also criticised Beria for 'capitulation' to imperialism and for 'activating bourgeois-nationalist elements in the republics'.[12]

The most dramatic event of these months was the arrest of Beria on 26 June and his execution in December. For many years most commentators accepted the view that Beria was simply a ruthless police chief who had been seeking autocratic power.[13] But as more information became available, some Western historians came to the conclusion that he had also seriously undertaken economic and political reforms.[14]

Thanks to the opening of the archives, the view that Beria was both a reformer and a ruthless police chief can now be confirmed. The main new sources of information are the verbatim reports of the central committee plenums of 5 March held while Stalin was on his death-bed, and of 2–7 July 1953, at which Beria was condemned.[15] Beria's lengthy, ungrammatical, hysterical and informative letter to Malenkov, dated 1 July, pleading for his life, has also been published.[16] The Politburo papers for this period have not been released to historians, but they have been extensively cited by the fortunate staff of the Presidential Archive.[17] In addition, useful memoirs have appeared from the surviving participants – and from the sons of Beria, Khrushchev and Malenkov.[18]

The March plenum, a joint session with the Council of Ministers and the Presidium of the Supreme Soviet, assembled at 8 p.m., 1 hour 50 minutes before Stalin's death. The proceedings lasted only forty minutes, but in that time Molotov and Mikoyan were restored to the Presidium of the central committee (the new name adopted for the Politburo in October 1952 – not to be confused with the Presidium of the Supreme Soviet), Malenkov was appointed Prime Minister (chair of the Council of Ministers), and Beria, Molotov, Bulganin and Kaganovich as his deputies.[19] The plenum also resolved that Khrushchev should 'concentrate on work in the central committee' – foreshadowing his appointment as party General Secretary on 21 March.

The course of the reforms following Stalin's death as revealed by the archives has been described by several Russian historians,[20] and by Beria's American biographer Amy Knight.[21] The records show that Beria took much of the initiative; the period between 5 March and his arrest on 26 June is often now referred to as Beria's '113 days'. It was Beria who proposed to the Presidium of the central committee the majority of the reforms announced in the press. Beria's proposals were often based on documentation prepared in his Ministry, the MVD (Ministry of Internal Affairs). These included the Amnesty decree, which resulted in the release of 1.2 million prisoners (see p. 183 above); and the release of the doctors, on which Beria sent a memorandum to the Presidium stating that the 'Doctors' Plot' 'from beginning to end is a provocative invention'. Following memoranda to the Politburo by Beria, several other notorious political cases were also denounced as fabrications, including the charges against the great Jewish actor Mikhoels.[22]

Beria was also responsible for the transfer of the major construction departments manned by forced labour from the MVD to the economic ministries (this did not include the camps for exceptionally dangerous state prisoners – for which see p. 178 above). The Chief Administration for the Camps (GULAG), was transferred to the Ministry of Justice.[23] Simultaneously, following a memorandum from Beria, about twenty expensive major projects began in Stalin's last years were brought to a halt.[24]

All these measures were adopted within a month of Stalin's death. In May Beria embarked on the extension of the rights of the areas annexed to the Soviet Union in 1939–41: the Baltic republics, Western Ukraine and Belorussia. In regard to Lithuania, for example, the Presidium decided on

26 May, on the basis of a memorandum by Beria, that the practice of appointing senior government and party officials who did not know Lithuanian should be stopped. All business should be conducted in Lithuanian rather than Russian. Senior officials who were recalled because they did not know Lithuanian should be allocated to new jobs by Moscow.[25] Perhaps the most remarkable decision of the 113 days was symbolic: on 9 May, Victory Day, the Presidium resolved that henceforth portraits of the leaders should not be carried in demonstrations or erected on buildings on festival days.[26]

This was clearly a coordinated programme. In important respects Beria wanted to take reform further. Thus he prepared proposals for the release of the special settlers; 1.7 million were to be released immediately, the remaining one million within a couple of years. These proposals were cancelled after Beria's arrest and execution.[27] Russian historians have also claimed that he wanted to extend the amnesty, and to limit the extraordinary powers of arrest and sentence introduced by Stalin. This remains uncertain; archival references have not been provided.[28]

Beria also sought to strengthen the state against the party. In discussions with the Hungarian communist leaders about the role which should be played by the central committee of the party in relation to the Council of Ministers, he brusquely commented: 'Why the central committee? The Council of Ministers should decide everything, and the central committee should be concerned with personnel and propaganda.'[29] He also criticised the inactivity of the trade unions.[30] He made hostile remarks about Stalin, and sought to make his critical view of Stalin widely known: his memorandum on the doctors' plot, circulated to party organisations, stated that those under arrest had been beaten on Stalin's orders.[31] All these statements were ostensibly directed towards establishing a less arbitrary regime. Beria also wanted to make sweeping changes in Eastern Europe. When the situation in the GDR, the German Democratic Republic, was discussed on 27 May Beria proposed a resolution which boldly declared that 'the policy of constructing socialism is mistaken in present conditions' in the GDR. Molotov proposed to insert the word 'forced' before 'socialism', making it clear that socialism remained the long-term aim. Beria explained that his view was that 'all we need is a peaceful Germany; we are indifferent whether there is socialism there or not'(though he conceded to Molotov in conversation that he thought socialism should not be constructed 'at the present time'). Khrushchev supported Molotov, and Beria dropped his proposal.[32] But on his own initiative he decided to reduce the number of 'plenipotentiaries' of the MVD in the GDR to a mere one-seventh of their previous number, and replace Soviet 'instructors' by advisers.[33]

Then on 25 June, the day before his arrest, he proposed to Malenkov that the connections of the MVD should be used to facilitate the normalisation of relations with Yugoslavia. A letter from Beria to the Yugoslav politician Rankovich, found in Beria's papers after his arrest, asked Rankovich to tell Tito in strict confidence that 'Beria and his friends support the necessity of a fundamental reconsideration and improvement in the relations between the two countries'.[34]

By this time opinions within the Soviet party leadership had hardened against Beria. A popular uprising in East Berlin had been suppressed by Soviet tanks, and the leaders of the DDR blamed Beria's policies for the crisis.[35] These events may have provided the other Soviet leaders with the final pretext for arresting Beria.

Far more compelling reasons for his arrest emerge from his letter to Malenkov of 1 July and from the proceedings of the July plenum of the central committee. The other leaders feared his growing power. Molotov complained that Beria had insisted on being the person who proposed Malenkov as Prime Minister to the Supreme Soviet. He also reported other cases of Beria's unilateral actions, including his decision to explode the hydrogen bomb without consulting the Presidium. Bulganin explained at length that the other members of the Presidium had found out that Beria's staff were spying on them and reporting their activities to Beria (the same complaint was made by Yeltsin about Gorbachev nearly 40 years later).[36]

Above all, in pressing for reforms, Beria wielded the sinister and ruthless authority of the MVD, which he controlled (the same pattern was followed on a far more modest scale by Andropov a generation later). In March he re-appointed officials loyal to himself, who had been dismissed in 1951, to senior posts in the MVDs of the USSR and the republics.[37] And although he had initiated the transfer of the GULAG to the Ministry of Justice, key powers remained firmly in the hands of the MVD and therefore of himself. In particular, the MVD retained control of the 'Special Camps for particularly dangerous state criminals' established in 1948.[38]

Beria went out of his way to stress publicly the importance of the MVD. For example, the decision on the Doctors' Plot was published as a 'Communication of the Ministry of Internal Affairs', not as a decision of the central committee. In his letter to Malenkov, Beria admitted:

your criticism, the criticism of cde. Khrushchev N. S. and the criticism of other comrades at the Presidium was completely correct . . . of my incorrect wish to circulate with the decisions of the central committee the memoranda of the MVD. Of course this to a considerable extent lessened the importance of the decisions of the CC [Central Committee] itself.

Beria also acknowledged, obviously in reply to criticism, that in the party Presidium and the Council of Ministers 'my conduct was very often incorrect and impermissibly gave rise to nervousness and I was too sharp . . . sometimes going as far as impermissible crudeness and effrontery on my part towards comrades Khrushchev N. S. and Bulganin N. A.'[39]

The common thread of all the speeches against Beria at the July plenum was alarm at the past, present and possible future power of Beria and the secret police. Khrushchev denounced the methods of the MVD as 'terror directed against the government and against our people'. 'Beria, Yagoda, Ezhov, Abakumov [the past secret police chiefs] – all those plants grew in the same field'.[40] Kaganovich pointed out that the MVD as an organisation 'is partly spoiled because for many years it has been polluted by bad people – Yagoda, Ezhov and Abakumov – but also because it is polluted by its method' – the MVD had been out of control, with no supervision by the party.[41]

Beria was also frequently accused in the course of the campaign against him of seeking to free state agencies from party supervision – a matter which particularly concerned Khrushchev as General Secretary of the party. He was held responsible for the recent practice of discussing foreign policy at the Council of Ministers without previously referring the issues to the party Presidium.[42]

The party leaders also unanimously condemned Beria's national policy. The decisions about Lithuania and the other republics were cancelled on 2 July, the day the plenum opened.[43]

The plenum resolution adopted on 7 July particularly emphasised three transgressions. He had attempted to 'use the apparatus of the Ministry of Internal Affairs to advance his criminal machinations to seize power'. He had sought to 'sow discord and enmity among the peoples of the USSR, and to activate the bourgeois-nationalist elements in the Union republics'. His proposals on the German question 'amounted to a policy of transforming the GDR into a bourgeois state'.[44]

Some speakers at the plenum strongly attacked Beria's reform programme in general and his criticisms of Stalin in particular. The party leader Andreev, who had been a full or candidate member of the Politburo from 1927 until 1952, said that Beria had 'cast a shadow on the name of comrade Stalin' in order to 'bury the name of comrade Stalin and come to power more easily'.[45] The veteran industrial administrator Tevosyan took the same line, and also criticised economic measures adopted since March 1953.[46] According to Khrushchev, several people who did not speak held similar views.[47]

In contrast the members of the Presidium made it abundantly clear at the plenum that they supported most of the reform measures, including the steps towards a more law-governed society.[48] Bulganin even claimed that Beria's initiative on the Doctors' Plot was worthless because the members of the Presidium had realised that the charges were 'rubbish' as soon as they were announced.[49]

The other members of the Presidium went a long way towards agreeing with Beria's policies even on issues about which they criticised him. Kaganovich admitted that there had been faults in the policy towards the Baltic and other republics. Malenkov strongly criticised the 'forced construction of socialism' in the GDR. Molotov announced that the USSR wanted to establish the same relationship with Yugoslavia as with 'other bourgeois states'.[50]

In his reply to the discussion Malenkov said almost nothing about Beria. Instead he rounded on Andreev and Tevosyan for their uncritical attitude to Stalin, and presented a hard-hitting reform programme of his own. He began by criticising the cult of Stalin, the exclusion of the Politburo from important decisions and the failure to call a party Congress between 1939 and 1952. He drew the conclusion:

> the cult of the personality of cde. Stalin in the daily practice of leadership took morbid forms on a large scale, the collective method in work was discarded, criticism and self-criticism at the higher level of leadership were completely absent.
>
> We do not have the right to conceal from you that such a deformed cult of personality led to personal decisions from which there was no appeal; criticism and self-criticism in our highest level of leadership were completely absent.

Malenkov refrained from attributing responsibility for the repressions to Stalin, even at this closed meeting of the plenum. But in significant respects this speech sounds like a rehearsal for Khrushchev's secret speech three years later . . .

Malenkov also made it absolutely clear to the assembled central committee members that the reforms must be extended to the economy. He pointed out that 'we have a substantial number of backward enterprises and even whole branches of industry . . . A substantial number of collective farms and whole agricultural districts are in a neglected condition.' Against this background he inveighed against the overtaxation of the peasantry, the decision to build the Great Turkmenian Canal without a proper economic assessment, Stalin's support for 'product-exchange' rather than trade, and the lack of economic incentives to collective farmers.[51]

The biographies of their fathers by Sergo Beria and Andrei Malenkov are entirely unconvincing when they attempt to defend their fathers' conduct

212 The New Soviet History

as associates of Stalin in terror and political murder.[52] But they present a persuasive portrait of men who genuinely wanted to bring about substantial changes in the system.

The archival evidence shows that Malenkov had himself initiated significant reform proposals long before Beria's arrest. On 10 March 1953, the day after Stalin's funeral, he told the party Presidium that 'we consider it essential to cease the policy of the cult of personality'.[53] Khrushchev supported this move. An editorial in the literary newspaper *Literaturnaya gazeta* on 19 March declared that it was 'a holy duty of writers' to present an image of 'the greatest genius of all times and peoples – the immortal Stalin'. Khrushchev strongly objected, and threatened to dismiss the editor of the newspaper.[54]

With Beria out of the way, Malenkov launched important economic policy initiatives in August 1953, including the switch of resources towards agriculture and consumer goods. After much manoeuvring and infighting among the party leaders, which included the dismissal of Malenkov from the post of Prime Minister, the banner of reform was raised still higher in 1956 by Khrushchev and Mikoyan. Like Beria and Malenkov, they were both potential reformers who had kept their jobs and their lives by obeying Stalin unconditionally.

Hostility to reform was widespread in the party among both the leadership and sections of the rank and file. The archives have revealed how bitter the other party leaders were about Khrushchev even twenty years after his fall.[55] At a meeting of the Politburo held on 12 July 1984, eight months before Gorbachev was appointed General Secretary of the party, Chernenko reported that he had informed Molotov of the decision to reinstate him in the party. The Politburo then discussed whether Malenkov and Kaganovich should also be reinstated. No-one (and this includes Gorbachev) found a good word to say about Khrushchev, but there were plenty of kind words about Stalin:

Ustinov [Minister of Defence] . . . I will say frankly, that if not for Khrushchev, then the decision to expel these people from the party would not have been taken. And in general those scandalous disgraces which Khrushchev committed in relation to Stalin would never have occurred. Stalin, no matter what is said, is our history. No one enemy brought us so much harm as Khrushchev did in his policy towards the past of our party and state, and towards Stalin . . .

Tikhonov [Prime Minister]. Yes, if not for Khrushchev, they would never have been expelled from the party. He soiled and stained us and our policies in the eyes of the whole world.

Chebrikov [head of KGB]. Besides that, a whole list of individuals were illegally rehabilitated. As a matter of fact they were rightly punished. Take, for example, Solzhenitsyn . . .

Gorbachev. Concerning Malenkov and Kaganovich, I would also support their restoration in the party . . .

Gromyko [Minister of Foreign Affairs]. He [Khrushchev] rendered an irreversible blow to the positive image of the Soviet Union in the eyes of the outside world . . . Basically thanks to him the so-called 'Eurocommunism' was born.

Tikhonov. And what he did to our economy! I myself have had to work in a Sovnarkhoz [regional economic council under which industry was placed in 1957].

Gorbachev. And to the party, breaking it into industrial and agricultural party organisations! . . .

These unbusinesslike proceedings degenerated into farce. Ustinov proposed that the name of Stalingrad should be restored to Volgograd (an issue which was not on the agenda). On this Gorbachev commented cautiously (the only sign of differing from his aged colleagues which he manifested at the meeting) 'this proposal has positive and negative sides'. Then Tikhonov remarked that there was a very good new film about Zhukov 'in which Stalin is portrayed rather fully and positively'. Chernenko agreed the film was good. Ustinov commented 'I really should see it'. The proceedings ended with the distinguished comrades wishing Chernenko a good rest during the recess.[56] These were men quite incapable of governing a great country.

Views about Khrushchev continue to be sharply divided. At the conference held in Moscow in 1994 on the occasion of the centenary of his birth, the historians present were mainly reformist contemporaries of Khrushchev, and spoke about him with nostalgic enthusiasm (see pp. 54–5 above). Simultaneously, other historians (including some of those presenting Beria as a great reformer) published articles extremely hostile to both Khrushchev and his reforms. Anatolii Ponomarev concluded:

He was little different from Stalin's closest entourage in bullying and high-handedness to his subordinates, and in open flattery of the 'boss'. But he was superior to them in other respects, primarily in his ability to bang the heads of his rivals. The latter was the crucial factor in the Khrushchev phenomenon.[57]

Ponomarev is the historian who gained some notoriety in 1987 by the extremely conservative article attacking the re-evaluation of Soviet history which he wrote jointly with Vaganov, then head of the state archives.[58] But his own work is competent and interesting: he was one of the three editors of *Moskva Voennaya 1941–1945* (see p. 198 above).

Not surprisingly, Malenkov's assessment of Khrushchev followed similar lines. His son reported that after *perestroika* got under way, his father commented bitterly that 'our country could have followed the road of *perestroika* in the 1950s if the partocracy headed by Khrushchev had not triumphed.'[59]

The memoirs and archival documents all confirm the view that a substantial number of leading politicians recognised the necessity of reform. The trouble was not the absence of leaders committed to reform but the resistance of the system to reform – as the Politburo discussion of July 1984 demonstrates – and the inability of all the reforming leaders, including Khrushchev, Beria and Malenkov, to cast off Stalinism morally and intellectually. This rendered them incapable of designing a viable model of 'reformed Communism.'

18 The Future of the Soviet Past

In the years of Brezhnev and Andropov most Soviet historians were tamed and silenced by the orthodoxy imposed by the party. With few exceptions, they remained quite passive in 1987, when writers and journalists were already calling for a profound reassessment of the Soviet past. But in 1988 they became leading actors in the drama of rival ideas. In the autumn *Pravda* published an important series of articles by Danilov, Lel'chuk, V. A. Kozlov and others, based on their work for the never-to-be-completed party history. Throughout the next three years substantial articles by historians about the Soviet past appeared in periodicals and newspapers. The most prominent historians frequently appeared on TV.

The division of opinion among historians did not correspond to that among other Moscow and Leningrad intellectuals. Before the collapse of the Soviet Union few historians concerned with the Soviet period were hostile to the October Revolution and the Soviet regime as such; and those few were by no means the most serious. Both the main groups were committed Leninists. One group – the most prominent were Danilov and Volobuev, both in trouble under Brezhnev for their views – argued that Stalin's 'great breakthrough' at the end of the 1920s had destroyed the possibility of democratic socialism and betrayed the revolution.

The other group, mainly working in the Institute of Marxism–Leninism, included Vladimir A. Kozlov, Nikolai Simonov and Mikhail Gorinov.[1] They stressed the 'objective' factors, both international and internal, which had led to Stalinism. They did not seek to defend the purges or the camps, but they placed more emphasis than the first group on the achievements of the Stalin period.[2]

In 1989 and 1990 historians from both these groups played an independent and constructive role in the re-examination of the Soviet past. It was historians rather than publicists who ensured that Trotsky was treated justly as a historical figure, and that his analysis of the Stalinist regime received proper attention (see pp. 14–16 above).

In these years pronouncements by historians were often more influential than speeches by political leaders. In the autumn of 1991, however, the collapse of the Soviet Union was accompanied by a precipitate decline in public interest in history. A leading historian from the former Institute of Marxism–Leninism commented to me in 1992 that it felt very strange to

215

have been suddenly withdrawn from centre stage after having been thrust there equally suddenly only a year or two before. The complete rejection of the Soviet past fashionable in the year or so after the collapse of the USSR meant that historians who had been near-dissidents under Brezhnev were temporarily cast out of the media as stubborn Leninists.

Public interest declined, but was certainly not absent altogether. In every country political leaders appeal to the image of their nation's past to justify their own actions. In post-Communist Russia public utterances and private conversations are spiced with far more references to history than in Britain or the United States. Politicians of all shades of opinion – and ordinary citizens – refer to Yeltsin's era as a 'Time of Troubles' (*smutnoe vremya*), the period in the early Seventeenth Century when Pretenders vied for the Russian throne in conditions of civil strife and foreign intervention. Yeltsin's entourage talk about him as 'the Tsar'. One of Yeltsin's former associates claimed that Korzhakov, the influential head of the Presidential bodyguard dismissed in June 1996, behaved towards the President like a pre-revolutionary manservant: 'side by side with a president who is like a democrat there is also a president living like the Russian gentleman Trayekurov' – a high-handed nobleman, a character in Pushkin.[3]

The speeches of most Presidential candidates abounded in references to the Russian and Soviet past. Zyuganov, for example, condemned Yeltsin's excessive Presidential powers as 'those of the Tsar and the [party] General Secretary combined', and claimed that the ideas and concepts imposed on Russia 'had a worse effect than Goering's Luftwaffe and Guderian's tanks'.[4]

Gaidar, a minor Presidential candidate now that his popularity and that of his party had waned into insignificance, sought after he lost office to justify his policies in government by a sophisticated account of Russian history. He argued that under various guises the Russian and Soviet past had always been ruled by the same phenomenon: 'the mercenary and predatory arbitrariness of bureaucracy, concealed by demagogy'. In the 1990s the pressure of the past had driven Russia towards a form of bureaucratic capitalism dominated by the old *nomenklatura*. According to Gaidar, his attempt at shock therapy in 1992 had been the best that could be done to introduce as much as possible of a genuine market so that Russia would have the chance to become a proper market economy in the future.[5]

In an atmosphere in which history is frequently invoked to control the future, some historians will always gain temporary fame by providing the current political master with an appropriate account of the past. At the same time the public interest in the past, and the deep-rooted social desire to learn from past tragedies, tempts historians to produce instant history designed to appeal to the general reader. A Russian reviewer of two recent books on the secret police under Stalin complained that, like many recent publications, they used what he described as the 'decorative' method. Articles and books are provided with lively illustrative facts more or less at random, preferably from the archives, and the author juggles the facts to advocate some striking picture of the past which will attract the reader.[6] I need hardly add that it is not hard to find historians in Europe and North America who pontificate about politics or write poor instant history intended for the masses . . .

Many Russian historians have been far more responsible. They have reconsidered the past in an endeavour to offer fresh understanding. Thus Yurii Polyakov, in a thoughtful article on 'Russian Spaces: an Advantage or a Curse?', traces the history of the Russian Empire before 1917 as a story of colonisation and expansion over centuries, involving a high level of militarisation. The expansion of the state offered a vast potential, but 'the country was not in a position to handle this potential rationally'. Russian economic development was extensive rather than intensive; and Russians became convinced that their resources were inexhaustible. After 1917 development was again extensive in character, even in the 1960s when the West was mastering a new scientific and technical revolution. And with the collapse of the Soviet Union 'a gigantic break has taken place in the historical development of Russia', which requires a fundamental shift in 'the whole conception of the historical development of the country'. 'There is no way out except a real turn to intensive development, in deeds and not just in words.'[7]

Another senior historian, A. N. Sakharov, Director of the Institute of Russian History (no connection with the famous physicist), has examined the long-term history of the numerous nationalities which made up the Russian Empire, many of which are still located within the Russian Federation. The title of his article reflects its pessimistic conclusions: 'The Middle Ages on the Threshold of the Twenty-first Century: the Tragic Regularities of Nationalism'. He emphasises that in Eastern Europe the formation of nation states took place many centuries later than in Western Europe. Within the Russian Empire itself self-determination was delayed. Then in the Soviet period nations were subordinated to political control and class ideology. But at the same time industrialisation and agricultural transformation, and the rapid development of education, encouraged national consciousness and national movements. For every nationality within the USSR the Stalin regime created a new intelligentsia which supported and developed national ideals. At the same time the stormy growth of Soviet industry meant that towns in the national regions and republics emerged as 'huge contemporary villages' into which people brought their national customs and traditions. With the overthrow of the Communist regime, the nationalities are now confident that they are masters of their own fate. But their level of civilisation is often extremely low, and many years will be needed before they can turn into modern nations.[8]

The publication of articles on broad historical themes written from independent positions will not seem remarkable to Western readers unless it is placed in the context of the ideological controls which prevailed before *perestroika*. Such publications are playing an important role in broadening the understanding of the past by the Russian public, and by historians themselves.

Until the end of the 1980s most Soviet historians were isolated from the historical profession in the rest of the world. As late as the spring of 1988 Soviet historians attending a conference in London were not permitted to accept private dinner invitations from their British hosts. In my experience very few historians working on the Soviet period were acquainted either with debates about Soviet history taking place in the West or with the major Western publications in their own field. Historians living in Moscow and Leningrad could, with some difficulty, obtain Western publications from the *spetskhran* of the Lenin Library or the library of the Institute of Marxism–Leninism. But nearly all historians concerned with the Soviet period lacked sufficient knowledge of foreign languages; and only a privileged few were able to see the special translations available to the top party élite.

Now Russian historians can attend international conferences and visit the West, and these barriers are rapidly breaking down – at least for the minority of historians who can obtain foreign financial support. Within Russia several initiatives are spreading knowledge of Western historiography far more widely. The most important is the Seminar on Contemporary Concepts of Agrarian Development organised by Viktor Danilov, which has been meeting twice or three times a year since February 1992. Each session is devoted to a major Western work on the peasantry. A comprehensive Russian précis, some 5 000 words in length, is circulated to the seminar. Books so far discussed include J. C. Scott, *Moral Economy of the Peasant* (1976), about South-East Asia, T. Shanin, *Defining Peasants* (1990), E. R. Wolf, *Peasants* (1966), R. Redfield, *The Little Community and Peasant Society and Culture* (1960), R. E. Seavoy, *Famine in Peasant Societies* (1986), H. Hunter and J. M. Szyrmer, *Faulty Foundations: Soviet Economic Policies, 1928–1940* (1992), and a famous book on the Soviet peasantry, M. Lewin, *Russian Peasants and Soviet Power* (1975, first published in French, 1966). Shanin and Lewin personally participated in the sessions concerned with their own books.

The discussions were at a high level, and placed the study of the Russian and Soviet peasantry in a comparative context. Both précis and discussions are published in full in a major historical journal, and therefore have a considerable impact on the profession.[9] As Danilov has pointed out, this is not the first attempt to organise a high-level peasant seminar in Russia. In the late 1960s and early 1970s a series of seminars discussed the village commune (*obshchina*) in a comparative context. These studies tended to contradict the orthodox view of agrarian development, and in particular the insupportable view of S. P. Trapeznikov, long-term head of the science and education department of the central committee, that during collectivisation the communes were not destroyed, but transformed into collective farms. The 1976 session was banned.[10]

The new research discussed in Part III illuminates the past fitfully and incompletely. Sometimes existing knowledge is complemented by new information. Sometimes we learn about a new aspect of the past which was previously unknown or misunderstood. This is no rounded, systematic or even consistent version of the past. It is history, not propaganda. One day a Gibbon or a Kluchevsky may transform our understanding with a fresh paradigm. But the prerequisite for this is the kind of work now taking place in post-Soviet Russia.

These new developments provide grounds for optimism about the future of professional history. A minority of senior historians – such as Danilov and Ivnitskii – have produced major studies based on archival materials which they previously had not seen or could not cite. And a new generation is gradually coming to the fore – relatively small in number, but creative, open-minded and hard-working. The vast majority of the historians whose books and articles have been discussed here did not even feature in the index or the references of my *Soviet History in the Gorbachev Revolution*, published in 1989. These include, for example, Babichenko, Goland, Gorelik, Gorinov, Khlevnyuk, Osokina, Tsakunov, Vatlin, Zemskov and Zubkova – and many talented young historians for whom I have not managed to find space. (I should explain that, being aged myself, I use the term 'young historian' to mean someone under forty . . .)

The concluding section of the book by Bordyugov and Kozlov on historiography during *perestroika*, published in 1991, is entitled 'Farewell Politics?' and insists that 'professional history must no longer accept evaluations and quality marks from the politicians'. 'Only non-dogmatic history . . . can educate active, well-informed, adult citizens, capable of managing their own affairs and resisting the long arm of the bureaucracy'

– past, present and future.[11] Perhaps the most encouraging of all the developments in history since the end of the 1980s is that to a large extent professional history is now separated from politics.

Historians are deeply divided in their political allegiances. But many historians now seek to write history which is informed but not distorted by their outlook on the world. And – perhaps most important of all – historians of different outlooks, at least in the younger generation, respect each others' professional competence. European and North American historians would often fail this test.

Appendix 1: Print Runs of Newspapers and Periodicals, 1985–95

(a) Periodicals (thousands)	1985	1988	1989	1990	1991	1992	1993	1995
Istoriya SSSR/ Otechestvennaya istoriya	10	13	25	26	26	23	17	8
Kommunist/ Svobodnaya mysl'	944	1025	935	615	178	26	10	5
Nash sovremennik	220	220	245	482	275	205	88	31
Novyi mir	430	1150	1560	2660	958	250	74	25
Ogonek	1500[a]	1770	3200	4451	1800	1840	300	43
Rodina	–	–	300[b]	450	120	80[c]	80[c]	90[d]
Voprosy istorii	16	19	75	106	92	108	40	12

[a] 1987 [b] May [c] April 1993 [d] December 1994

(b) Newspapers (millions)	1985	1988	1989	1990	1991	1992	1993	1995
Argumenty i fakty (weekly)	?	9.2	20.5	33.0	23.8	25.7	12.1[e]	4.2[f]
Izvestiya	?	?	10.1	10.0	4.7	3.8	?	.6[g]
Pravda	11.0[h]	10.7	9.7	6.8	3.1	1.5	.6	.2
Trud	16.7	18.7	20.2	20.9	18.2	13.5	4.0	1.5[i]

[e] Dropped to 5.1 in July [f] Dropped to 3.0 in July [g] December [h] 1987
[i] Dropped to 1.2 in October

Note: Throughout the table the print run is for the first available issue in each year

Appendix 2: Major Events in Russian and Soviet History

988		Adoption of Christianity by Kievan Rus'
1240–1380		Mongol domination of Russia
1533–84		Reign of Ivan IV ('the Terrible')
1648–54		Ukrainian revolt under Bohdan Khmelnitsky
1694–1725		Reign of Peter I ('the Great')
1825	December	Decembrist rising against Nicholas I
1861		Emancipation of serf peasantry
1890s		First industrialisation drive
1905		First Russian revolution
1906		First Duma elected on limited franchise
1906–11		Stolypin's agrarian reforms
1909–13		Industrial boom
1914	July	Outbreak of first world war
1917	February/March	Liberal-democratic Revolution overthrows Tsar; establishment of Provisional Government
1917	October/November	Bolshevik ('October') Revolution
1918–20		Civil War/'War Communism'
1921–9		New Economic Policy
1924	21 January	Death of Lenin
1926–8		Pre-1914 industrial and agricultural output restored
1927–8	Winter	Grain crisis
1928	October	First five-year plan begins (up to December 1932)
1929	Autumn	Defeat of Bukharin group
1929	End of year	Mass collectivisation of agriculture and 'dekulakisation' began
1932–3		Widespread famine
1933	January	Hitler appointed Chancellor of German Reich

1933–7		Second Five-Year Plan
1934	January–February	XVII Party Congress
1934	1 December	Murder of Kirov in Leningrad
1936–8		'Ezhovshchina' (Great Purge); execution of Zinoviev, Kamenev, Rykov and Bukharin
1939	23 August	Soviet–German Pact
1941	22 June	Nazi Germany invades USSR
1941	October	Moscow under siege
1942	November	Soviet victory at Stalingrad
1945	9 May	Victory over Germany
1952	October	XIX Party Congress
1953	5 March	Death of Stalin
1953	26 June	Arrest of Beria
1956	February	XX Party Congress: Khrushchev denounces Stalin
1964	14 October	Khrushchev dismissed; replaced as First (General) Secretary by Brezhnev
1985	11 March	Gorbachev appointed party General Secretary
1988	June–July	XIX Party Conference
1990	July	XXVIII Party Congress
1991	12 June	Yeltsin elected President of Russian Federation
1991	19–21 August	Coup by State Committee for State of Emergency
1991	December	Soviet Union dissolved
1992	January	'Shock therapy' launched
1993	September–October	Yeltsin closes down Supreme Soviet; siege of White House
1993	December	First elections to State Duma
1995	December	Second elections to State Duma
1996	June–July	Re-election of Yeltsin as President of Russian Federation

Glossary

APRF (Arkhiv prezidenta Rossiskoi Federatsii)
: Archive of the President of the Russian Federation

Bolsheviks
: More revolutionary section, headed by Lenin, of Russian Social-Democratic Labour Party (later Communist Party)

Constituent Assembly
: Parliament established in 1917, dissolved by Bolsheviks in January 1918

Council of People's Commissars (SNK) (later Council of Ministers)
: Government of the Soviet Union, in practice subordinate to Politburo (q.v.)

fond
: (In archives) collection of materials, group of records

frontoviki
: Front-line soldiers

GARF (Gosudarstvennyi arkhiv Rossiskoi Federatsii) – formerly TsGAOR
: State Archive of the Russian Federation

Gosplan (Gosudarstvennaya planovaya komissiya)
: State Planning Commission

GPU*
: see OGPU

GULAG/GULag/Gulag (Glavnoe upravlenie lagerei)
: Chief Administration of Corrective-Labour Camps, responsible for forced labour – hence used to mean the camps themselves

KGB (Komitet gosudarstvennoi bezopasnosti)*
: Committee of State Security

Mensheviks
: Less revolutionary section of Russian Social-Democratic Labour Party

MVD (Ministerstvo vnutrennikh del)*
: Ministry of Internal Affairs

NKVD (Narodnyi komissariat vnutrennikh del)*
: People's Commissariat of Internal Affairs

nomenklatura
: List of key posts subject to higher approval – hence used to refer to the élite

OGPU (Ob'edinennoe gosudarstvennoe politicheskoe upravlenie)*
: Unified State Political Administration

Politburo	Political committee of Communist Party central committee, effectively supreme organ of power
RGAE (Rossiskii gosudarstvennyi arkhiv narodnogo khozyaistva) – *formerly* TsGANKh	Russian State Archive of National Economy
Rosarkhiv (Gosudarstvennaya arkhivnaya sluzhba Rossii)	State Archival Service of Russia
Roskomarkhiv (Rossiskii komitet po arkhivnym delam)	Russian Committee for Archival Affairs
RSFSR (Rossiskaya Sovetskaya Federativnaya Sotsialisticheskaya Respublika) (until end of 1991)	Russian Soviet Federative Socialist Republic
RTsKhIDNI (Rossiskii tsentr khraneniya i izucheniya dokumentov noveishei istorii)	Russian Centre for the Preservation and Study of Documents of Recent History
SNK (Sovet narodnykh komissarov)	Council of People's Commissars (q.v.)
SR (Sotsialist-revolyutsioner)	Socialist Revolutionary (member of peasant revolutionary party)
STO (Sovet truda i oborony)	Council for Labour and Defence (economic committee of SNK)
TsGANKh (Tsentral'nyi gosudarstvennyi arkhiv narodnogo khozyaistva) – *now* RGAE	Central State Archive of National Economy
TsGAOR (Tsentral'nyi gosudartvennyi arkhiv Oktyabr'skoi revolyutsii) – *now* GARF	Central State Archive of the October Revolution
TsKhSD (Tsentr khraneniya sovremennoi dokumentatsii)	Centre for the Preservation of Contemporary Documentation (post-1952 archive of party central committee)
TsPA (Tsentral'nyi partiinyi arkhiv) – *now* RTsKhIDNI	Central Party Archive

* In charge of secret police.

Notes

Place of publication is Moscow or Moscow/Leningrad unless otherwise stated.

PART I THE POLITICS OF SOVIET HISTORY

1. R. W. Davies, *Soviet History in the Gorbachev Revolution* (London and Indiana, 1989).
2. *Rodina*, no. 11, 1995.
3. For the changing Ukrainian view of the past, see A. Wilson, *Ukrainian Nationalism in the 1990s: a Minority Faith* (forthcoming).
4. *Istoriya Kazakhstana s drevneishikh vremen do nashikh dnei (ocherk)* (Almaty, 1993); 100 000 copies.
5. *East–West Education*, vol. 15, no. 2 (Fall 1994, published 1995), pp. 165–70 (S. Nettleton).
6. *Moscow Times* (weekly edition), 20 August 1995; *Transition*, 22 September 1995, p. 40.
7. Information from Andrew Wilson.

1 The Onslaught on Leninism

1. *Nauka i zhizn'*, no. 11 (November), 1988, pp. 45–55; no. 12, 1988, pp. 40–8; no. 1, 1989, pp. 46–56; no. 2, 1989, pp. 53–61.
2. On the Andreeva affair, see Davies (1989), pp. 141–6.
3. Private communication.
4. *Kuda idet Rossiya? Alternativy obshchestvennogo razvitiya*, vypusk 2 (1995), pp. 327–8.
5. *Rodina*, no. 7, 1989, pp. 80–4; another article by Khanin on the same theme appeared in *EKO*, no. 10, 1989, pp. 66–83.
6. For this controversy see R. W. Davies (ed.), *From Tsarism to the New Economic Policy* (1990), where both views are represented.
7. *The Guardian*, 30 November 1988 (from AP in Moscow).
8. *Moscow News*, no. 29, 16 July 1989.
9. For earlier favourable comments on Stolypin, see Davies (1989), p. 24.
10. *Sovetskaya Moldaviya*, cited in *Radio Liberty Report*, no. 30, 28 July 1989.
11. Cited by G. L. Smirnov (Director of the Institute of Marxism–Leninism), *Pravda*, 1 February 1990.
12. The letter appeared in *Izvestiya TsK*, no. 4, 1990, pp. 190–5, with extensive annotations, and accompanied by several previously unpublished Lenin documents from this period. According to the party archivists (*ibid.*, p. 174), the letter was published 'from a copy not known to us in the newspaper *Russkaya mysl'* (Paris), of 1 April 1971, which stated that it was reprinted from *Vestnik russkogo studencheskogo dvizheniya*, no. 98'; the latter journal was also published in Paris. The mass-circulation Young Communist weekly *Sobesednik*, no. 16, 1990, and the Russian nationalist journal *Nash*

sovremennik also published the letter. See Radio Liberty, *Report on the USSR*, no. 18, 4 May 1990 (V. Tolz).

13. For 1987–8, see Davies (1989), pp. 197–8.
14. *Sovetskaya Rossiya*, 19 September 1989.
15. See for example the article by G. Bordyugov, V. Kozlov and V. Loginov in *Kommunist*, no. 14, 1989, and their reply to critics in *ibid.*, no. 5, 1990, and the commemorative but not uncritical article by the respected Leningrad historian V. Startsev 'We are with Lenin', published on the occasion of the 120th Anniversary of Lenin's birth in *Pravda*, 3 April 1990.
16. The most important are N. I. Bukharin, *Izbrannye proizvedeniya* (1988), *Put' k sotsializmu* (Novosibirsk, 1990), and *Problemy teorii i praktiki sotsializma* (1989); his plenum speech appears on pp. 253–308 of the latter volume.
17. 'Evgenii Alekseevich Preobrazhenskii: shtrikhi k portretu', ms., 26 pp. A revised English-language version of this paper appeared in *Slavic Review*, vol. 50 (1991), pp. 286–96.
18. *Molodoi kommunist*, no. 8, 1989; *Voprosy istorii*, nos. 7, 8 and 9, 1989.
19. These included four volumes from the Trotsky archive in the United States, published by a Soviet cooperative in 100 000 copies: *Arkhiv Trotskogo: kommunisticheskaya oppozitsiya v SSSR, 1923–1927*, vols 1–4 ('Terra', 1990 – these were reprints of the Chalidze Publications edition, NY, 1988), and a selection of Trotsky's writings covering 1903–1939, the reprint of which alone was issued in 150 000 copies by the official publishing house Gospolitizdat: L. D. Trotsky, *K istorii russkoi revolyutsii* (1990). I am indebted to Darron Hincks for drawing my attention to these volumes.
20. *EKO*, no. 1, 1990, pp. 47–62; the same number contains (pp. 63–6) an article by A. V. Pantsov, 'Trotskii i Preobrazhenskii'.
21. The full text of the notes on Trotsky's speech by Bazhanov (who later emigrated), with full explanatory notes, was later published by V. P. Vilkova and V. P. Danilov in *Voprosy istorii KPSS*, no. 5, 1990, pp. 32–43.
22. *Voprosy istorii KPSS*, no. 3, 1990 (N. S. Simonov). For a similar approach, see M. M. Gorinov, *NEP: poisk putei razvitiya* (1990) – Znanie, Istoriya series, no. 2, 1990, and his article in *Voprosy istorii KPSS*, no. 1, 1990.
23. See *Izvestiya TsK*, no. 9, 1990, pp. 29–31.
24. *Pravda*, 6 June 1990.
25. *Pravda*, 31 May 1990.
26. For the proceedings, see *BBC Summary of World Broadcasts*, former Soviet Union (hereafter known as SWB), SU/0650, 30 December 1989 and *Izvestiya*, December 1989; for the Congress resolution, see *Pravda*, 28 December 1989.
27. *God krizisa, 1938–1939: dokumenty i materialy*, vol. 2 (1990), doc. 603; see *Soviet Studies*, vol. 44 (1992), p. 78, n. 51 (G. Roberts).
28. TASS statement, 23 December 1989 (see SWB, SU/0650, p. C/7).
29. *Izvestiya*, 6 November 1988 (V. Anan'ev, a chief inspector of the Ministry of Culture of the RSFSR).
30. *Moscow News*, no. 18, 1990 (this account by a journalist has several important inaccuracies); *Mezhdunarodnaya zhizn'*, no. 5, 1990, pp. 112–30 (in Russian) and *International Affairs*, June 1990, pp. 98–115, 144 (in English).
31. *Voenno-istoricheskii zhurnal*, no. 6, 1990, pp. 47–9 (Yu. N. Zorya); this is followed on pp. 49–57 by the texts of relevant documents, with specific

references to file numbers, prepared for publication by the Director of the
Central State Special Archive A. S. Prokopenko.
32.   TASS Report, 13 April 1990, cited in Radio Liberty *Report on the USSR*,
no. 16, 20 April 1990.

2   The XXVIII Party Congress

1.   *Pravda*, 26 November 1989 (this statement appears in Gorbachev's lengthy
article 'The Socialist Idea and Revolutionary *Perestroika*').
2.   *Pravda*, 6 February 1990 (report of 5 February).
3.   *The Sunday Telegraph*, 11 February 1990.
4.   *Pravda*, 11 April 1990.
5.   *Pravda*, 21 April 1990 (address of April 20).
6.   *The Guardian*, 20 June 1990 (report by Paul Quinn-Judge).
7.   *Izvestiya TsK KPSS*, no. 6, 1990, pp. 69–70 (speech of 25 December 1989).
8.   *Pravda*, 16 April 1990.
9.   'Diskussionyi listok' 11, *Pravda*, 3 March 1990 (Platform adopted 20–21
January 1990).
10. *Pravda*, 3 July 1990.
11. *Pravda*, 4 July 1990.
12. *Pravda*, 4 July 1990.
13. *Pravda*, 5 July 1990.
14. *Pravda*, 11 July 1990.
15. *Pravda*, 8 July 1990.
16. *Pravda*, 8 July 1990. See also the speech by the author Chingis Aitmatov
(a member of the Presidential Council) in *ibid.* 9 July 1990; he implicitly
rejects the whole course of development since 1917.
17. *Pravda*, 7 July 1990 (A. I. Teplenichev).
18. *Pravda*, 11 July 1990.
19. *Kommunist*, no. 10, 1990, pp. 7–8.
20. For the April 1987 questions see Davies (1989), p. 131.

3   The Leninist Counter-Offensive

1.   Reminiscences of Andrei Belyi, written just after Blok's death in August
1921; the sentence about 'The Twelve' is crossed out in the original
(*Literaturnaya gazeta*, 1 August 1990).
2.   *Literaturnaya gazeta*, 17 October 1990.
3.   *Literaturnaya gazeta*, 5 September 1990.
4.   *Literaturnaya gazeta*, 22 August 1990 (Karen Khachaturov).
5.   *Literaturnaya gazeta*, 4 July, 18 July 1990 (V. Golovanov).
6.   *Literaturnaya gazeta*, 29 August 1990.
7.   See *Pravda*, 13 February 1991 (V. Sokolov), citing N. Berdyaev, *The Fate
of Russian Communism* (1937).
8.   *Literaturnaya gazeta*, 7 November 1990.
9.   Reported in *Pravda*, 23 October 1990.
10. See Davies (1989), pp. 138–9.
11. See reports in *Pravda*, 11, 16 August 1990.
12. *Pravda*, 14 October 1990.

13. See Davies (1989), p. 4, and p. 7 above.
14. *Pravda*, 23 October 1990. *Kommunist*, no. 16, 1990, pp. 76–83, published a thoughtful discussion by Ioffe and the American historian Alex Rabinowitch about the historical choices in October 1917. For Brusilov, see Yu. V. Sokolov, *Krasnaya zvezda ili krest? (Zhizn' i sud'ba generala Brusilova)* (1994; 1000 copies).
15. *Pravda*, 1 December 1990.
16. *Pravda*, 17 January 1991.
17. *Komsomol'skaya pravda*, 16 January 1991. Readers will have noticed that, in common with many other Western historians, I simply call it 'the October revolution' . . .
18. *Pravda*, 21 January 1991.
19. *Pravda*, 4 February 1991; the other three were Burbulis, Sobchak and Starovoitova.
20. Cited from I. K. Polozkov, first secretary of the central committee of the party for the Russian republic, and E. I. Kalinina, a secretary of the Leningrad party regional committee – *Pravda*, 4 February 1991.
21. *Pravda*, 1 February 1991.
22. *Sovetskaya Rossiya*, 23 July 1991.
23. *Komsomol'skaya pravda*, 2 October 1991.
24. *Nezavisimaya gazeta*, 18 June 1991.
25. See Pikhoya's article in *Istochnik*, trial number (no. 0, 1993), p. 4.
26. *Pravda*, 1 March 1991.
27. See *Europe–Asia Studies* (formerly *Soviet Studies*), vol. 46 (1994), pp. 478–9 (J. Surovell).
28. *Pravda*, 25 April 1991.
29. *Pravda*, 26, 29 April 1991.
30. *Pravda*, 26 July 1991.
31. *Pravda*, 27 July 1991.
32. *Pravda*, 30 July 1991 (A. A. Prigarin).
33. *Pravda*, 30 July 1991 (M. N. Kachanov).
34. There are exceptions in both directions. The circulation of *Trud*, which was on the whole a pro-Gorbachev paper, kept up, while that of the more liberal *Literaturnaya gazeta* greatly declined.
35. *Chas pik* (Leningrad), 23 July 1990.

4 The Drive against Communism, 1991–2

1. *Pravda*, 8 August 1991.
2. *Pravda*, 15 August 1991. The document was headed 'Treaty on the Union of Sovereign States' – without the word 'Soviet', but the full title was used throughout the text.
3. Raisa Gorbacheva's diary entries for 5 and 7 August 1991, published in *Komsomol'skaya pravda*, 12 December 1991.
4. Diary entry for 13 August, *loc. cit.*
5. *Moskva*, no. 5, 1991.
6. *Pravda*, 20 August 1991; see also documents and statements in *ibid*. 21 August 1991.
7. See *Pravda*, 10 September 1991; the decree was issued on 29 August.

8. *Pravda*, 24 September 1991; *Nazavisimaya gazeta*, 17 September 1991.
9. *Summary of World Broadcasts* (henceforth SWB), 30 August 1991, reporting broadcast of 28 August.
10. *Guardian*, 31 January 1992.
11. B. El'tsin, *Zapiski prezidenta* (1994), p. 67; the preface is dated October 1993.
12. See E. Hobsbawm, *Age of Extremes: the Short Twentieth Century, 1914–1991* (London, 1994).
13. SWB, 19 November 1993 (interview, 16 November).
14. El'tsin (1994), p. 181.
15. *Literaturnaya gazeta*, 6 November 1991.
16. El'tsin (1994), pp. 121–5. The Yeltsin file was discovered by a Kazan' historian (*Izvestiya*, 28 September 1993).
17. Korolenko's letter to Lunacharsky, an old friend, cited by I. Dedkov in *Kommunist*, no. 1, 1991, p. 8. The letter, written on 4 August 1920, may be found in *V. G. Korolenko v gody revolyutsii i grazhdanskoi voiny: biograficheskaya khronika* (Benson, Vermont, 1985), pp. 395–404.
18. S. V. Kuleshov, *Velikii Oktyabr' i torzhestvo leninskoi natsional'noi programmy partii* (1987).
19. Private communication, courtesy of Guin Glasford.
20. *Komsomol'skaya pravda*, 21 September 1991 (letter dated 1–5 September).
21. *Rodina*, nos 6–7, 1991, p. 56; for his anti-semitism, see *Détente*, no. 8 (1987), pp. 5–7.
22. *Literaturnaya gazeta*, 6 November 1991.
23. *Sovetskaya Rossiya*, 3 August 1991.
24. *Pravda*, 5 October 1991; for Yakovlev's general views on social and economic issues at this time, see *Literaturnaya gazeta*, 28 August, 25 December 1991.
25. *Komsomol'skaya pravda*, 24 August 1991 (letter dated 19 August).
26. *Svobodnaya mysl'*, no. 18, 1991, pp. 30, 33 (Boris Grushin).
27. *Nezavisimaya gazeta*, 4 December 1991; Topolyansky drew on a respectable source – the émigré poet and writer Ivan Bunin, who received the Nobel Prize for Literature in 1933.
28. S. Selivestrov in *Nezavisimaya gazeta*, 17 November 1991.
29. Mary Dejevsky in *The Times*, 14 May 1992.
30. J. Steele, *Eternal Russia: Yeltsin, Gorbachev and the Mirage of Democracy* (1994), p. xiii. For a Russian criticism of the film, see A. Nemzer in *Nezavisimaya gazeta*, 27 June 1992.
31. *Modus vivendi*, June 1993, p. 5 (Yu. Polyakov).
32. *Komsomol'skaya pravda*, 12 February 1992.
33. See, for example, R. Hingley, *Stalin: Man and Legend* (London, 1974), p. 304; A. Werth, *Russia at War, 1941–1945* (1965 edn), p. 602.
34. *Izvestiya*, 15 October, 19 November 1992; the accompanying letter was also endorsed by Voroshilov, Molotov, Mikoyan, Kaganovich and Kalinin. The Beria letter and Politburo minute may also be found in *Voprosy istorii*, no. 1, 1993.
35. See V. Tolz, 'The Katyn Documents and the CPSU Hearings', Radio Free Europe/Radio Liberty *Research Report*, vol. 1, no. 44, 6 November 1992, pp. 27–33.

36. V. I. Boldin, *Krushenie p'edestala: shtrikhi k portretu M. S. Gorbacheva* (1995), pp. 257–8.
37. Poltoranin in *L'Unità*, 6 June 1992, and Radio Free Europe/Radio Liberty *Research Report*, 23 October 1992.
38. *Izvestiya*, 14 July, 8 October 1992.
39. *Izvestiya*, 30 May 1992.
40. *Pravda*, 23 August 1991 (conference of 22 August).
41. The other signatories were Butenko, prominent in 1988–91 as a fierce socialist critic of Stalinism (see *ibid.*, pp. 95–7), and V. Kelle, a philosopher.
42. See criticism in *Izvestiya*, 11 April 1992.
43. For Prokhanov, see Davies (1989), pp. 142–3; for Shafarevich and Sterligov see Chapters 1 and 5 of the present book.
44. Steele (London, 1994), pp. 324–5.
45. *Izvestiya*, 27 April 1992.
46. Radio Free Europe/Radio Liberty *Research Report*, no. 7, 12 February 1993.

5 The Mental Revolution after the First Decade

1. *Izvestiya*, 20 July 1993.
2. *Izvestiya*, 24 April 1993.
3. *Izvestiya*, 22 June 1993 (V. Izmozik).
4. *Izvestiya*, 30 October 1993.
5. *Izvestiya*, 17 July 1993.
6. *Izvestiya*, 24 April 1993.
7. *Izvestiya*, 16 November 1993.
8. *Nezavisimaya gazeta*, 4 June 1994 (Mariya Svidneva).
9. See for example *Moskovskaya pravda*, 14 June 1994, one of a series of articles by Lev Kolodnyi entitled 'Lenin Without a Mask'.
10. *Rossiiskaya gazeta*, 27 March 1993 (Anatolii Latyshev); see also pp. 137–8 below.
11. *Izvestiya*, 29 May 1993.
12. *Rossiiskaya gazeta*, 27 February 1993.
13. Lenin's Jewish origins were discussed in the émigré press in 1960 (*Novyi zhurnal*, no. 61 (1960), pp. 220–4), and first reported in the Soviet press in 1990 and 1991 (see for example *Ogonek*, no. 25, 1991 – Yu. Gavrilov; *Izvestiya*, 26 August 1991 – L. Osherova). Original documents and articles based on the archives appeared in 1992: *Otechestvennye arkhivy*, no. 2, 1992, pp. 38–45 (V. V. Tsaplin); no. 4, 1992, pp. 76–83 (documents). The issue continued to reverberate: see for example *Izvestiya*, 27 February 1993.
14. See Davies (1989), pp. 41–3.
15. D. Volkogonov, *Triumf i tragediya: politicheskii portret I. V. Stalina*, kniga 1, i–ii, kniga 2, i–ii (1989).
16. D. Volkogonov, *Lenin: politicheskii portret*, vols 1 and 2 (1994); 30 000 copies. See also the somewhat abridged English translation, D. Volkogonov, *Lenin: Life and Legacy* (London, 1994).
17. *Nezavisimaya gazeta*, 4 March 1993.
18. See Davies (1989), pp. 139–40.
19. *Sunday Telegraph*, 9 April 1995.
20. *Moskovskaya pravda*, 18 February 1994.

21. *Svobodnaya mysl'*, no. 6, 1995, pp. 111–12 (E. Zubkova).
22. *Izvestiya*, 16 October 1993 (Sergei Zhdakaev).
23. *Izvestiya*, 23 October 1993.
24. V. Suvorov (pseudonym of V. Rezun), *Ledokol* (1992) (first published in Stuttgart in German in 1989), and *Den'-M* (1994).
25. See *Rodina*, no. 5, 1994, p. 70.
26. The first instalment appeared on 20 October, the final instalment a couple of weeks before the election on 26 November.
27. *Otechestvennaya istoriya*, no. 4, 1993, pp. 19–31.
28. *Istoriya SSSR*, no. 3, 1991, pp. 16–28.
29. For Mel'tyukhov's article, see *Otechestvennaya istoriya*, no. 3, 1994, pp. 4–22; for the editorial discussion, see *ibid.*, nos 4–5, 1994, pp. 277–84. Publication was supported by A. N. Sakharov, V. S. Lel'chuk, L. N. Nezhinskii, the editor K. F. Shatsillo, Yu. S. Kukushkin and (with reservations) by S. V. Tyutyukhin and M. A. Rakhmatullin; and opposed by V. N. Bovykin, V. P. Dmitrenko, V. A. Fedorov, and L. V. Milov; Yu. A. Polyakov strongly criticised the articles, but did not commit himself on the publication issue.
30. *Prepodavanie istorii v shkole*, no. 3, 1993, pp. 23–7, no. 5, 1994, pp. 8–14; *Voprosy istorii*, no. 8, 1994, pp. 164–70; *Rossiskaya gazeta*, 21 September 1994; *Otechestvennaya istoriya*, no. 2, 1995, pp. 53–85. See also the collection of articles edited by Nevezhin and dominated by his own point of view: *Gotovil li Stalin nastupatel'nuyu voinu protiv Gitlera?: nezaplanirovannaya diskussiya: sbornik statei* (1995).
31. *Isskustvo kino*, no. 5, 1993, pp. 10–16; *Novaya i noveishaya istoriya*, no. 3, 1993, pp. 29–45; *Istoricheskii arkhiv*, no. 2, 1995, pp. 23–31.
32. For the Russian translation of these documents, and a careful commentary on the Western literature entitled 'Strategic Planning of Aggression against the USSR', by V. I. Dashichev, see *Voenno-istoricheskii zhurnal*, no. 3, 1991, pp. 10–38.
33. G. Gorodetskii, *Mif 'Ledokola': nakanune voiny* (1995).
34. *Rodina*, no. 6, 1995, pp. 67–72.
35. BBC SWB, 6 October 1993 (broadcast 4 October). (BBC SWB here and elsewhere refers to the British Broadcasting Corporation *Daily Summary of World Broadcasts: the former Soviet Union*.)
36. BBC SWB, 8 October 1993 (broadcast 6 October).
37. *Izvestiya*, 23 September 1993 (Leonid Nikitinskii). The slogan 'Stalin is Lenin Today' was a cliché in Stalin's time.
38. *Izvestiya*, 16 November 1993.
39. SWB, 11 November 1993 (statement of 9 November).
40. SWB, 8 October 1993 (statement of 5 October).
41. SWB, 8 October 1993.
42. SWB, 9 and 10 November 1993 (despatches of 7 and 8 November).
43. *The Guardian*, 20 October; *Izvestiya*, 21 October 1993.
44. *Rodina*, no. 1, 1994, p. 39.
45. *Guardian*, 20 October 1993.
46. *Izvestiya*, 23 October 1993.
47. *Izvestiya*, 3 December 1993 (decree of 30 November).
48. *Istoriya sovremennoi Rossii* (1994), pp. 202–3. The Emblem is depicted on the front cover of *Rodina*, no. 1, 1994.

49. A. L. Khoroshkevich, *Simvoly russkoi gosudarstvennosti* (1993, 10 000 copies), p. 79.
50. N. Ryzhkov, *Perestroika; istoriya predatel'stv* (1992), p. 129.
51. 'Social Snobbism as a Russian Phenomenon', in *Svobodnaya mysl'*, no. 11, 1995, pp. 3–4.
52. See *Svobodnaya mysl'*, *op. cit.* p. 4, citing *Nezavisimaya gazeta*, December 11, 1992, and *Literaturnaya gazeta*, 12 May 1993.
53. K. Marx, *The Eighteenth Brumaire of Louis Bonaparte* (London, 1926), p. 83.
54. *Izvestiya*, 17 November 1993.
55. For a similar point of view to mine, see *Svobodnaya mysl'*, no. 11, 1995, pp. 3–15.
56. *Svobodnaya mysl'*, nos 17–18, 1993, p. 13.
57. See *Svobodnaya mysl'*, no. 11, 1995, p. 7.
58. On *vintiki*, see Davies (1989), pp. 80–1.
59. V. Rogovin, *Stalinskii Neonep* ([1995]), p. 347.
60. G. Zyuganov, *Derzhava* (1994), p. 5.
61. *Ibid.*, pp. 102, 79.
62. *Ibid.*, pp. 14–16.
63. *Ibid.*, pp. 18–20.
64. *Ibid.*, p. 66.
65. *Sovetskaya Rossiya*, 31 August 1995.
66. *Pravda*, 5 May 1993 ('A Satanic Tribe', by D. Gerasimov) and 17 June 1993.
67. *Pravda*, 20 September 1995.
68. R. I. Kosolapov (ed.), *Slovo tovarishchu Stalinu* (1995); see also the extremely critical review by L. Onikov, also a former party official, *Nezavisimaya gazeta*, 26 December 1995.
69. *Financial Times*, 11/12 November 1995 (John Lloyd).
70. *Pravda*, 29 June 1993; *Izvestiya*, 3 July 1993.
71. *Zavtra*, no. 19, May 1994. In recent years some objective studies by historians of the role of the Masons have also been published.
72. For fascist extremism in Russia, see *Transition*, 23 June 1995, pp. 2–15.
73. See *Transition*, 8 September 1995, p. 35.
74. See the acid comments by Academician Volobuev in *Pravda*, 15 March 1995.
75. BBC SWB, Soviet Union, 1 December 1993 (broadcast of 26 November).
76. Zhirinovskii, *O sud'bakh Rossii*, vol. 2, *Poslednii nabrosok na yug* (1994), pp. 35–6.
77. Zhirinovskii, vol. 1, p. 29.
78. A. Lebed', *Za derzhavu obidno . . .* (1995), p. 423.
79. *Ibid.*, pp. 434–5.
80. *Ibid.*, pp. 440–1.
81. *Nezavisimaya gazeta*, 28 November 1992; see also Steele (1994), pp. 303–5.
82. See Davies (1989), pp. 187–8, and p. 9 above.
83. Private conversation, September 1994.
84. A. Zinoviev, *Katastroika: Legend and Reality of Gorbachevism* (London and Lexington, 1990).

85. *Pravda*, 11 March 1993.
86. *Pravda*, 17 May, 19 July 1995.
87. *Izvestiya*, 21 September 1993.
88. *Izvestiya*, 12 December 1993.
89. *Izvestiya*, 28 May, 21 September 1995.
90. *Meeting Report*, Kennan Institute for Advanced Russian Studies, vol. xii, no. 8 [1995] (lecture on 8 December 1994).
91. *Svobodnaya mysl'*, nos. 17–18, 1994, pp. 5, 13–15.
92. SWB, 17 December 1993 (statement of 15 December).
93. *Izvestiya*, 25 August 1993.
94. Private communication. The Gorki museum had already been renamed a museum of popular history in 1993, but continued to exhibit the Leniniana from Lenin's stay there in his last years.
95. *Argumenty i fakty*, no. 33, August 1995.
96. *St Petersburg Press*, 7–13 February 1995, Supplement.
97. *The Guardian*, 15 March 1996.
98. *The Guardian*, 28 February 1995.
99. *Krasnaya zvezda*, 18 March 1995; *Istoricheskii arkhiv*, no. 3, 1995, pp. 84–110.
100. *Nezavisimaya gazeta*, 8 October 1995.
101. *Sunday Times*, 9 April 1995.
102. *The Guardian*, 4 May 1995.
103. BBC SWB, Soviet Union, 28 December 1995 (statement on 26 December).
104. Davies (1989), p. 199.
105. *The Guardian*, 6 May 1995; *International Herald Tribune*, 10 May 1995; BBC TV transmission, 9 May 1995.
106. *International Herald Tribune*, 10 May 1995.
107. M. S. Gorbachev, *Zhizn' i reformy*, vol. 1 (1995), p. 333.
108. *Iskusstvo kino*, no. 5, 1993 (Olga Kuz'mina).
109. *Novoe vremya*, no. 6, 1996, pp. 40–1.
110. *Iskusstvo kino*, no. 5, 1995, pp. 59–60.
111. *Transition*, 22 September 1995, pp. 63–5.
112. See BBC SWB, Soviet Union, January 1, 1996 (statement of 29 December 1995).
113. *The Economist*, 27 January 1996.
114. BBC SWB, Soviet Union, 28 December 1995 (statement on 26 December).
115. *Rossiskaya gazeta*, 27 February 1996.
116. BBC SWB, Soviet Union, 21 December 1995 (statement of 20 December).
117. *Rossiskaya gazeta*, 27 February 1996.
118. BBC SWB, Soviet Union, 2 December 1995 (instruction of 30 November).
119. SWB, 21 February 1996.
120. BBC SWB, 13 February 1996 (interview on 11 February).
121. BBC SWB, 14 February 1996 (statement of 13 February).
122. *Kuda idet Rossiya?: alternativy obshchestvennogo razvitiya*, vypusk 2 (1995), p. 221 (Yu. A. Levada).
123. See p. 48 above. The April 1992 survey was in Moscow alone; attitudes in Moscow were likely to be more unfavourable to Lenin than in the country as a whole, so the shift against Lenin was probably greater than these figures indicate.
124. *Ibid.*, p. 195 (L. A. Sedov).

125. SWB, 5 December 1995 (Moscow radio, 3 December).
126. *Izvestiya*, 24 July 1993.

PART II   THE BATTLE FOR THE ARCHIVES

6   Before Perestroika: The Historical Background

1. For Lenin's decree and an account of earlier Soviet discussions see the article by Patricia Grimsted in *American Archivist*, vol. 45 (1982), pp. 429–43.
2. P. K. Grimsted, *Intellectual Access and Descriptive Standards for Post-Soviet Archives* (IREX, Princeton, NJ, 1992), pp. 9–10.
3. *Otechestrennye arkhivy*, no. 3, 1992, pp. 19, 22–3 (V. E. Korneev and O. N. Kopylova).
4. See *Sovetskie arkhivy*, no. 5, 1990, pp. 37–44 (O. N. Kopylova).
5. For example, *Materialy po istorii SSSR*, vol. 7 (1959); *Pervye shagi industrializatsii SSSR (1926–1927gg.)* (1959).
6. *Voprosy istorii KPSS*, no. 1, 1990, p. 56 (V. V. Tsaplin).
7. *Krokodil'*, no. 26, 1989, p. 4 (R. Petrov).
8. *Literaturnaya gazeta*, 16 August 1989 (V. P. Kozlov).
9. *Voprosy istorii KPSS*, no. 1, 1990, p. 54.
10. *Voprosy istorii KPSS*, no. 1, 1990, p. 4.
11. *Dokumenty vneshnei politiki SSSR*.
12. *V. I. Lenin i VChK: sbornik dokumentov (1917–1922gg.)* (1975) is the most important collection; it was competently edited by S. K. Tsvigun, a deputy head of the KGB who was later in disgrace and committed suicide.
13. See the account in *Izvestiya*, 17 February 1990 (E. Maksimova) and in *American Archivist*, vol. 55 (1992), pp. 108–10.
14. *Literaturnaya gazeta*, 28 August 1991 (E. Kuz'min).
15. *Literaturnaya gazeta*, 28 August 1991 (E. Kuz'min).
16. GARF, fond 5446, op. 27, d. 23, ll. 140, 139, 139ob (a printed 'List of Information Constituting a State Secret (in Peacetime)', a 149-page document).

7   The Opening of the Archives

1. *Pravitel'stvennyi vestnik*, no. 5, January 1990; *Voprosy istorii KPSS*, no. 7, 1990, pp. 46–50.
2. *Sovetskie arkhivy*, no. 4, 1990, p. 37.
3. See Davies (1989), pp. 171–3. For an informative memoir about Vaganov and his predecessors as director of Glavarkhiv, see *Otechestvennye arkhivy*, no. 5, 1995, pp. 11–23 (V. V. Tsaplin).
4. See for example *Sotsiologicheskie issledovaniya*, no. 10, 1991, pp. 3–21 (Zemskov). The NKVD *fond* was located in TsGAOR (now GARF).
5. *Literaturnaya gazeta*, 19 July 1989.
6. D. N. Nokhotovich, from TsGAOR (now GARF) – *Sovetskie arkhivy*, no. 4, 1990, p. 35.
7. *Voprosy istorii*, no. 4, 1989, pp. 175–81.

8. *Sovetskie arkhivy*, no. 6, 1990, p. 12.
9. *Komsomol'skaya pravda*, 17 October 1990.
10. V. Shentalinsky, *The KGB's Literary Archive* (London, 1995).
11. *Loc. cit.*; see also *Sovetskie arkhivy*, no. 6, 1990, p. 10.
12. 'Loi sur le Fonds d'Archives de l'Etat de l'URSS' (mimeographed [1990]), arts. 5, 20. The word *'fond'* was used to refer both to all archival material relating to the USSR, and to mean a group of records – e.g. the *fond* of Gosplan or the NKVD. For comments on the draft Law, see *Voprosy istorii KPSS*, no. 1, 1990, p. 59.
13. *Vestnik Akademii Nauk SSSR*, no. 10, 1989, pp. 75–87.
14. *Pravitel'stvennyi vestnik*, no. 5, January 1990.
15. *Sovetskie arkhivy*, no. 1, 1991, pp. 17, 18.
16. *Sovetskie arkhivy*, no. 1, 1991, p. 16. For further details, see *American Archivist*, vol. 55 (1992), pp. 96–7 (Grimsted).
17. *Izvestiya*, 28–29 August 1991; *Otechestvennye arkhivy*, no. 1, 1992, p. 3.
18. Interview with Pikhoya, Autumn 1991.
19. *Otechestvennye arkhivy*, no. 1, 1992, p. 6.
20. *Rodina*, no. 1, 1992, p. 81.
21. See *American Archivist*, vol. 55 (1992), pp. 101–2 (Grimsted).
22. *Otechestvennye arkhivy*, no. 1, 1992, pp. 23, 28.
23. A brief polite obituary appeared in *Otechestvennye arkhivy*, no. 6, 1993, p. 120.
24. *Otechestvennye arkhivy*, no. 2, 1992, p. 16.
25. *Otechestvennye arkhivy*, no. 1, 1992, p. 4.
26. *Ibid.*, no. 2, 1992, pp. 3–4; *Izvestiya*, 25 February 1992.
27. See E. Bacon, *The Gulag at War: Stalin's Forced Labour System in the Light of the Archives* (1994) and Getty, Rittersporn and Zemskov in *American Historical Review*, October 1993, both based on material collected before the end of 1992.

8 Persistent Problems

1. *Izvestiya*, 18 September 1991 (E. Maksimova).
2. *Sunday Times*, 3 November 1991.
3. *American Archivist*, vol. 56 (1993), p. 618 (Grimsted).
4. *Otechestvennye arkhivy*, no. 5, 1993, pp. 11–13.
5. See *Bulletin*, Cold War Project, no. 5 (1995), pp. 1–9 (K. Weatherby).
6. *Slavic Review*, vol. 52 (1993), p. 102 (J. A. Getty). For an authoritative report on access, see the final report of the American 'task force', *Slavic Review*, vol. 54 (1995), pp. 407–26.
7. *Stalinskoe Politbyuro v 30-e gody: sbornik dokumentov*, compiled by O. V. Khlevnyuk, A. V. Kvashonkin, L. P. Kosheleva and L. A. Rogovaya (1995). The coordinator of the project is Andrea Graziosi. The book's findings are discussed in Chapter 12 below.
8. *Annali* of the Feltrinelli Institute, vol. 30 (1994): *The Cominform: Minutes of the Three Conferences 1947/1948/1949*, ed. G. Procacci with G. Adibekov, A. Di Biagio, L. Gibianskii, F. Gori, S. Pons.
9. *Slavic Review*, vol. 52 (1993), pp. 82–3; Cold War *Bulletin*, no. 3 (1993),

pp. 23, 36–7. And see Martin Walker's report of Washington press conference, *The Guardian*, 25 June 1992. For further details see *American Archivist*, vol. 56 (1993), p. 639 (Grimsted).

10. *Nezavisimaya gazeta*, 20 December 1995.
11. Cold War *Bulletin*, no. 3 (1993), p. 23 (Mark Kramer).
12. J. Costello and O. Tsarev, *Deadly Illusions* (1993).
13. *Nezavisimaya gazeta*, 20 December 1995.
14. M. D. Steinberg and V. M. Khrustalev, *The Fall of the Romanovs: Political Dreams and Personal Struggles in a Time of Revolution* (New Haven and London, 1995).
15. *The Secret World of American Communism*, ed. H. Klehr, J. E. Haynes and F. I. Firsov (New Haven and London, 1995).
16. *Slavic Review*, vol. 54 (1995), pp. 429–30; and see the exchange between Klehr and Rieber in *ibid.*, pp. 1154–5.
17. See *American Archivist*, vol. 56 (1993), p. 640 (Grimsted).
18. See p. 109 below and *Segodnya*, 7 October 1995 (O. Shishkin).
19. See *Slavic Review*, vol. 52 (1993), p. 88; Cold War *Bulletin*, no. 3 (1993), pp. 24–5; *AAASS Newsletter*, November 1992.
20. *Rossiskaya gazeta*, 15 May 1992.
21. *Izvestiya*, 9 March 1992; see Pikhoya's reply, 'Facts and Inventions', *ibid.* 17 March 1992.
22. Further discussion about the Hoover project in the Russian press is summarised in *American Archivist*, vol. 56 (1993), pp. 643–5 (Grimsted).
23. See *Izvestiya*, 24 January 1992.
24. *Izvestiya*, 17 January 1996 (E. Maksimova).
25. *Rossiiskie vesti*, 23 January 1996.
26. *Times Literary Supplement*, 31 March 1995. For a critical review of Volkogonov's books, claiming – rightly, but sometimes over-pedantically – that he made many factual errors, see for example *Svobodnaya mysl'*, no. 3, 1993, pp. 44–51 (A. Maksimenko).
27. *The Independent*, 4 July 1992; the official concerned was V. Tarasov.
28. 12 April 1993.
29. The 'Morris affair' is fully described by Mark Kramer in Cold War *Bulletin*, no. 3 (1993), pp. 18, 28–31. Kramer points out that the tightening up was not entirely due to the Morris affair: Vladimir Chernous, one of Pikhoya's deputies and a man with a liberal approach to access, had already been dismissed in February 1993 – though his dismissal was also accompanied by charges of shady financial dealings.
30. *Ibid.*, p. 18. Prokopenko was in turn succeeded by Natalya Tomilina in the autumn of 1993.
31. *Izvestiya*, 6 February 1992.
32. *The Guardian*, 6 February, 25–6 April 1992. The latter group of documents was shown 'exclusively' to *The Guardian*.
33. Dr Silvio Pons kindly helped me to untangle the intricacies of this affair.
34. *Otechestvennye arkhivy*, no. 3, 1992, pp. 89–97, which prints Russian translations of Togliatti's and Bianco's letters. The letters are preserved in the Togliatti files (fond 527), and Bianco's memorandum to the NKVD in the files of the Executive Committee of Comintern (fond 495).

35. *La Stampa*, 14 February 1992, claimed to have found twelve errors in the *Panorama* extract, and reproduced both the *Panorama* text and the original version.
36. *Otechestvennye arkhivy*, no. 2, 1992, p. 14.
37. *Ibid.*, no. 3, 1992, p. 89.
38. *Ibid.*, no. 2, 1992, p. 14.
39. *Voprosy istorii estestvoznaniya i tekhniki*, no. 3, 1992, pp. 103–34.
40. See the commentary by David Holloway, the historian of the Soviet bomb project. He concluded that the document 'might help someone who wished to build' a bomb: *The Bulletin of Atomic Scientists*, vol. 50, no. 1, pp. 62–3; Cold War *Bulletin*, no. 4, pp. 4, 8–9.
41. See the decree of the Supreme Soviet of 19 June 1992 'On the Provisional Procedure for Access to Archival Documents and their Utilisation'; and also the 'Principles of the Legislation of the Russian Federation on the Archival Fund of the Russian Federation and the Archives', approved by Yeltsin on 7 July 1993 (*Otechestvennye arkhivy*, no. 5, 1992, p. 3; *ibid.*, no. 5, 1993, p. 9).
42. *Slavic Review*, vol. 54 (1995), p. 415; and personal communication.
43. 27 April 1995.
44. For the directive and the names of members of the Commission see *Otechestvennye arkhivy*, no. 1, 1995, pp. 3–4.
45. *Rossiskaya gazeta*, 22 February 1995; and see Cold War *Bulletin*, no. 5 (1995), p. 77.
46. *Rossiiskaya gazeta*, 27 December 1995.
47. *Rossiskie vesti*, 23 January 1996.
48. *Rossiiskaya gazeta*, 1 February 1996.
49. *International Herald Tribune*, 27 April 1995.
50. A. Vatlin in G. Bordyugov, ed., *Istoricheskie issledovaniya v Rossii* (forthcoming); *Segodnya*, 7 October 1995 (O. Shishkin).
51. Private communications.
52. Vatlin, *loc. cit.*
53. *Izvestiya*, 28 August 1991 – statement by V. I. Abramov.
54. *Krasnaya zvezda*, 13 November 1991.
55. *Izvestiya*, 24 January 1992.
56. See Cold War *Bulletin*, no. 3 (1993), p. 24.
57. Information from Patricia Grimsted.
58. *Izvestiya*, 9 June 1992.
59. See for example *Izvestiya*, 26 November 1992.
60. See Cold War *Bulletin*, no. 4 (1994), p. 9 (D. Holloway).
61. *Organy gosudarsvennoi bezopasnosti v Velikoi Otechestvennoi Voine*, vol. 1, *Nakunune*, books i–ii (1995); *Sekrety Gitlera na stole u Stalina: razvedka i kontrrazvedka o podgotovke Germanskoi agressii protiv SSSR, mart-iyun' 1941g.* (1995).
62. *Otechestvennye arkhivy*, no. 1, 1992, p. 6; *Svobodnaya mysl'*, no. 14, 1992, p. 120n.
63. See the Politburo decision of 23 June 1990, reprinted in *Istochnik*, no. 1, 1995, p. 115.
64. *Istochnik*, no. 1, 1995, p. 115.
65. *Izvestiya*, 6 June 1992.

66. *Rossiiskaya gazeta*, 10 June 1992.
67. *Svobodnaya mysl'*, no. 14, 1992, pp. 120–1 (the letter is cited in full in an article by A. Chechevishnikov).
68. *Izvestiya*, 26 November 1992.
69. 13 July 1994.
70. *Rossiiskaya gazeta*, 27 August 1994 (interview with A. Batygin).
71. Tikhvinskii, Rzhevskii and Sevastyanov. Pikoya was himself engaged in personal research on post-war political history in the Presidential Archive, although he is primarily a pre-revolutionary historian, and in any case as head of Rosarkhiv was supposed to be securing the transfer of the Archive to state archives where its materials could be used by historians without special privileges (see his article on the XX Party Congress in *Rossiiskie vesti*, 21 February 1996).
72. *Otechestvennye arkhivy*, no. 1, 1995, p. 3. For other aspects of this directive, see p. 108 above.
73. *Istochnik*, no. 1, 1995, pp. 113–60; the announcement appears on p. 114. Further inserts of the *Vestnik* appear in each subsequent issue.

PART III   THE NEW SOVIET HISTORY

1. *Zvezda*, no. 1, 1996, pp. 186–7.
2. E. Karr, *Bol'shevistskaya revolyutsiya, 1917–1923* (1990).
3. O. Khlevnyuk, *1937-i: Stalin, NKVD i sovetskoe obshchestvo* (1990).
4. O. Khlevnyuk, *Stalin i Ordzhonikidze: konflikty v Politbyuro v 30-e gody* (1993).
5. Goland (1993); for this book see Chapter 11 below.
6. This work is surveyed in G. Bordyugov, ed., *Istoricheskie issledovaniya v Rossii* (forthcoming). Unfortunately Elaine McClarland's Emory College dissertation on Soviet history writing was available too late to be used here.

9   Teaching about the Soviet Past

1. For a careful account of history teaching and textbooks in 1989–92 see Janet G. Vaillant's chapter in A. Jones (ed.), *Education and Society in the New Russia* (Armonk, NY and London, 1994), pp. 141–68.
2. Yu. S. Borisov, *Istoriya SSSR: materialy k uchebniku dlya devyatogo klassa srednego shkoly* (1989).
3. See Davies (1989), pp. 169–70.
4. Yu. I. Korablev, I. A. Fedosov, Yu. S. Borisov, *Istoriya SSSR: uchebnik dlya desyatogo klassa srednei shkoly* (1989). For a similar approach in the syllabus for students applying for entry into higher education establishments in 1990, see *Spravochnik dlya postupayushchikh v vysshie uchebnye zavedeniya v 1990 godu* (1990), p. 388.
5. See Harold Shukman's account of history lessons which he attended in Moscow schools in September 1989 (*The Times Higher Educational Supplement*, 2 March 1990).
6. See Davies (1989), p. 184.
7. *Prepodavanie istorii v shkole*, no. 2, 1989, pp. 3–4; *Uchitel'skaya gazeta*, 31 January 1989.

8. *Pravda*, 13 January 1989 (G. V. Klokova).
9. *Nashe otechestvo: opyt politicheskoi istorii*, vols 1 and 2 (1991), edited by S. V. Kuleshov, O. V. Volobuev and E. I. Pivovar; signed for the press on 28 June 1991.
10. L. N. Zharova, I. A. Mishina, *Istoriya otechestva, 1900–1940: uchebnaya kniga dlya starshikh klassov srednikh uchebnykh zavedenii* (1992). This textbook is discussed together with others by A. P. Ševyrev in *Internationale Schulbuchforschung*, no. 4, 1995, pp. 397–424.
11. Zharova and Mishina (1992), p. 162.
12. *Ibid.*, pp. 293–5.
13. *Ibid.*, p. 305.
14. *Primernye voprosy po predmetam dlya provedeniya itogovoi attestatsii vypusknikov XI (XII) klassa srednei (polnoi) obshcheobrazovatel'noi shkoly v 1993/94 uchebnom godu* (1993), pp. 8–9.
15. *Programma dlya obshcheobrazovatel'nykh uchebnykh zavedenii: istoriya, 6–11 klassy* (1992), pp. 58, 66–9; *Primernye voprosy* (1993), pp. 8–9.
16. *ISSE Newsletter* (Indiana University), vol. 1, no. 2 (July 1992), pp. 25–9 (J. Vaillant).
17. R. Lewis, M. Newitt and A. Sokolov, *Reform of Teaching and Research in Russia: a Report to the Nuffield Foundation on a Pilot Project* (Exeter, 1993), pp. 24–7 (report by John Laver).
18. *Otechestvennaya istoriya*, no. 6, 1994, p. 142 (L. S. Leonova).
19. 'The Strategy of Development of Historical and Social Education in General Educational Establishments', *Ministerstvo Obrazovaniya Rossiiskoi Federatsii: reshenie kollegii*, no. 24/1, 28 December 1994.
20. Information from Russian teachers.
21. A. A. Danilov, L. G. Kosulina, *Istoriya Rossiya: XX vek: uchebnaya kniga dlya 9 klassa obshcheobrazovatel'nykh uchrezhdenii* (1995); signed for the press 23 May 1995; 275 000 copies.
22. V. P. Ostrovskii, A. I. Utkin, *Istoriya Rossii: XX vek; 11 klass: uchebnik dlya obshcheobrazovatel'nykh uchebnykh uchrezhdenii* (1995); signed for the press 27 July 1995; 300 000 copies.
23. I. I. Dolutskii, *Otechestvennaya istoriya XX vek: uchebnik dlya X klassa srednei shkoly*, chast' I (1994); 200 000 copies.
24. *Prepodavanie istorii v shkole*, nos 1 and 2, 1996.
25. Ostrovskii and Utkin (1995), pp. 130, 189–90.
26. P. N. Zyryanov, *Istoriya Rossii: XX vek: uchebnaya kniga dlya 9-ogo klassa srednei shkoly* (1994), pp. 43, 105 (the textbook was evidently written before Twentieth-Century Russian history was transferred to Year IX). See also *Svobodnaya mysl'*, no. 11, 1995, p. 120.
27. Ostrovskii and Utkin (1995), p. 210.
28. *Ibid.*, pp. 244–5.
29. D. I. Ilovaiskii, *Kratkie ocherki russkoi istorii: kurs starshego vozrasta* (1992).
30. *The Harriman Institute Forum*, vol. 6, no. 8 (April 1993), pp. 4, 7 (E. K. Valkenier).
31. V. O. Kluchevskii, *Kratkoe posobie po russkoi istorii* (1992).
32. A. K. Sokolov, *Lektsii po sovetskoi istorii, 1917–1940* (1995); published by the enterprising Mosgorarkhiv, which also issued the new book on Moscow in 1941–5 (see pp. 198–200 above).

33. *Istoriya sovremennoi Rossii, 1985–1994: eksperimental'noe uchebnoe posobie* (1995); sent to press 9 November 1994; 50 000 copies. This institute is also issuing textbooks on general history, from the Stone Age onwards, for primary schools (*Po sledam proshlogo*) – see *Prepodavanie istorii v shkole*, no. 8, 1995, 43–4 (L. N. Dobrokhotov).
34. See *Prepodavanie istorii v shkole*, no. 6, 1994, pp. 27–36 (A. Polonskii).
35. See *Education*, vol. 184, no. 25 (16 December 1994), p. 509.
36. On this, see A. Jones (ed.) (1994), pp. 151–2 (Vaillant).
37. Visited by Stephen Webber, December 1995.

10 Lenin and the Civil War

1. See the discussion in *Svobodnaya mysl'*, no. 10, 1994 (V. Zotov), no. 8, 1995 (P. Lukichev and A. Skorik) and no. 11, 1995 (V. Tishkov).
2. For the information in the previous two paragraphs see *Voprosy istorii*, no. 10, 1990, pp. 108–12 and no. 1, 1994, pp. 42–4; *Izvestiya TsK*, no. 6, 1989, pp. 177–8.
3. V. L. Genis, 'Razkazachivanie v Sovetskoi Rossii', *Voprosy istorii*, no. 1, 1994, pp. 42–55; the material in this section is taken from this article unless otherwise stated. See also R. A. Medvedev and S. P. Starikov, *Zhizn' i gibel' Filippa Kuz'micha Mironova* (1989), and E. Losev, *Mironov* (1991).
4. This directive was first published in full in *Moskva*, no. 2, 1989; see also *Izvestiya TsK*, no. 6, 1989, pp. 177–8.
5. See *Pravda*, 1 April 1991 (E. Losev).
6. *Krest'yanskoe vosstanie v Tambovskoi gubernii v 1919–1921gg. ('Antonovshchina'): dokumenty i materialy* (Tambov, 1994) – 334 pp., 3025 copies. For the standard Western history of the uprising, which fits in well with the Russian version based on the archives, see O. H. Radkey, *The Unknown Civil War in Russia: a Study of the Green Movement in the Tambov Region* (Stanford, 1976), and the shorter account in C. Read, *From Tsar to Soviets* (London, 1996), pp. 266–72.
7. *Krest'yanskoe vosstanie* (1994), pp. 14, 150 (Cheka report of April 1921).
8. *Ibid.*, p. 95 (Statute of 9 January 1921).
9. *Ibid.*, p. 181; see also p. 85. For an example of torture, see *ibid.*, p. 187.
10. See for example Order No. 130, dated 12 May 1921 (*ibid.*, p. 162).
11. *Ibid.*, pp. 178–9.
12. For a Tambov example, see the Order of 25 July 1919, *ibid.*, p. 33.
13. *Ibid.*, p. 57.
14. *Ibid.*, pp. 186, 238 (dated 22 June 20 July 1921).
15. *Ibid.*, p. 188 (report of June 1921).
16. *Voenno-istoricheskii zhurnal*, no. 1, 1993, p. 53 (P. A. Aptekar').
17. *Krest'yanskoe vosstanie* (1994), p. 16; see also p. 185. No further details are provided.
18. *Ibid.*, pp. 226–7 (doc. 271) – the VTsIK proposal is reported in a letter to Trotsky by Rykov, dated 18 July.
19. *Ibid.*, pp. 16–17.
20. *Ibid.*, pp. 226–7 (docs. 270, 272).
21. *Ibid.*, p. 228 (dated 20 July).

242   *Notes to pp. 132–41*

22. *Ibid.*, pp. 223–4 (report from S. S. Kamenev, Commander in Chief of Red Army, dated 16 July).
23. *Vek*, 7 April 1995.
24. See the biographies of Antonov and others in *Krest'yanskoe vosstanie* (1994), pp. 309–10.
25. See the declaration by the SR leader Yu. N. Podbel'skii, *ibid.*, pp. 244–6 (dated July 1921) – reprinted from publication of Institute of Social History, Amsterdam. See also the editors' comments, *ibid.*, pp. 11–12.
26. *Vek*, 7 April 1995.
27. Cited in S. Tsakunov, *V labirinte doktriny: iz opyta razrabotki ekonomicheskogo kursa strany v 1920-e gody* (1994), p. 59.
28. *Krest'yanskoe vosstanie* (1994), pp. 79–80; this is the version of the programme of the Union of Labouring Peasantry adopted by the Tambov provincial committee in December 1920.
29. *Otechestvennaya istoriya*, no. 4, 1993, pp. 60–72, especially p. 71 (S. A. Esikov and V. V. Kanishchev); see also *Voprosy istorii*, nos 6–7, 1992, pp. 47–57 (Esikov and L. G. Protasov).
30. *Krest'yanskoe vosstanie* (1994), pp. 67–8, 76.
31. See for example *ibid.*, pp. 120–1.

11 Lenin, Stalin and the New Economic Policy

1. Tsakunov (1994), p. 56.
2. Cited from the account in Tsakunov, *op. cit.*, pp. 55–9 and R. Service, *Lenin: a Political Life*, vol. 3 (1995), pp. 207–11.
3. *Izvestiya TsK*, no. 12, 1989, p. 200.
4. *Rossiiskaya gazeta*, 27 March 1993 (Anatolii Latyshev).
5. *Izvestiya TsK*, no. 12, 1989, p. 198.
6. L. Trotski, *Stalin: an Appraisal of the Man and his Influence* (1947), pp. 376–8, 381.
7. *Izvestiya TsK*, no. 12, 1989, pp. 197–8.
8. See M. Lewin, *Lenin's Last Struggle* (1969), ch. 4 and Appendices I–III.
9. See the documents for the period August–October 1922 in *Izvestiya TsK*, no. 9, 1989, pp. 191–218.
10. See the Politburo decision of 18 December, Lenin and Krupskaya's note to Trotsky of 21 December, Kamenev's note to Stalin [21 or 22 December], Stalin's note to Kamenev of 22 December, Krupskaya's note to Kamenev of 23 December, in *Izvestiya TsK*, no. 12, 1989, pp. 189–92. The documents of 21 December and (in part) of 23 December were previously available.
11. *Ibid.*, p. 198.
12. *Ibid.*, pp. 198–9.
13. *Ibid.*, p. 199.
14. *Ibid.*, pp. 192–3. Lenin's letter has been available since 1956, Stalin's reply was first published in 1989.
15. *Izvestiya TsK*, no. 9, 1989, pp. 208–9.
16. *Izvestiya TsK*, no. 9, 1990, pp. 152–3.
17. *Izvestiya TsK*, no. 4, 1991, p. 171 – the first publication of the proceedings of this section.
18. *Izvestiya TsK*, no. 4, 1991, pp. 179–91.

19. *Socialism in One Country, 1924–1926*, vol. 1 (1958), p. 186.
20. The documents are printed from the Gosplan archives with a commentary by E. A. Tyurina, now director of RGAE, the economic archive, in *Izvestiya Akademii Nauk: seriya ekonomicheskaya*, no. 2, 1991, pp. 128–40. See also *Svobodnaya mysl'*, no. 3, 1992, pp. 57–67 (V. Mau).
21. Yu. Goland, *Valyutnoe regulirovanie v period NEPa* (1993); 300 copies. Most of this study has been published in English translation in *Europe–Asia Studies*, vol. 46 (1994), pp. 1251–96.

12 Stalin and his Entourage

1. O. V. Khlevnyuk, A. V. Kvashonkin, L. P. Kosheleva, L. A. Rogovaya, compilers, *Stalinskoe Politbyuro v 30-e gody: sbornik dokumentov* (1995), p. 10.
2. *Ibid.*, pp. 20–1, 74–7.
3. *Stalin's Letters to Molotov, 1925–1936*, edited by L. T. Lih, O. V. Naumov and O. V. Khlevniuk (1995); L. Kosheleva, V. Lel'chuk, V. Naumov, O. Naumov, L. Rogovaya and O. Khlevnyuk, *compilers, Pis'ma I.V. Stalina V.M. Molotovu, 1925–1936gg.: sbornik dokumentov* (1995) (10 000 copies). I shall cite here the Russian edition (referred to as *Pis'ma Stalina*), as the English translation is sometimes inaccurate.
4. *Pis'ma Stalina* (1995), pp. 51–2, 72–4.
5. *Ibid.*, p. 36.
6. *Ibid.*, pp. 192–209. Bazarov was a leading economist of independent views; Ramzin an engineer and industrial administrator who was the principal defendant in the 'Industrial Party' trial in November 1930.
7. *Ibid.*, pp. 187–8; this letter was first published in *Kommunist*, no. 11, 1990, pp. 99–100. Yurovsky had been the principal official concerned with the currency (see p. 143 above); Chayanov was the leading agricultural economist; and Larichev an engineer who was a senior administrator in Gosplan.
8. *Pis'ma Stalina*, p. 217.
9. *Ibid.*, pp. 222–4 (letter dated 22 September).
10. *Stalinskoe Politbyuro* (1995), pp. 107–12.
11. *Ibid.*, pp. 30–2.
12. Estimated from data in *ibid.*, pp. 93–4, 183–255.
13. *Ibid.*, p. 16.
14. *Ibid.*, p. 55. A second five-member commission prepared urgent economic questions for the Politburo, but without the formal power to take decisions.
15. *Za industrializatsiyu*, 22 August 1933.
16. RTsKhIDNI, fond 17, op. 3, d. 929, l. 121; confirmed at the session of 29 August.
17. *Pis'ma Stalina* (1995), p. 247.
18. RTsKhIDNI, f. 17, op. 3, d. 930, l. 13; confirmed at the session of 13 September.
19. *Pis'ma Stalina* (1995), pp. 248–9.
20. Reprinted in *Izvestiya*, 10 June 1992.
21. *Trud*, 4 June 1992.
22. *Stalinskoe Politbyuro* (1995), pp. 90–1.
23. O. Khlevnyuk, *Stalin i Ordzhonikidze: konflikty v Politbyuro v 30-e gody* (1993), p. 141.

24. See the evidence in *ibid.*, pp. 48–142.
25. *Kommunist*, no. 13, 1991, pp. 56–7.
26. The correspondence is reprinted from the Presidential Archives in *Voprosy istorii*, no. 3, 1994, pp. 3–25.
27. *Pravda*, 23 March 1933.
28. *Pravda*, 10 March 1963.
29. *Pis'ma Stalina* (1995), pp. 178–9.
30. *Ibid.*, pp. 193–4, 202–3, 211–2, 216–7.
31. See R. W. Davies, *The Soviet Economy in Turmoil, 1929–1930* (1989), p. 415.
32. *Ibid.*, pp. 431–3. This account was written before we knew about Pyatakov's memorandum and Stalin's attitude to it.
33. See R. W. Davies, *Crisis and Progress in the Soviet Economy, 1931–1933* (1996), p. 204.
34. D. Volkogonov, *Triumf i tragediya: politicheskii portret I. V. Stalina*, vol. 1, part 2 (1989), pp. 122–3.
35. *Rodina*, nos. 8–9, 1992, pp. 156–7.
36. *Izvestiya TsK*, no. 7, 1989, p. 68 (a report of the Politburo commission on repressions).
37. *Svobodnaya mysl'*, no. 8, 1992, p. 64 (L. Rogovaya). On the work of the Commission, see also *Rossiskie vesti*, 21 February 1996 (R. Pikhoya).
38. See A. Kirilina, *Rikoshet* (1993), p. 99; for this book see n. 43 below.
39. For the memorandum see *Svobodnaya mysl'*, no. 8, 1992, pp. 64–71.
40. Cited by Kirilina (1993), p. 100.
41. *Pravda*, 28 January 1991.
42. *Pravda*, 28 January 1991.
43. A. Kirilina, *Rikoshet, ili skol'ko chelovek bylo ubito vystrelom v Smol'nom* (St. Petersburg, 1993), 134 pp., 10 000 copies. Unfortunately this booklet contains no specific references to the archives from which her rich materials were obtained.
44. *Istochnik*, no. 1, 1993, p. 9. This informal diary, which she did not show to her family, was kept in various exercise books and notebooks, and on loose sheets of paper (*ibid.*, p. 5).
45. *Ibid.*, p. 14.
46. O. Khlevnyuk, *1937-i: Stalin, NKVD i sovetskoe obshchestvo* (1992), p. 64; 100 000 copies.
47. *Stalin's Letters to Molotov, 1925–1936* (1995), p. x.
48. *Iosif Stalin v ob"yatiyakh sem'i* (1993), p. 18 (dated 9 October [1936]).
49. *Ibid.*, pp. 14 (dated 25 April 1929), 16–17 (24 March 1934), 19 ([May 1937]).
50. *Ibid.*, pp. 16–17 (24 March 1934).
51. *Ibid.*, pp. 24–5 (16 September 1929), 22 (9 April 1928).
52. *Ibid.*, pp. 35, 37 (9, 14 September 1931), 29 (21 June [1930]).
53. *Ibid.*, pp. 31–3 (8, 24 September 1930).
54. *Pis'ma Stalina* (1995), p. 71 (15 June 1926), 204 (24 August 1930), 252 (5 August 1935); *Iosif Stalin* (1993), p. 23 (1 September 1929).
55. *Ibid.*, p. 31 (8 September 1930).
56. *Pis'ma Stalina* (1995), p. 194 ([August 1930]).
57. *Ibid.*, pp. 216–18 (letter of [13 September 1930] and note 2).

13 The Secret Police and the Camps

1. *Istochnik*, no. 1, 1993, pp. 83–4. The provisions of the memorandum were evidently put into practice, but no central committee decision about this is recorded on the document.
2. *Kniga pamyati* (Ekaterinburg, 1994), appendix 2 (unnumbered).
3. The most important work was N. A. Ivnitskii, *Klassovaya bor'ba v derevne i likvidatsiya kulachestva kak klassa* (1972). The standard work on Soviet agricultural history contained a chapter on similar lines; this was sent to press after Gorbachev took office but before the press began to be more frank about the past (*Istoriya sovetskogo krest'yanstva*, vol. 2 (1986), chapter 7).
4. Z. Fazin, *Tovarishch Sergo: stranitsy bol'shoi zhizni* (1970), p. 125; the three dots are in the original.
5. For sources, see S. G. Wheatcroft in *Soviet Studies*, vol. XXXIII (1981), pp. 265–95.
6. R. Conquest, *The Great Terror: Stalin's Purge of the Thirties* (London, 1968), pp. 531–3, and *The Harvest of Sorrow: Soviet Collectivization and the Terror Famine* (London, 1986), p. 305.
7. S. G. Wheatcroft, R. W. Davies and J. M. Cooper, *Economic History Review*, 2nd series, vol. XXXIX (1986), pp. 264–94.
8. S. F. Cohen, *Bukharin and the Bolshevik Revolution: a Political Biography* (London, 1974), p. 341.
9. S. F. Cohen (ed.), *An End to Silence* (NY, 1982), p. 23, and *Slavic Review*, vol. 45 (1986), 299.
10. M. Malia, *The Soviet Tragedy: a History of Socialism in Russia, 1917–1991* (London, 1994), p. 263.
11. A. Bullock, *Hitler and Stalin: Parallel Lives* (London, 1993), p. 543.
12. J. Hough and M. Fainsod, *How the Soviet Union is Governed* (Cambridge, Mass., 1979), pp. 176–7.
13. *The Nation*, 7/14 August 1989, p. 184.
14. *New York Review of Books*, 28 April, 13 October 1983.
15. *Commission on the Ukraine Famine: Report to Congress* (Washington DC, April 1988), p. vii.
16. *Moscow News*, 27 November 1988; *Argumenty i fakty*, no. 5, 1989; *Delovoi mir*, 3 March 1995.
17. See Davies (1989), ch. 6.
18. *Literaturnaya gazeta*, 3 August 1988.
19. Compare for example *Neva*, no. 10, 1988, pp. 154–8 (A. Chalikov) and Conquest (1968), p. 533.
20. *Soyuz*, no. 9, February 1990; *Sotsial'no-politicheskie nauki*, no. 7, 1990, pp. 90–101 (articles by A. Dugin).
21. J. A. Getty and R. T. Manning (eds), *Stalinist Terror: New Perspectives* (Cambridge, 1993), pp. 261–274, and Nove's supplementary article in *Europe–Asia Studies* (formerly *Soviet Studies*), vol. 46 (1994), pp. 535–7; J. A. Getty, G. T. Rittersporn, V. N. Zemskov, in *American Historical Review*, vol. 98 (1993); E. Bacon, *The Gulag at War: Stalin's Forced Labour System in the Light of the Archives* (Basingstoke and London, 1994).
22. *Soyuz*, 18 May 1990 (Zemskov); *Raduga* (Tallin), no. 6, 1990, pp. 43–8

(Zemskov). Even before the labour legislation of 1940, some citizens were sentenced to 'corrective labour without deprivation of liberty'; there were 312 800 in this category in March 1940 (*Sotsiologicheskie issledovaniya*, no. 10, 1991, p. 17).

23. Sources of table in text are as follows:
   [a] May 1933: See M. Fainsod, *Smolensk under Soviet Rule* (1958), p. 186.
   [b] *Sotsial'no-politicheskie nauki*, no. 7, 1990, p. 91.
   [c] *Sotsiologicheskie issledovaniya*, no. 6, 1991, p. 11 (Zemskov). The figure for colonies in the 1933 column is for 1 January 1935.
   [d] *Sotsiologicheskie issledovaniya*, no. 11, 1990, pp. 6, 16 (Zemskov).
   [e] *Sotsiologicheskie issledovaniya*, no. 2, 1991, p. 75 (Zemskov). The prisons' figure for 1937 refers to 1 February.
   [f] 15 January 1948.
   Note: the data for 1939 in my article in *New Left Review*, no. 214 (1995), p. 67, are wrong. In particular, the figure for those confined in camps should read 1 317 000 not 1 718 000.

24. See Getty, Rittersporn and Zemskov (1993), p. 1025, data for 1940.
25. *Sotsiologicheskie issledovaniya*, no. 2, 1992, p. 18. These figures are mistakenly stated to be for 1 October 1944, but they obviously refer to 1 October 1941.
26. Ivnitskii, *Kollektivizatsiya i raskulachivanie (nachalo 30-kh godov)* (1994), p. 257; R. W. Davies, M. Harrison and S. G. Wheatcroft (eds), *The Economic Transformation of the Soviet Union, 1913–1945* (Cambridge, 1994), p. 68. The total number 'dekulakised', including those who left for the towns, may have amounted to five or six million persons. The book by Ivnitskii is a new edition of the volume referred to in note 3 above.
27. *Istoriya SSSR*, no. 6, 1989, p. 136 (Bugai); *Otechestvennaya istoriya*, no. 6, 1992, pp. 140–68 (Bugai).
28. See R. Conquest, *The Nation Killers* (London, 1972).
29. *Istoriya SSSR*, no. 6, 1989, p. 135; *Voprosy istorii*, no. 7, 1990, p. 44.
30. Malia (1994), p. 287.
31. *Rossiya XXI*, no. 5, 1993, p. 80 (Zemskov).
32. *Sotsiologicheskie issledovaniya*, no. 7, 1991, pp. 4–5 (Zemskov).
33. *Istoriya SSSR*, no. 4, 1990, p. 36 (Zemskov).
34. *Istoriya SSSR*, no. 4, 1990, pp. 39–40.
35. 'Assessing the Victims of Repression 1930–45' (unpublished working paper, 1995).
36. See Getty, Rittersporn and Zemskov (1993), pp. 1048–9.
37. *Sotsiologicheskie issledovaniya*, no. 11, 1990, p. 6. USSR death rates in special settlements have been available only for 1932–40.
38. *Voprosy istorii*, no. 7, 1990, p. 33 (Bugai); *Istoriya SSSR*, no. 1, 1992, p. 130.
39. According to an MVD document dated 10 April 1953, the 145 000 died 'after exile to special settlement' (*Istoriya SSSR*, no. 1, 1992, p. 142).
40. See Bacon (1994), p. 36.
41. *Otechestvennye arkhivy*, no. 2, 1992, pp. 28–9 (V. P. Popov). For details about this and other reports prepared at the beginning of 1954 see *Rossiya*, nos. 1–2, 1994, pp. 107–111.
42. V. I. Ivnitskii, *Kollektivizatsiya i raskulachivanie* (1994), pp. 103–4.

43. *Istochnik*, no. 4, 1994, p. 8.
44. Conquest (1968), pp. 228, 485; J. Erickson, *The Soviet High Command* (London, 1962), pp. 449, 451–2.
45. For details see *Izvestiya TsK*, no. 1, 1990, pp. 188–9; Getty and Manning, eds. (1993), pp. 199–201. The report states that only 9506 officers were arrested; but as a further 18 822 were discharged 'for links with the plotters' or for being of foreign nationality or having links with abroad, it seems mostlikely that the 9701 of these who were not reinstated were arrested.
46. *Soviet Studies*, vol. 42 (1990), p. 366.
47. *Vestnik statistiki*, no. 7, 1990, p. 41 (E. Andreev, L. Darskii and T. Khar'kova).
48. A. Blum, *Naitre, vivre et mourir en URSS* (Paris, 1994), p. 243.
49. Getty and Manning (eds) (1993), p. 268.
50. *Vestnik statistiki*, no. 10, 1990 (Andreev, Darskii and Khar'kova). Their estimate, 26.7 million, does not allow for the net emigration, about one million.
51. *Rossiya*, nos. 1–2, 1994, p. 110.
52. *Times Literary Supplement*, 24 February 1995.
53. *Sotsiologicheskie issledovaniya*, no. 6, 1991, p. 10.
54. *Komsomol'skaya pravda*, 4 June 1991.
55. See *Spetspereselentsy v zapadnoi Sibiri, 1930-vesna 1931g* (Novosibirsk, 1992), p. 13.
56. See Bacon (1994), pp. 48–9.
57. *Svobodnaya mysl'*, no. 13, 1992, p. 75 (Khlevnyuk).
58. *Spetspereselentsy* (1992), pp. 14–15.
59. *Spetspereselentsy v zapadnoi Sibiri, vesna 1931-nachalo 1933 goda* (Novosibirsk, 1993), p. 5.
60. RTsKhIDNI, fond 17, op. 162, d. 9, 11, 138 (20 February 1931), 174–8 (20 March 1931), d. 10, 11. 46–54 (20 May 1931).
61. *Otechestvennye arkhivy*, no. 2, 1992, p. 28 (V. P. Popov).
62. Getty and Manning (eds) (1993), pp. 116–17.
63. *Svobodnaya mysl'*, nos. 7–8, 1994, pp. 123–4.
64. *Bulletins on Soviet Economic Development*, no. 7 (1952), pp. 31, 36 (Baykov).
65. See for example *Voprosy istorii*, no. 6, 1994, p. 189 (S. G. Ebedzhans and M. Ya. Vazhnov); *Svobodnaya mysl'*, no. 13, 1992, pp. 79–80 (Khlevnyuk).
66. See Bacon (1994), p. 144.
67. *Bulletins on Soviet Economic Development*, no. 7 (1952), p. 31.
68. Bacon (1994), pp. 136–7; *Sotsiologicheskie issledovaniya*, no. 6, 1991, p. 26 (Zemskov); *Soyuz*, no. 38, 1990 (A. Emelin and V. Litovkin).
69. *Kniga pamyati* (Ekaterinburg, 1994), pp. 72–86.
70. *Istochnik*, no. 6, 1994, pp. 112–15.
71. *Izvestiya*, 16 May 1992 (N. Burlyga). For further fascinating and unpleasant details, see the not always reliable memoirs: P. and A. Sudoplatov, *Special Tasks: the Memoirs of an Unwanted Witness* (London, 1995). They claim that the laboratory was at work from Lenin's time until the 1980s.
72. *Istochnik*, no. 1, 1993, pp. 74–7; this is a top-secret memorandum prepared by the Commission of Party Control and the department of administrative agencies of the party central committee, dated 4 October 1956.
73. *Istoricheskii arkhiv*, no. 3, 1994, pp. 128–38.
74. *Otechestvennye arkhivy*, no. 4, 1994, pp. 33–4.

75. *Ibid.*, p. 33; these are included in the total for 1953 on p. 166 above.
76. *Ibid.*, pp. 50–1, 57.
77. A. Solzhenitsyn, *The Gulag Archipelago*, vol. 3 (London, 1978), pp. 285–331.
78. *Otechestvennye arkhivy*, no. 4, 1994, pp. 33–87.
79. These doocuments are discussed (in Russian) by an Italian historian, M. Kraveri, in *Cahiers du Monde Russe*, vol. 36 (1995), pp. 319–44.
80. Kraveri reports archival evidence that a further five death sentences were carried out (*Cahiers, op. cit.*, pp. 333–4).
81. For details of these war-time developments, see *Sotsiologicheskie issledovaniya*, no. 2, 1992, pp. 3–26 (Zemskov).
82. See *Sotsiologicheskie issledovaniya*, no. 8, 1992, pp. 18–37 (Zemskov); the figure for 1953 is from *ibid.*, no. 1, 1991, p. 8.
83. *Sotsiologicheskie issledovaniya*, no. 1, 1991, pp. 5, 18, 23 (for special settlers), no. 7, 1991, pp. 14–15 (for camps and colonies). Figures for the number in prisons have not been available.
84. *Sotsiologicheskie issledovaniya*, no. 7, 1991, p. 12 (Zemskov).
85. See *Sotsiologicheskie issledovaniya*, no. 1, 1991, pp. 5–26 (Zemskov).

14 Opposition to Stalinism

1. See Davies (1989), pp. 83–5. For the text of Ryutin's platform and declaration see *Izvestiya TsK*, no. 6, 1989, nos. 3 and 8–12, 1990; *Yunost'*, no. 11, 1988.
2. See Davies (1989), p. 85; Volkogonov, vol. 1, pt. 2 (1989), pp. 77–9. For the official report see *Izvestiya TsK*, no. 7, 1989, pp. 114–21.
3. Cited in Pospelov's memorandum, *Svobodnaya mysl'*, no. 8, 1992, p. 66, and in Kirilina, *op. cit.*, pp. 49–50. These materials have not been generally available to historians, and as in other cases they may have been partly or wholly forged by the OGPU.
4. *Istochnik*, no. 1, 1993, p. 26.
5. See for example L. R. Graham, *The Soviet Academy of Sciences and the Communist Party, 1927–1932* (Princeton, 1967), p. 201.
6. *Istochnik*, no. 1, 1995, pp. 139–40; the letter, from the Presidential Archive, was first published in *Sovetskaya kul'tura*, 14 January 1989.
7. *Istochnik*, no. 1, 1995, pp. 140–4. See also V. Tolz's study of Pavlov in 'Russian Academicians under Soviet Rule', Ph. D. thesis, Centre for Russian and East European Studies, University of Birmingham, 1994.
8. *Izvestiya TsK*, no. 8, 1991, pp. 146–7.
9. *Svobodnaya mysl'*, no. 1, 1992, pp. 48–52. Gorelik has now moved to the Dibner Institute at the Massachusetts Institute of Technology.
10. *Izvestiya TsK*, no. 8, 1991, pp. 136, 151–2, 154; the Danish physicist Niels Bohr also appealed to Stalin (*ibid.*, pp. 149–50).
11. *Voprosy istorii estestvoznaniya i tekhniki*, no. 3, 1993, pp. 123–31.
12. *Voprosy istorii estestvoznaniya i tekhniki*, no. 2, 1994, pp. 3–17 (Ya. S. Lur'e, L. S. Polak).
13. *Izvestiya*, 16 July 1992 (E. Maksimova). For further information about their trial and rehabilitation, see *Izvestiya TsK*, no. 8, 1991, pp. 215–21.

14. See Davies (1989), pp. 86–7, and R. Marsh, *History and Literature in Contemporary Russia* (Basingstoke and London, 1995), pp. 88–91.
15. See R. W. Davies, *The Socialist Offensive: the Collectivisation of Agriculture, 1929–1930* (Basingstoke and London, 1980), pp. 255–61.
16. See *Dokumenty svidetel'stvuyut: iz istorii derevni nakanune i v khode kollektivizatsii 1927–1932 gg.* (1989), p. 265, and N. A. Ivnitskii, *Kollektivizatsiya i raskulachivanie (nachalo 30-kh godov)* (1994), pp. 138–51.
17. *Dokumenty svidetel'stvuyut* (1989), pp. 424–5, 430, 435, 446–53, 457–8, 491–3.
18. On the textile strikes, see *Svobodnaya mysl'*, no. 17, 1991, pp. 77–8 (Khlevnyuk). The party reports are in GARF, f. 374, op. 27s, d. 1988, ll. 93–82, 70–57; I am grateful to Nicolas Werth for drawing my attention to these documents.
19. E. A. Osokina, *Ierarkhiya potrebleniya: o zhizni lyudei v usloviyakh stalinskogo snabzheniya, 1928–1935gg.* (1993), p. 26.
20. *Istoricheskaya pravda o Sovetskom Soyuze 20–30 godov* (Alma-Ata, 1991), pp. 61–3 (Khlevnyuk).
21. The relevant documents are reprinted in *Istoricheskii arkhiv*, no. 2, 1994, pp. 111–36 (annotated jointly by French and Russian historians). They are located in the files of the Organisation-Instructor Department of the party central committee in RTsKhIDNI.
22. *Rodina*, no. 5, 1992, pp. 54–5 (documents from RTsKhIDNI files).

15 Science and Stalinism

1. *Voprosy istorii estestvoznaniya i tekhniki*, no. 3, 1993, p. 125.
2. *Ibid.*, no. 2, 1993, pp. 116–18.
3. *Svobodnaya mysl'*, no. 1, 1992, pp. 45–6, 51–2. See also his articles in *Priroda*, no. 1, 1990, pp. 123–8, no. 11, 1991, pp. 93–104, and in *Voprosy istorii estestvoznaniya i tekhniki*, no. 1, 1992, pp. 15–32.
4. *Voprosy istorii estestvoznaniya i tekhniki*, no. 3, 1993, p. 123 (Yu. N. Krivonosov).
5. See for example the articles in *ibid.*, no. 2, 1994, pp. 125–30 (Yu. Smirnov), no. 4, 1994, pp. 89–97 (L. P. Golesova), 97–107 (V. E. Kondrashov and I. D. Sofronov) and 107–110 (I. S. Drovenikov).
6. D. Holloway, *Stalin and the Bomb: the Soviet Union and Atomic Energy, 1939–1956* (New Haven, 1994). Holloway discusses his sources in Cold War *Bulletin*, no. 4 (1994), pp. 1–9.
7. The published discussions on physics are described in detail in L. Graham, *Science and Philosophy in the Soviet Union* (London, 1973), chapters III and IV.
8. *Krasnyi flot*, 13 June 1952. In the same year he published an authoritative collection of essays, A. A. Maksimov *et al.* (eds), *Filosofskie voprosy sovremennoi fiziki*.
9. *Voprosy istorii estestvoznaniya i tekhniki*, no. 1, 1992, p. 31.
10. For the correspondence about Fock's article, taken from the central committee repository TsKhSD, see *Istoricheskii arkhiv*, no. 3, 1994, pp. 215–23.

16   Soviet Society in the Stalin Era

1. *Vsesoyuznaya perepis' naseleniya 1937g.: kratkie itogi* (1991); *Vsesoyuznaya perepis' naseleniya 1939 goda: osnovnye itogi*, compiled by Yu. A. Polyakov, V. B. Zhiromskaya, A. A. Isupov and I. N. Kiselev (1992, 1350 copies).
2. E. A. Osokina, *Ierarkhiya potrebleniya: o zhizni lyudei v usloviyakh stalinskogo snabzheniya, 1928–1935gg.* (1993).
3. *Ibid.*, p. 64.
4. *Ibid.*, p. 70.
5. *Ibid.*, pp. 66–7. A later article by Osokina analyses the food crisis of 1939–41 (*Otechestvennaya istoriya*, no. 3, 1995, pp. 16–32).
6. *Moskva Voennaya: memuary i arkhivnye dokumenty, 1941–1945* (1995), compiled by K. I. Bukov, M. Gorinov and A. N. Ponomarev; 674 pp., 60 000 copies.
7. *Ibid.*, p. 158.
8. *Ibid.*, p. 355.
9. *Ibid.*, pp. 173–4.
10. *Ibid.*, pp. 203, 205.
11. *Ibid.*, p. 160.
12. *Ibid.*, pp. 116–19 (NKVD report dated 18 October 1941).
13. *Ibid.*, pp. 352–3.
14. *Ibid.*, pp. 456–8.
15. *Ibid.*, pp. 657–87.
16. M. M. Gorinov, 'Dinamika nastroenii Moskvichei: 22 iyunya 1941g. – mai 1942g.', Working Paper presented to the V World Congress of the International Council for Central and East European Studies, Warsaw, 6–11 August 1995.
17. *Meldungen aus dem Reich. Die geheimen Lageberichte des Sicherheitsdienstes der SS, 1938–1945*, 17 vols (Herrsching, 1984).
18. *Istochnik*, no. 3, 1995, pp. 88–90; *Meldungen*, vol. 11, pp. 4081–105. I have translated these passages from the Russian version, but Dr Steven Welch, a specialist in German history, has kindly checked them with the German original.
19. *Istochnik*, no. 3, 1995, pp. 90–6; *Meldungen*, vol. 13, pp. 5124–44.
20. E. Yu. Zubkova, *Obshchestvo i reformy, 1945–1964* (1993; 1000 copies).
21. For this speech see Davies (1989), pp. 80–1.
22. For a careful study of the role of the party and Stalin in literature, based on a wealth of archive material, see D. L. Babichenko, *Pisateli i tsenzory: sovetskaya literatura 1940-kh godov pod politicheskim kontrolem TsK* (1994, 1000 copies) and D. L. Babichenko, compiler, *'Literaturnyi front': istoriya politicheskoi tenzury, 1932–1946gg.: sbornik dokumentov* (1994, 2000 copies).
23. The central committee documents in the Lysenko affair, deposited in RTsKhIDNI, were published in *Izvestiya TsK*, nos. 4, 1991, pp. 125–41; 6, 1991, pp. 157–73; 7, 1991, pp. 109–21 (compiled by V. Esakov, S. Ivanova and E. Levina).

17 Stalin's Entourage at the End

1. See Davies (1989), p. 73.
2. F. Chuev, *Sto sorok besed s Molotovym* (1991), p. 297.
3. *Nezavisimaya gazeta*, 4 March 1993 (Volkogonov).
4. Chuev (1991), p. 271.
5. See Davies (1989), p. 63.
6. *Svobodnaya mysl'*, no. 2, 1995, p. 101 (L. Maksimenkov).
7. Chuev (1991), p. 332. See also F. I. Chuev, *Tak govoril Kaganovich* (1992), p. 193.
8. Chuev (1991), p. 271.
9. K. Simonov, *Glazami cheloveka moego pokoleniya: razmyshleniya o I. V. Staline*, pp. 240–1; and see Shelepin's imprecise account in *Neizvestnaya Rossiya XX vek*, vol. 1 (1992), p. 275. The proceedings of this plenum have not been available.
10. See Davies (1989), pp. 63–4.
11. Based on statements by Mikoyan, Khrushchev and Malenkov (*Izvestiya TsK*, no. 2, 1991, pp. 154, 196); direct documentary evidence has not been available.
12. See the pioneering article by J. Miller in *Soviet Studies*, vol. v, no. 4 (April 1954), pp. 357–401.
13. See for example R. Medvedev, *Khrushchev* (Oxford, 1982), chapter 7.
14. See for example the articles by Robert Service: *Soviet Studies*, vol. XXXIII (1981), pp. 232–45; and 'De-Stalinisation in the USSR before Khrushchev's "Secret Speech"', unpublished Working Paper, October 1986.
15. For March plenum see *Istochnik*, no. 1, 1994, pp. 106–11; for July plenum see *Izvestiya TsK*, no. 1, 1991, pp. 139–214, no. 2, 1991, pp. 141–208.
16. *Istochnik*, no. 4, 1994, pp. 3–9.
17. *Ibid.*, pp. 10–14; unusually, the names of the archivists are not given.
18. S. N. Khrushchev, *Pensioner soyuznogo znacheniya* (1991); A. G. Malenkov, *O moem ottse – Georgii Malenkov* (1992); S. L. Beriya, *Moi otets – Lavrentii Beriya* (1994).
19. *Istochnik*, no. 1, 1994, pp. 108–11. Many other major appointments were also agreed. The large new Presidium of the central committee and the smaller 'bureau of the Presidium', instituted at the October 1952 plenum, were replaced by the traditional Politburo (at this time known as Presidium) of 11 members (including for his remaining 1 hour 10 minutes Stalin) and four candidate members. For the plenum and the appointments which followed, see *Slavic Review*, vol. 54 (1995), pp. 16–17 (Y. Gorlizki).
20. The most succinct Russian account for the general reader is 'Neizvestnaya perestroika' ('The Unknown Perestroika') by Aleksandr Frolov (*Sovetskaya Rossiya*, 11 April 1992).
21. A. Knight, *Beria: Stalin's First Lieutenant* (Princeton, 1993), pp. 183–94.
22. *Istochnik*, no. 4, 1994, p. 11; *Sovetskaya Rossiya*, 11 April 1992; *Argumenty i fakty*, no. 19, 1992 (Beria's memorandum on Mikhoels dated 2 April 1953). On the destruction of the Jewish anti-fascist committee, see *Nepravednyi sud: poslednii Stalinskii rasstrel* (1994).
23. *Istochnik*, no. 4, 1993, p. 85 (B. Starkov), apparently citing the MVD archives.
24. See Knight (1993), pp. 184–5.

25. *Istochnik*, no. 4, 1994, p. 11.
26. *Izvestiya TsK*, no. 2, 1991, p. 185. This decision was rescinded on 2 July after Beria's arrest.
27. *Sotsiologicheskie issledovaniya*, no. 7, 1991, p. 14.
28. *Sovetskaya Rossiya*, 11 April 1992; *Istochnik*, no. 4, 1993, pp. 84–5; no. 4, 1994, p. 11.
29. *Izvestiya TsK*, no. 1, 1991, p. 153.
30. *Ibid.*, no. 1, 1991, p. 191.
31. *Ibid.*, no. 2, 1991, p. 187.
32. This account was given by Molotov to the July plenum, using the word 'rapid' instead of 'forced', and apparently conforms to the archives (see *Izvestiya TsK*, no. 1, 1991, p. 163; Knight (1993), pp. 193–4; *Istochnik*, no. 4, 1994, pp. 11–12). But in Molotov's later account to Chuev, Molotov and the Ministry of Foreign Affairs put forward a draft memorandum including the word 'forced', and Beria attempted to modify it! (Chuev (1991), pp. 332–5).
33. *Izvestiya TsK*, no. 1, 1991, p. 213.
34. *Izvestiya TsK*, no, 1, 1991, p. 143.
35. See Knight (1993), pp. 191–4, and *Soviet Studies*, vol. XXVII (1974–5), pp. 381–95 (V. Baras).
36. *Izvestiya TsK*, no. 1, 1991, pp. 145, 161, 173.
37. *Slavic Review*, vol. 54 (1995), p. 20 (Y. Gorlizki); N. A. Barsukov, *XX s"ezd KPSS i ego istoricheskie realnosti* (1991), p. 15.
38. *Sovetskaya militsiya*, no. 4, 1990, p. 41 (V. Nekrasov); for the Special Camps, see pp. 178–9 above.
39. *Istochnik*, no. 4, 1994, pp. 4–5.
40. *Izvestiya TsK*, no. 1, 1991, p. 154.
41. *Ibid.*, no. 1, 1991, p. 195.
42. *Ibid.*, no. 1, 1991, pp. 161–2.
43. *Istochnik*, no. 4, 1994, p. 11.
44. *Izvestiya TsK*, no. 2, 1991, pp. 203–4.
45. *Ibid.*, p. 185.
46. *Ibid.*, pp. 186–9.
47. *Ibid.*, p. 195.
48. See for example *ibid.*, no. 1, 1991, pp. 170 (Molotov on Turkmenian canal), no. 2, 1991, p. 176 (Voroshilov on amnesty).
49. *Ibid.*, no. 1, 1991, p. 175.
50. *Ibid.*, no. 1, 1991, 192, 144, 164.
51. *Ibid.*, no. 2, 1991, pp. 195–200. For the personal rivalry between Malenkov and Khrushchev, see *Otechestvennaya istoriya*, no. 4, 1995, pp. 103–15 (Zubkova).
52. See the reviews in *Svobodnaya mysl'*, no. 2, 1995, pp. 103–10 (O. Khlevnyuk), and no. 6, 1995, pp. 106–17 (E. Zubkova).
53. Barsukov (1991), p. 13.
54. Barsukov (1991), p. 14.
55. The proceedings of the October 1964 plenum at which Khrushchev was disposed were published in *Istoricheskii arkhiv*, no. 1, 1993, pp. 3–19.
56. Translated from the Russian in Cold War *Bulletin*, no. 4 (Fall 1994), pp. 80–1.

57. *Rodina*, no. 10, 1994, pp. 82–8; see also his article in *Neizvestnaya Rossiya*, no. 3 (1993), pp. 119–42.
58. See Davies (1989), pp. 171–3.
59. Malenkov (1992), p. 118.

18   The Future of the Soviet Past

1. The Institute of Marxism–Leninism was first renamed the Institute for the Theory and Practice of Socialism, and is now known as the Russian Independent Institute of Social and National Problems. Gorinov at that time worked in the Institute of the History of the USSR, which has been renamed the Institute of Russian History.
2. See Davies (1989), pp. 98–9.
3. BBC SWB, 6 February 1996 (TV interview with V. Kostikov, 4 February).
4. BBC SWB, 8 February 1996 (broadcast of 6 February); asked whether the ideas imposed on Russia today or fascism were worse, he replied 'they are both worse'.
5. E. Gaidar, *Gosudarstvo i evolyutsiya* (1995); 10 000 copies.
6. *Svobodnaya mysl'*, no. 1, 1996, pp. 125–8 (Khlevnyuk). He was criticising V. F. Nekrasov, *Trinadtsat' 'zheleznykh' narkomov* (1994) and V. A. Kovalev, *Dva stalinskikh narkoma* (1995).
7. *Svobodnaya mysl'*, no. 12, 1992, pp. 17–22.
8. *Svobodnaya mysl'*, no. 6, 1994, pp. 13–26.
9. *Otechestvennaya istoriya*, no. 5, 1992, nos 2 and 6, 1993, nos 2, 4–5 and 6, 1994, nos 3, 4 and 6, 1995.
10. *Otechestvennaya istoriya*, no. 6, 1994, pp. 3–31.
11. G. Bordyugov and V. A. Kozlov, *Istoriya i kon"yunktura: sub"ektivnye zametki ob istorii sovetskogo obshchestva* (1992), pp. 345–7; they invoke the French historian Coquin in their support.

Index